Advice Online

Pragmatics & Beyond

Volume 149

Advice Online: Advice-giving in an American Internet health column
by Miriam A. Locher

Advice Online

Advice-giving in an
American Internet health column

Miriam A. Locher

University of Berne

John Benjamins Publishing Company
Amsterdam / Philadelphia

™ The paper used in this publication meets the minimum requirements
of American National Standard for Information Sciences – Permanence
of Paper for Printed Library Materials, ANSI z39.48-1984.

Library of Congress Cataloging-in-Publication Data

Miriam A. Locher
    Advice online : advice-giving in an American Internet health column /
    Miriam A. Locher.
       p. cm. (Pragmatics & Beyond, New Series, ISSN 0922-842X ; v. 149)
    Includes bibliographical references and indexes.
       1. Health--Computer network resources. 2. Medical care--Computer
    network resources. I. Title.

    RA773.6.L63 2006
610'.285--dc22   2006047706
ISBN 90 272 5392 7 (Hb; alk. paper)

John Benjamins Publishing Co. · P.O. Box 36224 · 1020 ME Amsterdam · The Netherlands
John Benjamins North America · P.O. Box 27519 · Philadelphia PA 19118-0519 · USA

Table of contents

Part IV

Acknowledgments

My first thanks go to the Internet advice column that is the subject of this study for allowing me to investigate the language used on their site. The people involved in the production of 'Lucy Answers' expressed genuine interest in my research and I hope that the results may prove helpful to them.

This study would not have been possible without the help of many colleagues and friends to whom I am deeply grateful. I would first like to thank Gunnel Tottie and the students of her seminar on "Speech Events" in Zurich (Leata Kollaart, Marylène Lüscher, Jacqueline von Arx, and Michael Wenziger) who gave me the idea to work on advice columns. Thanks also to Anita Kaufmann, who told me about 'Lucy Answers' in particular.

Sebastian Hoffmann helped me in compiling the corpus for this study and worked with me on the topic of *Lucy*'s advisor voice in the initial pilot phase of this project (Locher & Hoffmann 2003, 2006), the results of which have found their way into Chapter 8. I am particularly indebted to him for the comparisons with data of the British National Corpus. Thanks also to Iman Makeba Laversuch, who read critically through initial drafts of the paper on *Lucy*'s voice and to Benjamin Ruef, who introduced me to XML programming, which proved invaluable for my analysis.

I have written this study while working at the English Department in Berne, where I found many much appreciated colleagues. I wish to thank Richard Watts for his feedback and support. Without the generous amount of time he allowed me to take for my research, this study could not have been completed in the time it was. I am grateful to Anouk Hiedl and Margaret Mace-Tessler for checking the manuscript carefully. The members of the Berne Research Colloquium deserve an especially heartfelt thanks: Anne-Françoise Baer-Boesch, Mathias Kimmich, Danièle Klapproth, Nicole Nyffenegger, Adrian Pablé, Lukas Rosenberger, Philipp Schweighauser and Margun Welskopf. They have accompanied this project throughout with constructive criticism, support and friendship. This study was submitted as a post-doctoral thesis ('Habilitationsschrift') to the University of Berne, where it was reviewed by Sandra Harris, Elke Hentschel, Bruno Moretti, Peter Trudgill and Richard Watts. I wish to express my gratitude to them and to Adreas Jucker and the two anonymous reviewers from Benjamins for their constructive criticism. I should stress, of course, that I am fully responsible for all shortcomings that remain in this study.

I would also like to thank all those friends and family members who supported me with their love, warmth, and generosity, especially my parents and brother, my cousin Anna, and Lukas. I dedicate this study to my family.

List of tables and figures

Chapter 6

Chapter 7

CHAPTER 1

Introduction*

Human beings give and take advice almost on a daily basis: sometimes we seek and offer advice in private and personal settings, or we turn to professional institutions for help; sometimes advice is specifically requested, and at other times it is given without any explicit prompting from the advisee. There is thus great variation in advice-giving contexts as well as in the way advice is given. This study offers an analysis of solicited advice-giving in 'Lucy Answers' (LA) – a popular and professional Internet health advice column run by a large American educational institution (hereafter referred to as AEI; the names are pseudonyms).[1] The subject of study is thus expert advice-giving in written form in the context of health counseling. I focus on 'Lucy Answers' as a specific 'Community of Practice' (Eckert & McConnell-Ginet 1992a), which involves the team of professionals who stand for *Lucy* and the health service of AEI, the questioners who ask for advice, and the Internet readership which uses this site as a resource for information. Every Community of Practice deserves to be studied in its own right, taking into account the specifics that make it unique. By analyzing the question-answer[2] units in depth, I hope to identify the strategies used in this particular social practice and to contribute to the understanding of advice-giving in general and of advice-giving in the context of professional Internet health sites in particular.

In 'Lucy Answers' a team of professional health educators using the alias *Lucy* answers questions from the anonymous Internet readership. Topics that are covered on this web site include issues of sexuality, sexual health, relationship problems, emotional health, drug use and abuse, fitness and nutrition, and general health. 'Lucy Answers' was chosen because of its professionalism and popularity, which I take to explain its success. It is part of the conventional problem-page genre in that an advice-seeker describes a problem and asks for advice in the form of a 'letter' and receives an answer by an expert which is also in letter format. The notion of a 'letter' will be retained for this study despite the fact that we are dealing with Internet communication, simply because the general format of the problem and response texts corresponds best to the well-established pattern of a simplified letter (see (1.1) below). I will refer to these letters as 'texts' that are produced in the particular discourse of Internet health counseling (cf. van Dijk 1997).

In (1.1) we can see a question-answer exchange that is typical for 'Lucy Answers'. An anonymous questioner describes a problem and asks for advice.

Lucy takes up the questioner's narrative, analyses the problem and proceeds to give advice.

(1.1)   "Talking to yourself" (LA 626, emotional health)*

> Lucy,
>
> I frequently drift into talking to myself when alone or even when walking on the street. Is this healthy? I find that so long as I don't talk for a long time, it leaves a good effect on me. However, sometimes it's just a sub-conscious way of wasting time. Should I actively try to stop myself from this self-talking, or should I let myself "be natural"? I am twenty-four!
>
> – Self-Talker
>
> ---
>
> Dear Self-Talker,
>
> Most people talk to themselves quite regularly, even when walking down the street; but, it is primarily done silently so it's not evident to onlookers. Whether or not we talk out loud, or silently, when we talk to ourselves, we are processing our thoughts, solving our problems, or just deciding what we will eat for lunch that day.
>
> Some people have difficulty in making the transition from speaking to themselves out loud when they are alone, to speaking silently when they are in public. This is purely an issue of societal norms. Speaking to yourself out loud is not unhealthy behavior, but it does run counter to what is considered normal in American society. You can either try to speak to yourself silently when you're in public, or you can continue talking out loud and risk some stares – your choice!
>
> *Lucy*

* The record number refers to its call number in my database. This information is included to make transparent when examples come from the same record. The title of the record and the topic category in 'Lucy Answers' are included to contextualize the examples for the benefit of the reader. The texts of all examples of problem and response letters of 'Lucy Answers' are taken over as they appear on the site and are not edited for typing or any other grammatical inconsistencies.

The core 'piece of advice' in (1.1) can be located in *Lucy*'s last sentence which contains a suggestion introduced with *can*. However, you could also argue that the entire answer constitutes advice since the final suggestion largely obtains its full scope from being embedded in its context. The pieces of information delivered reassure the advice-seeker that the fears expressed in his or her question (*Is this healthy?*) are unwarranted. In many instances, offering advice is therefore not a matter of giving straightforward imperatives for instruction, but a complex interplay of linguistic realizations of different discursive moves.

According to Searle (1969:67), who contrasts advice with the speech act of request, the former "is not a species of requesting. .... Advising you is not trying to get you to do something in the sense that requesting is. Advising is more like telling you what is best for you." Advice has thus a weaker directive force than requests. Advice is also closely linked to the speech act type of assessments and judgments. However, advice-giving contains an additional element: a future action is recommended by the advice-giver. It is this combination of assessing, judging and directing that characterizes advice-giving. The *Oxford English Dictionary* defines advice as an "[o]pinion given or offered as to action; counsel" (OED, sense 5), the *Collins Concise Dictionary* defines it as a "recommendation as to appropriate choice of action" (1989:17) and the *American Heritage Dictionary* as an "[o]pinion about what could or should be done about a situation or problem; counsel" (2000, online). The advice-giver offers an opinion about how to solve a particular problem and by doing so implies that the suggested course of action is beneficial to the advice-seeker. In this study, it is my aim to find the particular strategies employed to give advice in 'Lucy Answers'.

This study is organized in four parts (Part I – Part IV) which each include one or several chapters. In Part I, Chapter 2, I will introduce the reader to 'Lucy Answers'. The site with its various functions will be explained in detail and I shall describe the set of question-answer sequences that form the linguistic corpus for this study, as well as explain how this data was prepared for analysis. This material is presented early in the book so that the reader can keep this particular site and its context in mind when being introduced to the literature on advice-giving in different situations.

Part II contains the literature review (Chapter 3) and the research questions (Chapter 4). Previous research on advice has focused on specific contexts that covered areas as varied as phone-in radio shows, medical and student counseling, therapy, or printed advice columns, among others. In Chapter 3, I will give an overview of the variety of advice-giving reported on in these studies. This overview will serve as background against which I can compare the patterns and strategies found in the analysis of 'Lucy Answers'. Chapter 4 will then outline the particular research questions to be explored in the study. They are partly derived from a synthesis of the literature review and partly developed from studying 'Lucy Answers' itself.

Part III contains the analysis chapters. Chapters 5 to 8 focus on the answers by *Lucy*. Chapter 5 deals with the content structure of the problem letter and the linguistic realization of advice in *Lucy*'s answers. The methodology employed will be both quantitative and qualitative. The qualitative component consists of close readings of individual question-answer sequences in order to establish the discursive moves that make up the answer; the quantitative aspect enters the analysis when the results of these close readings are compared in order to identify patterns of advice-giving.

Relational work – the "work" individuals invest in negotiating relationships with others – is at the heart of Chapter 6. In some cultures advice-giving can be a rapport-building strategy and a sign of solidarity or interest. Hinkel (1994, 1997) offers examples of this in his reports on studies of Japanese, Korean, Chinese and Indonesian speakers as well as speakers from Arabic countries.[3] Conversely, within an Anglo-Western context, giving and seeking advice is generally considered to be face-threatening,[4] because of the challenge to "the hearer's identity as a competent and autonomous social actor" (Goldsmith & MacGeorge 2000:235). The asymmetry between the interactants is thus perceived as threatening and, depending on the context in which the advice-giving takes place, it will require mitigation rather than a straightforward realization. Such mitigation may, for example, occur in the form of humor and empathy or lexical hedges such as *maybe* or *perhaps*. This is not to say, however, that advice is linked to mitigation by definition. In some contexts, advice in the form of an unmitigated imperative may be more appropriate than an indirect and/or downtoned rendition of the same content. The realization of advice can be manifold and is neither limited to the performative verb *advise*, nor to any other linguistic realization. Moreover, the appropriate level of relational work accompanying advice will be negotiated on the spot in the interaction in question. In a discursive practice such as 'Lucy Answers', in which the makers have an interest in their advice being taken seriously and readers returning to their site, it will be especially important to look at relational work in detail.

Chapter 7 deals with an aspect that is specific to public advice columns: the site uses a question-answer exchange in letter format to address the issues at hand, rather than, for example, offering a list of problems and their solutions. In other words, the site chooses to imitate a 'private' and 'personal' exchange between an advice-seeker and an advice-giver to address the 'public' readership of the Internet community. I will study how 'Lucy Answers' deals with this clash between the personal and the public dimension. In other words, I will investigate how the site meets its aim to be as relevant as possible to the public readership, while it still keeps up the appearance of a private and personal exchange.

Identifying the linguistic strategies that contribute to the construction of the particular advisor voice employed in 'Lucy Answers' will be central to Chapter 8. The act of giving advice involves asymmetry with respect to authority and expertise. Hutchby (1995:221) maintains that advice-giving "involves a speaker assuming some deficit in the knowledge state of a recipient, advice-giving is an activity which assumes or establishes an asymmetry between the participants". This asymmetry is also part of DeCapua and Dunham's (1993:519) definition of advice. They maintain that advice consists of "opinions or counsel given by people who perceive themselves as knowledgeable, and/or who the advice seeker may think are credible, trustworthy and reliable". Because advice in 'Lucy Answers' is solicited (i.e., readers who have a problem specifically ask for advice), *Lucy*, the fictive advisor, is already granted an authoritative position of expert with respect to the questioner, the advisee, at the outset of the question-answer exchange. In what way *Lucy* emerges as having an advisor-identity will be considered in this chapter.

While the main part of this study focuses on advice and thus on the responses given in 'Lucy Answers', Chapter 9 will look at the problem letters by the anonymous advice-seekers. In analogy to the analysis of the discursive moves in the response letters, the problem letters will be studied by looking at the linguistic realization of questions and requests for advice as well as at the level of relational work. In addition, the textual connections between question and answers will be investigated. In Part IV, I will pull together the lines of argumentation developed in this study and discuss the factors that constitute the discursive practice 'Lucy Answers'.

PART I

CHAPTER 2

Material description

'Lucy Answers', an American Internet advice column

2.1 The site

In this chapter the health question and answer service site called 'Lucy Answers' is described in more detail. The aim is to give the reader an impression of how this Internet site is organized and to explain from where the data for this study is taken. 'Lucy Answers' started in the early 1990s. For its tenth anniversary, a brief historical sketch was published on the Internet. From this we can learn that 'Lucy Answers' started out aiming modestly at only the AEI community as its target audience. A year after its launch, it went online and thus 'global'. Three years later, it started appearing in other college news media, was then published in print, revised its net-appearance, and added an e-mailbox service. In the process of celebrating the tenth anniversary of 'Lucy Answers', yet another overhaul of the site's appearance was launched. The layout described below is of this latter period. The earlier layout (with further improvements) was the one in use while my data collection was under way. However, the actual question-answer sequences, i.e., my data, are not touched by the changes in the layout.

'Lucy Answers' is run by the health education program of AEI and its declared mission is

> to increase access to, and use of, health information by providing factual, in-depth, straight-forward, and nonjudgmental information to assist readers' decision-making about their physical, sexual, emotional, and spiritual health.
>
> (Lucy Answers 2004)

This mission statement is important for this site. As we can see, its aim is to provide information so that the advice-seekers can make up their own minds about issues that are covered in the topic categories. The 'Lucy Answers' team thus hopes to facilitate the readers' decision processes. As one of the 'Lucy Answers' team members states: "We aim to present information in a sophisticated, yet easy-to-comprehend manner, offering options and support, along with our researched content" (personal communication).

In response to 'Who answers the questions?' on the 'Lucy Answers' information site, there is a description of the team which reads as follows:

> ['Lucy Answers'] is supported by a team of [AEI] health educators and health care
> providers, along with information and research specialists from health-related
> organizations worldwide.   (Lucy Answers 2004)

This brief information is expanded if the 'AEI Health Care' icon at the top right-
hand corner of the home page is clicked on. We are taken to a site which is part of
the general Health Services at AEI that tells us more about the Health Education
Program of AEI to which 'Lucy Answers' belongs:

> The original staff numbered one health education professional, with assistance
> from students volunteering as peer educators. Since then, the department's staff
> and working space has grown to six full-time professionals, 7 workstudy students,
> and numerous consultants.   (Health Services 2004)

The professional staff consists of the director, three health educators, a communi-
cations manager, an administrative assistant and a technology coordinator (Health
Services 2004). We can read short biographies of the staff members and find
information on their education, publication, work experience, professional mem-
berships and committee work. The professional staff is supported by a team of
seven students who act as information specialists, project assistants, outreach co-
ordinators and are responsible for office operations. 'Lucy Answers', the website, is
only one responsibility of the Health Education Program team. Others entail "focused workshops and limited publications to comprehensive education and skill-
building via psycho-educational groups, events and campaigns, major on-line and
print publications [...] and other special projects" (Health Services 2004).

In order to fulfill the aim of 'Lucy Answers' to provide quality information
"[r]esponses undergo a standardized review process to insure high quality and ac-
curacy, and announcements of updated content are posted" (Lucy Answers 2004).
According to information which I obtained from one of the staff members, the
'standardized review process' entails that an answer to a question is checked by
several people before it is put online. The answer itself is signed with the name
Lucy, which is the alias for the 'Lucy Answers' team.

'Lucy Answers' is organized into seven different topic categories as presented
in Figure 2.1, which represents a part of the main site as it has been in use since
May 2004. (Since I am not allowed to show screenshots of 'Lucy Answers' for legal
reasons, I have used tabular presentations to explain how readers can navigate.)
The seven topic categories can be found on the left-hand side (Figure 2.1, ❷).
They are 'alcohol and other drugs' (drugs for short), 'fitness and nutrition', 'emotional health', 'general health', 'sexuality', 'sexual health', and 'relationships'. If one
clicks on these main categories, further subcategories will appear. They are listed in

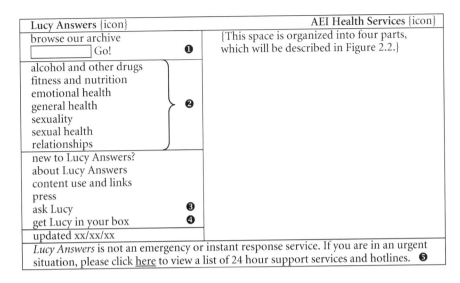

Figure 2.1 The main menu of 'Lucy Answers' (cf. Figure 2.2)

Table 2.1. By clicking on these subcategories, relevant question-answer sequences are opened, which in turn can link to previous questions and answers that are related to this topic. Alternatively, one can also click on the link entitled 'View all Q&As in this category' and see a list of all subject headings.

Questions by advice-seekers are entirely anonymous and come from all age groups, although the site originally was only aimed at students from AEI. Readers can ask their questions by clicking on the 'ask Lucy' link in the left-hand margin below the link for 'press' (Figure 2.1, ❸), which will take them to a question submittal site. There, after an explanatory text, they are asked to fill in two boxes for their subject and question, and they can choose the relevant topic category from a pop-up menu. Their computer identification is scrambled upon submitting their question. According to the fact sheet, 'Lucy Answers' receives nearly 2,000 inquiries a week (Lucy Answers 2004). While all of these are read, only five are answered every week. 'Lucy Answers' makes it clear that it is not an "emergency or instant response service" as indicated by a general disclaimer at the bottom of the main site (Figure 2.1, ❺).

Because 'Lucy Answers' is not a service which guarantees advice for every individual who posts a question, its archive is an integral part of the site since an advice-seeker is much more likely to find information in previous responses to similar questions than to receive a personalized reply. Readers of 'Lucy Answers' are explicitly encouraged to browse the archive in order to find an answer to their problem (e.g., in the instructions on the question submittal site). Searching the archive is made possible by typing in a keyword in the field labeled 'browse our

Table 2.1 Topic categories and their subcategories in 'Lucy Answers' (July 2004)

Category	Subcategories
relationships	'relationship stuff', 'gay, lesbian, bisexual, or questioning', 'nonconsensual relationships', 'talking with parents', 'friendship', 'roommate rumblings', 'miscellaneous'
sexuality	'genital wonderings', 'sexual questions', 'masturbation', 'orgasms', 'kissing', 'sexual secretions', 'tools and toys', 'fetishes and philias', 'erotica and pornography', 'sexual permutations', 'miscellaneous'
sexual health	'reproduction', 'contraception', 'sexually transmitted diseases', 'men's sexual health', 'women's sexual health', 'miscellaneous'
emotional health	'stress and anxiety', 'blues and depression', 'communication concerns', 'obsessive and compulsive behavior', 'child abuse', 'grief and loss', 'counseling', 'medications', 'miscellaneous'
drugs	'alcohol', 'nicotine', 'marijuana', 'club drugs', 'hard drugs', 'inhalants', 'prescription and over-the-counter drugs', 'caffeine and energy-boosting drugs', 'helping and getting help', 'miscellaneous'
fitness and nutrition	'fitness', 'optimal nutrition', 'weight gain and loss', 'food choices and health', 'eating disorders', 'body image', 'miscellaneous'
general health	'body maintenance', 'colds, aches, pains, and other ailments', 'stomach and other gastrointestinal grumblings', 'cancer', 'injuries', 'complementary medicine', 'skin conditions', 'hair', 'oral health', 'eyes', 'sleep', 'body decoration', 'miscellaneous'

archive' in the top left-hand corner of the start page (Figure 2.1, ❶). Results are presented as links to the question-answer sequences most relevant for the search.

The part to the right of the menu on the start page is divided into four sections (Figure 2.2). The first contains the new questions of the week which are displayed on the main site for one week ('new Q&As', ❶), before they are moved to an archive called 'recently posted Q&As' (❸), which is accessible by mouse click right below this section. After a month the questions are moved to the main archive. The five new questions can also be delivered to one's e-mailbox every week. The sign-up button for this service is located as the last option on the menu on the left-hand side ('get Lucy in your box', Figure 2.1, ❹). At times, the slot of 'new Q&As' is also taken up by 'retro Lucy', which means that five previously posted questions and answers are reposted there.

The questions and answers posted in the section called the 'theme of the week' (Figure 2.2, ❷) also appear on the main menu site. They are taken from the archive and are dedicated to one particular topic each week. Previously posted collections can be accessed by mouse click on the button below this category ('recently posted themes', ❺).

The link between 'recently posted Q&As' and 'recently posted themes' is called 'recently updated Q&As' (❹). The 'Lucy Answers' team regularly goes through its archive and updates information previously given. The link leads to such up-

new Q&As ❶	theme of the week ❷
• Healthy vs. unhealthy relationships • Switching birth control pills – Pregnancy risks? • Does my bisexual friend "like" me? • Why can't a women have sex for a few weeks after an abortion? • Sex offender … Forever?	sound of body • Help – My stomach rumbles and grumbles to no end • Stop snoring! • Why do people fart? • Knuckle cracking • During sex, you should: (a) grunt, (b) moan, or (c) talk? • Constant coughing keeps me up at night
recently posted Q&As ❸ recently updated Q&As ❹ recently posted themes ❺	
reader responses ❻	this week's poll ❼

• Ow! How do I deal with red ant bites?
• Natural highs
 	
• **Readers Rave**
	How many hours per weekday do you sit at a computer?
	  o Less than an hour
	  o 1–2
	  o 3–5
	  o 6–8
	  o More than 8 hours
	<div align="right">vote</div>

Figure 2.2 The menu of 'Lucy Answers', cont. (cf. Figure 2.1)

dated records. Information on updates can also be found in the question-answer sequence itself, where the dates of its first publication and possible updates are indicated. This practice means that the archive is not only constantly growing but also changing.

The third part, below the new questions and answers, contains the 'reader responses' with its latest contributions (❻). The links which appear in this section lead directly to the responses. A response archive as such is not directly available from the main menu. To the right of the 'reader responses', the site offers a poll, the topic of which changes every week (❼).

Let us now look at the layout of a question-answer sequence in more detail. If one clicks on any of the links provided in the sections 'new Q&As' or 'theme of the week', the entire space visualized in Figure 2.2 is taken up by the display of the question and answer chosen. One example has already been given in the introduction. Here I have chosen one from the category 'relationships' and the subcategory 'relationship stuff' entitled *Healthy versus unhealthy relationships*. The actual texts of the question and answer are omitted in Figure 2.3 as only the layout is of interest for the moment. As we can see, the advice subcategory is given directly at the top (Figure 2.3, ❶). It is followed by the title of the question-answer sequence (❷) and information about when it was first published and when it was updated (❸). To the right of this is a link which allows this exchange to appear in a printer-friendly format (❹). The texts of the question and answer follow in a separate box (❺). An

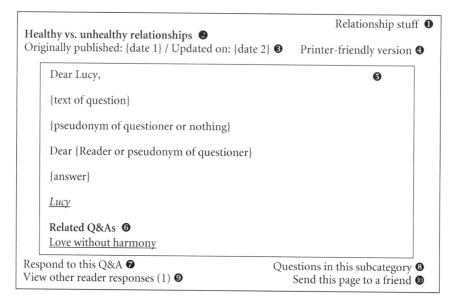

Figure 2.3 Layout of a question-answer sequence, abbreviated (LA 2457)

address form by the advice-seeker is followed by the text of the question. Readers can then use a pseudonym or leave their questions unsigned. *Lucy* will either adopt the pseudonym or use "Dear Reader" as her form of address. Then follows the main text of her answer, which is signed with *Lucy*, a hyperlink leading to the fact sheet of 'Lucy Answers'. After *Lucy*'s signature there is a category for links to related questions and answers (❻). Below this question-answer box are four further links: the first invites readers to react to this posting (❼), the second links back to further questions in this topic subcategory (❽), the third leads to previously posted responses by other readers (❾), and the last one allows you to send this question-answer sequence to a friend in the form of a hyperlink (❿).

2.2 The data for this study

The data for this study is taken from the 'Lucy Answers' web-archive. Data collection took place in August 2002 and in March 2004, which means that all question-answer sequences, or records, published up to this time are part of the corpus. This results in 2,286 question-answer sequences, the distribution of which can be seen in Table 2.2. The overall size of the corpus is 990,036 words, with the answers holding the larger share of 82 percent. The average length of the questions and answers per topic category can also be seen in Table 2.2. The standard deviations (sd) indicate that the lengths of questions and answers vary greatly. With respect to

Table 2.2 Question-answer records in 'Lucy Answers'

topic categories	no. of records	%	no. of words in all questions	average no. of words per question	standard deviation	no. of words in all answers	average no. of words per answer	standard deviation
drugs	155	7	11,673	75	74	65,126	420	233
fitness/nutrition	347	15	21,103	61	51	150,038	432	227
emotional health	150	7	16,069	107	95	65,214	435	277
general health	499	22	32,129	64	62	177,902	357	219
sexuality	392	17	30,199	77	67	104,268	266	171
sexual health	469	21	32,695	70	56	154,789	330	221
relationships	274	12	34,106	124	107	94,725	346	206
total	2,286	100	177,974	78		812,062	355	

content we can see that the category 'general health' has the most records (22%), closely followed by the category 'sexual health' (21%). Next follow the categories 'sexuality' (17%) and 'fitness and nutrition' (15%). This distribution is illustrated in Figure 2.4. Combining the related topics 'sexual health' and 'sexuality', we arrive at 38 percent. If we pair up the categories 'general health' and 'fitness and nutrition', the combined percentage is 37. These two themes are therefore given equal weight in the entire corpus. The other categories are smaller in comparison.

Table 2.2 captures the entire corpus containing the records from the early 1990s until 2004. However, some of the analysis chapters call for a qualitative interpretation of the question-answer sequences. For this reason a subcorpus was compiled with 40 records from each topic category. This corresponds to 12 percent of the entire corpus. I used the length of the answers as a criterion for inclusion. I established how many records occur within every window of 100 words and then calculated the percentage. As a second step, I randomly chose the corresponding number of records for the subcorpus. In other words, I tried to imitate the distribution of answers in each topic category by choosing a proportional number of records per 100 word steps. In this way, I obtained a sample of answers that is as representative as possible for each topic category.

As a case in point, let us look at Figure 2.5 which contains the graphs for the distribution of records in the topic category 'sexuality' for the entire corpus and for the subcorpus in percent. The graphs roughly correspond to each other. Taking the length of the answer in number of words into account when deciding which records to include in the subcorpus thus ensured that the largest number of records chosen for analysis does indeed come from the most representative set of answers with respect to answer length. In the case of the category 'sexuality' this means

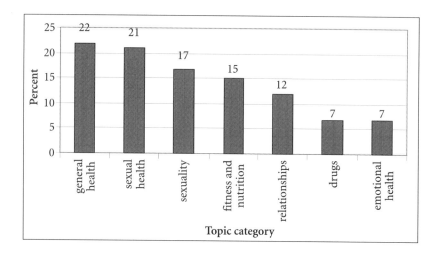

Figure 2.4 The distribution of records in the topic categories in percent in 'Lucy Answers' (100% = 2,286)

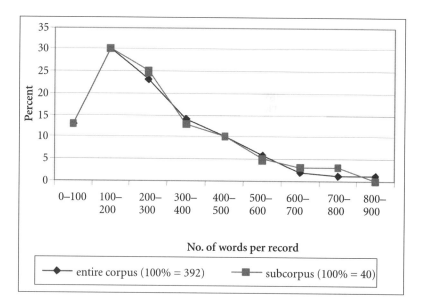

Figure 2.5 The distribution of records in the topic category 'sexuality' in the entire corpus of 'Lucy Answers' and in the subcorpus in percent

that 30 percent of the records analyzed were randomly chosen from answers of between 100 to 200 words. The same criterion for inclusion was applied in the other six topic categories as well.

Table 2.3 Question-answer records in the subcorpus of 'Lucy Answers'

categories	no. of records	no. of words in all questions	average no. of words per question	standard deviation	no. of words in all answers	average no. of words per answer	standard deviation
drugs	40	2,381	60	58	14,735	368	179
fitness/nutrition	40	2,327	58	55	17,037	426	212
emotional health	40	4,835	121	94	15,611	390	217
general health	40	2,632	66	57	13,499	337	191
sexuality	40	2,938	73	54	10,495	262	158
sexual health	40	2,648	66	55	13,017	325	214
relationships	40	3,611	90	76	14,100	353	202
total	280	21,372	76		98,494	352	
% of entire corpus	12	12			12		

Table 2.3 shows the distribution of words in the questions and answers per topic category in the subcorpus. Overall, the 280 records included in this subcorpus make up 12 percent of the entire corpus with respect to the total number of records, length of questions and length of answers. The average length of questions and answers is almost identical to the numbers given in Table 2.2 because of the method of record selection. The standard deviation again varies to a great extent.

In 'Lucy Answers' there is also a reader response section that contains 446 contributions. This corpus is much smaller than the collection of problem and response letters. The topic category that triggers most reader responses is 'relationships' (27%), followed by 'sexuality' (21%). *Lucy* only rarely reacts to the reader responses (n = 61) and if she does answer, the letter is addressed to more than one contributor in 50 percent of all cases. Since my main focus in this study is on the advice given by *Lucy*, I will only rarely refer to this corpus.

Summarizing the most important features of 'Lucy Answers', we can say that this discursive practice is part of a professional and institutional health service that uses the well-established genre of an advice column, i.e., the exchange of a problem letter and a response letter, to complement its services. The mission of 'Lucy Answers' is clearly defined and declares that it operates in the framework of this health education program. The main target readership consists of college students from the home university (AEI), but due to its public Internet appearance, this advice column is accessible to other people as well. Its design is more interactive than a print advice column, since the archive which contains all previously answered problem letters and their answers is an integral part of the site. Readers are encouraged to search this archive before they submit their questions. The content of the response letters stored in the archive is regularly updated to ensure quality advice.

In the next chapter, I will report on previous research on advice in many different contexts. As already pointed out, I see 'Lucy Answers' as presenting one particular form of social practice. Results from previous research will allow me to compare this specific discursive practice with other practices in other contexts.

PART II

CHAPTER 3

Literature review on advice

Giving advice is a common activity in daily life. It can occur on a private and personal level among friends, but it also occurs in institutional settings and often in institutionalized ways. Most studies on advice have been conducted in institutionalized contexts because, on the one hand, researchers can work towards a better understanding of how communication works in general and, on the other hand, such studies can ideally contribute to an amelioration of situations in which it is important that advice is followed, such as medical encounters. Furthermore, the literature on advice has mainly concentrated on spoken, face-to-face settings. Examples are studies dealing with advice in visits by health care nurses to first-time mothers (Heritage & Sefi 1992), HIV counseling sessions (Silverman 1997, among others), medical encounters more generally (e.g., Leppänen 1998; Pilnick 1999, 2001; Sarangi & Clarke 2002), student counseling (Bresnahan 1992; Erickson & Shultz 1982; He 1994) or advice on call-in radio (Gaik 1992; Hudson 1990; Hutchby 1995). However, the printed genre of advice columns has received some attention in the advice literature as well (Currie 2001; Franke 1997; Gough & Talbot 1996; Hendley 1977; Kreuz & Graesser 1993; Mininni 1991; Mutongi 2000; Talbot 1992, 1995; Thibault 1988, 2002). What all of these studies show is that every individual type of advice-giving deserves to be examined in its own right. In Leppänen's (1998:210) words, this means that "the study of advice should both carefully explicate the details of the production of advice and show how these details are systematic products of the interactants' orientations to specific features of the institutions". It is my aim in this study to approach 'Lucy Answers' in this manner.

The term 'Community of Practice' is particularly useful here. For my purposes, I follow Eckert and McConnell-Ginet (1992b) who define 'Community of Practice' as

> an aggregate of people who come together around mutual engagement in an endeavour. Ways of doing things, ways of talking, beliefs, values, power relations – in short, practices – emerge in the course of this mutual endeavour. As a social construct, a Community of Practice is different from the traditional community, primarily because it is defined simultaneously by its membership and by the practice in which that membership engages.
>
> (quoted from Sunderland & Litosseliti 2004:16)

The interactants who come together in the Community of Practice 'Lucy Answers' are the team of professionals who stand for *Lucy* and the health service of AEI, the questioners who ask for advice, and the Internet readership. What makes this practice different from many others previously investigated (cf. Meyerhoff 2002) is that the players do not meet in physical space, but use the Internet as a platform where they engage with each other and co-construct the social practice of advice-giving that is particular to them. This issue will be further discussed in the final chapter of this study.

In the first part of the literature review (Sections 3.1–3.5), I will report on results from the following fields of study: advice in face-to-face health care settings, advice in face-to-face educational counseling, radio advice programs, advice in therapeutic contexts and everyday advising. All of these fields are relevant to the present investigation because they touch on aspects that are important for 'Lucy Answers' as a public, institutionalized health care service that offers expert counseling and advice. In the second part of the literature review (Section 3.6), I will focus on previous research on advice columns in particular. This detailed literature review will allow me, as a next step, to understand better how advice is realized in 'Lucy Answers', the Community of Practice chosen for analysis in this study.

3.1 Advice in face-to-face health care settings

There are several important studies focusing on advice in medical settings that should be reported on in this section. A seminal study is Heritage and Sefi's (1992) investigation of the communicative practice of health visitors to first-time mothers in Britain. As their work inspired many other studies, I will talk about it in some detail. Then I will briefly look at research in connection with HIV counseling (e.g., Silverman et al. 1992a; Kinnell & Maynard 1996), Leppänen's (1998) study on patient-nurse interaction and Pilnick's (1999, 2001) work on patient-pharmacist interaction. Remarks on Sarangi and Clarke's research (2002) on genetics risk communication conclude this section.

Heritage and Sefi (1992) focus on the problematic of requesting, delivering and receiving advice in one specific situation of health visits. The data on which Heritage and Sefi base their study is a corpus of eight audio-tape recordings (4.5 hours) of the initial visits of health visitors to first-time mothers. These visits were unannounced, although they were expected to occur during the first days after a child's birth. Mothers dislike these unannounced visits, probably because they attribute the character of control and surveillance to them (1992:412). Mothers viewed their health visitors as "baby experts", and felt that their knowledge and competence as mothers were being evaluated (1992:366). A certain reluctance by the mothers to request advice can be accounted for by their fear of judgments about their mothering skills. Heritage and Lindström (1998), work-ing with the same data, point out the moral dimension of these advice encounters. While moral norms of what constitutes being a good mother are not *per se* a pri-mary topic of conversations, "these medical encounters are drenched with implicit moral judgments, claims and obligations" (1998: 398).

Health visitors gave advice in different ways. They could use overt recommen-dations (*"I would recommend giving her a ba:th every da:y."*), the imperative mood (*"No always be ve:ry very qui:et at ni:ght."*), modal verbs of obligation (*"And I think you should involve your husband as much as possible no::w."*), and less commonly factual generalization (*"Lots of mums do: progress to thuh terrries when they're a bit older."*) (Heritage & Sefi 1992: 368–369). However, in general, health visitors "delivered their advice explicitly, authoritatively and in so decided a fashion as to project their relative expertise on health and baby-management issues beyond any doubt" (1992: 369).

Heritage and Sefi (1992) identified several advice-giving patterns in their data. First they distinguished between mother-initiated advice and health visitor-initiated advice. Mother-initiated advice was relatively infrequent and could take the form of a direct and straightforward request, which generally took the pat-tern of question-answer sequences. Often mothers preferred to display certain knowledge in the problem area. This was frequently achieved through the use of 'closed' questions (yes/no), where the health visitor "is merely invited to confirm the viewpoint embedded in the mother's enquiry" (1992: 371). This procedure carries the risk that the health visitor will contradict the mother's point of view. Mothers could also solicit advice by describing "a state of affairs as problematic" (1992: 372). This is a more cautious and indirect way of requesting advice.

Heritage and Sefi found that advice-giving initiated by the health visitors pre-dominated in the corpus. Often the health visitors delivered advice without a clear indication that it was desired (1992: 377). Overall, Heritage and Sefi identified a stepwise entry into advice by health visitors:

Step 1: HV [Health visitor]: initial inquiry.
Step 2: M [Mother]:   problem-indicative response.
Step 3: HV: focusing inquiry into the problem.
Step 4: M: responsive detailing.
Step 5: HV: advice giving.   (Heritage & Sefi 1992: 379)

These five steps represent the most detailed pattern; in other words, some steps can be left out. Heritage and Sefi (1992: 389) observe that only minimal preparation for advice-giving occurs in the majority of advice-giving initiated by the health visi-tors. However, they suggest that "the extent of this preparation ... may strongly influence the subsequent reception of advice". They therefore also investigated the reception of advice by the mothers and distinguished between three different types: marked acknowledgment, unmarked acknowledgment and the assertion of knowledge or competence (1992:391). In marked acknowledgment, mothers respond by accepting the information they are presented with; they acknowledge its character of advice. A marked acknowledgement sometimes includes the repetition of elements of the advice given. Interestingly, Heritage and Sefi found that this type of reception is relatively rare. In unmarked acknowledgment, mothers avoid acknowledging that the information is helpful and thus do not openly accept the advice. Heritage and Sefi (1992:391) argue that this form of reception "may imply rejection of the advice that is given" and constitutes a passive form of resistance. Assertion of knowledge or competence was the third strategy observed. Mothers use this procedure of reception to give an assertion of their knowledge and competence, thus implying that the advice given by the health visitor is redundant.

In the discussion of their results, Heritage and Sefi (1992:409–410) point out that (1) health visitors initiated and delivered advice in a predominantly unilateral way, (2) little effort was made to acknowledge the competences that the mothers displayed and (3) three quarters of health visitors who initiated advice-giving met with either passive or active resistance on the part of the mothers. Finally, Heritage and Sefi offer four possible and partial explanations for the health visitors' persistence in the apparently unproductive process of self-initiated advice-giving. A first reason may be that the health visitors' background as trained nurses might incline them towards an "identification, diagnosis and treatment" approach (1992:411); secondly, health visitors are generally pessimistic about the knowledge of first-time mothers; thirdly, advice-giving offers the health visitors the possibility of displaying their expertise in contrast to the mothers'; and fourthly, health visitors are obliged to visit mothers with young children, advice-giving may thus serve as a legitimization approach or "ticket of entry" (1992:412).

From the late 1980s onwards, a group of researchers have dedicated their research efforts to optimizing counseling practices in the context of HIV centers and clinics (e.g., Bulcaen 1997; Kinnell 2002; Kinnell & Maynard 1996; Miller & Bor 1988; Peräkylä 1993, 1995; Peräkylä & Silverman 1991; Silverman 1989, 1990, 1994, 1997; Silverman & Peräkylä 1990; Silverman et al. 1992a, 1992b). Their methodology is predominantly conversation analytical combined with an ethnographic approach. This means that they study "special characteristics of counselling as a structure of communication" over a longer period of time and in detail (Peräkylä & Silverman 1991). From the description of the patterns they identify, they offer suggestions to improve counseling, to better render advice, and to contribute to the understanding of communication in general. Advice in the context of AIDS is especially delicate because of the taboo topic of sexuality and the seriousness of the illness. Furthermore, it is particularly difficult because counselors are pressed for time and cannot adjust to every patient in such a way that advice is rendered in the best way.

In their 1992b study of seven hospital centers in England and the USA, Silverman et al. summarize the overall structure of counseling observed in their previous research. They maintain that research "demonstrated that HIV counsellors use one of two kinds of communication formats as their 'home base': an Interview Format (in which Cs [counselors] asks [sic.] questions and Ps [patients] give answers) and an Information-Delivery Format (in which Cs deliver information and Ps are silent apart from small acknowledgment tokens)" (1992b: 176). They also maintain that advice-giving in itself is an unstable format in that counselors often switch between the different formats (Silverman et al. 1992b: 185). In the Information-Delivery format, patient acknowledgments are optional and when patients give any, "they do not implicate themselves in any future lines of faction [sic.] because they are only responding to what can be heard as information and not necessarily advice" (1992b: 184). Silverman et al. (1992b: 184) thus argue that "by constructing advice sequences that can be heard as information-delivery, counsellors manage to stabilize advice-giving". A further advantage of information-delivery is that "it neatly handles many of the issues of delicacy that can arise in discussing sexual behavior" (Silverman et al. 1992b: 185). Silverman and Peräkylä (1990: 300) thus report that "[m]uch of the talk about 'dreaded issues' in our corpus takes place within an Information Delivery footing".

The authors found that an interview format does not mean that the patient cannot be given the latest expert information. On the contrary, it "is highly compatible with delivering that information in a way specifically designed for its recipient, following a long question-answer sequence in the interview-format" (Peräkylä & Silverman 1991: 648). They also found that, because "[t]runcated, non-personalized advice sequences are usually far shorter", they may be the more efficient alternative for counselors than giving advice in a step-by-step manner (Silverman et al. 1992b: 185). In comparison to Heritage and Sefi's (1992) work, there were fewer cases of patient-initiated advice or demonstration of patient competence and seven cases where patients summarized the content of the sessions that did not contain any overt advice-giving (Silverman et al. 1992b: 179).

Basing their study of 25 HIV pretest counseling sessions in a clinic on the work by Heritage and Sefi (1992) and by Silverman et al., Kinnell and Maynard (1996) find similar patterns. In particular, they confirm the preference for non-personal recommendations (rather than making advice personally relevant to the particular client). Kinnel and Maynard (1996: 413) identified five strategies of giving advice, of which option 2b and 2c together constitute the majority (54 out of 72):

1. Client initiated
2. Counselor initiated
   a. Full stepwise entry (Heritage & Sefi 1992)
   b. Advice after information

c. Advice after proposing a hypothetical situation
d. Advice as information (Kinnel & Maynard 1996:413)

In particular, Kinnel and Maynard (1996:417) discuss hypothetical advice sequences which constitute an ambiguous way of giving advice in that "it is not
readily apparent whether the counselor is advising this client in particular or just
providing information that could and would be given to any person". The client
can therefore decide for him- or herself whether or not to reject the hypothetical
situation and the advice that is connected to it. The advantage of this strategy is
that delicate topics need not be personalized (Kinnel & Maynard 1996:430).

Leppänen (1998) also based her research question and methodology on Heritage and Sefi's (1992) study. She examined advice-giving interactions between
Swedish district nurses and patients with respect to initiation, rendition and up-
take of advice. 32 videotaped meetings were analyzed. Sixteen occurred at the
patients' homes, the others in a primary care center. She then compared her results
with the British findings. Leppänen (1998:218) identified four types of patient-
initiated advice: (1) proposing courses of action, (2) detailing problems within
topical environments already established by the nurses' questions, (3) detailing un-
toward states of affairs and (4) presenting parts of their bodies. A direct question
occurred only once.

Nurses initiated advice "after having *observed a possible problem* that indicated
that the patient was in need of medical advice" (Leppänen 1998:220, italics in
original). They could give advice immediately after a problem had appeared, talk
about some aspect of a problem before giving advice or give advice after other,
unrelated activities were completed (Leppänen 1998:223). Their advice "regularly
consists of three components: (a) a part that *proposes a course of action*, (b) a set
of characteristic *body movements* and (c) an *account* that supports the proposed
course of action" (Leppänen 1998:223, italics in original). Furthermore, courses
of action were proposed in four ways: (1) in an imperative mood, (2) with modal
verbs of obligation, (3) as "presentations of proposed actions as alternatives"
and (4) as "descriptions of patients' future actions" (Leppänen 1998:225). Body
movements were found to support the rendition of advice. Leppänen (1998:235)
summarizes that

> [i]n general, district nurses, like health visitors, designed advice in rather straight-
> forward ways. The straightforwardness of district nurses' advice is amplified by
> their use of accounts and body movements: Nurses postpone other activities, gaze
> at the patients, and wave their fingers back and forth as they give advice. District
> nurses used imperatives and modal verbs of obligation when patients seemed to
> understand that they had problems but not their solutions. District nurses did not
> form advice as recommendations or factual generalizations. Instead, they some-
> times designed advice as *alternatives* or as *descriptions of patients' future actions*.

> These two more mitigated forms were used when patients did not even seem to
> understand that there was an issue.   (Leppänen 1998:235; emphasis in original)

In examining their responses to advice, Leppänen (1998:237) found that Swedish
patients are straightforward and their answers are usually either in the form of
marked acknowledgments or overt rejections.

Pilnick (1999, 2001) investigates the counseling given by pharmacists to patients or carers in a hospital in the UK. Her data consists of 45 tape recorded
consultations. Like Heritage and Sefi or Silverman, Pilnick aims at identifying
the practice of this particular counseling situation. She identified the following
elements that occur in her data:

> Opening/Identification/Recognition/Acknowledgment
> Greeting
> Approach to advice giving
> Arrival at advice giving
> Acceptance/Rejection of Intention
> (Rearrival)
> Delivery of advice/information
> Response to advice/information
> Close implicature
> (Questions/Reclose implicature)
> Exit   (Pilnick 2001:1942)

The "approach to advice giving" could be accomplished by a question, a statement, or dispensed with altogether (2001:1939). Of special interest is her discussion of advice as opposed to information giving. This difference is not always clear-cut, neither in the literature nor in naturalistic data. Heritage and
Sefi (1992) argue that information is factual and non-normative, while advice
is normative and almost has a moral dimension (Pilnick 1999:614). Conversely,
Silverman (1997:154) maintains that non-personalized information can be interpreted as advice in the appropriate context. He maintains that this occurs within
the "Advice-as-Information" sequences. As we have seen earlier, this kind of advice is less face-threatening to the advisee because he or she can interpret it as not
relevant, or relevant for others rather than for the advisee him- or herself. Pilnick
(1999:616) concludes her discussion of advice as opposed to information giving
by saying that "the only valid distinction that can be made between 'information'
and 'advice' is a member's distinction". Therefore the responses by the clients need
to be included in an interpretation. The results of Pilnick's (1999:621) analysis
show that

> [p]rofessionals in any service encounter may package details as normative or
> nonnormative, as fact or opinion, and there are a range of responses that may

be forthcoming to both approaches. Thus, fact may be treated as opinion, and normative statements may receive only a very limited acknowledgement. Unfortunately for the professional, only some of these responses will actually indicate that the client has taken on board what has been said.   (Pilnick 1999:621)

The last study to be reported on in this section is by Sarangi and Clarke (2002), who investigate how genetic counselors and clients manage genetics risks communication. In this speech activity "professionals and clients discuss issues related to disorders that are, or may be, genetic in origin" (e.g., risks about a disease, about the likelihood of a future child being ill, etc.; 2002:143). They focus on the role of the counselors who are faced with a particularly challenging situation since they have to engage in "expert talk about uncertainty while assessing and communicating risk" (2002:145). In addition, there is a "tension between clients seeking an authoritative, definitive risk assessment" (139) and the experts, who, on the one hand, are aware of the limit of their professional knowledge, and, on the other hand, strongly adhere to "the slogan of nondirectiveness" (166). Sarangi and Clarke (2002:145) found that the counselors and the clients use a set of discursive resources such as "explicit formulations of claiming insufficient knowledge", "reference to other sources of expertise", "use of hedges", "rhetorical strategies such as contrast" and "reinforcement of mutual knowledge". The adherence to non-directiveness in counseling is said to benefit the counselors not only as a way of managing uncertainty, but also because it protects the counselors to a greater degree from clients who want to sue them, and because "it makes their work emotionally easier through discouraging overinvolvement with clients and by ensuring ... shared decision making" (2002:166; emphasis removed).

From the studies of advice in face-to-face health care environments mentioned in this brief overview, we can make use of several important findings and observations. Firstly, several researchers have pointed out the face-threatening character of advice to which some advisors try to adapt by adjusting their rendition of advice. Secondly, more neutral realizations of advice, such as information-delivery, leave it up to the advisee whether he or she recognizes it as advice. Information-delivery can thus be seen as one possible form of mitigation. Thirdly, there may be ideals of counseling such as non-directiveness which crucially influence the discursive practice. Fourthly, while the case studies mentioned have shown similarities in the rendition of advice, they did not identify one single and universal pattern of how advice is realized. The contexts of the studies differed, so that we cannot label them as representing 'advice in medical encounters' in general. Nevertheless, it was shown that the way in which advice is rendered, especially in the contexts concerned with AIDS, displayed topic sensitivity. Finally, the studies which took the reaction to advice into account mentioned a variety of possibilities for the advisees as well – from marked acknowledgement to silence – which differed from study to study.

3.2 Advice in face-to-face educational counseling

In an educational context, advising students is an important and integral part of everyday life. In this section, I will introduce the studies of three researchers who focus on advice in educational counseling: Bresnahan (1992), Vehviläinen (2001, 2003) and He (e.g., 1994).

Bresnahan (1992:22) studied fourteen advising interviews with respect to conflict of advisor roles and "use of foot-in-the-door (FITD) or door-in-the-face (DITF) strategies". I intend to focus on the conflicting advisor roles here. Bresnahan (1992:229) summarizes that "[m]oment by moment, [advisors] must decide whether their role as student advocate or institutional gatekeeper is paramount. Often, these roles are contradictory." Advisors can thus oscillate between a more integrative, collaborative style (student advocate) and a divisive, confrontational style (gatekeeper) (1992:232). Gatekeeping can be manifested by

> (a) invoking official rules and policies, (b) jumping-the-starting-gun tactics such as stating official positions before eliciting student premises, (c) "stopping and frisking" (Erickson & Shultz 1982:25), (d) advisor hyperexplanation (a verbal overpowering move) which invokes positional authority, (e) using other detrimental conversational strategies which cause the student to lose face, (f) limited concession making from the outset of negotiation, (g) using positive and negative altercasting (statements suggesting a course of action that might have better been followed), and (h) distributive orientation.   (Bresnahan 1992:231)

Bresnahan (1992:246) concludes that "[t]he transcripts repeatedly show that gatekeeping style, which is more dynamic, more intrusive, and more directly interventionist, accelerates interpersonal conflict and shifts focus from issues to personalities". This influenced the quality of advice-giving. In non-conflicting interviews, the quality and quantity of help was higher.

Vehviläinen (2001) analyses advice-giving within Finnish labor market training. She observes that "elicitation of the advisee's perspective enables the professional to fit their advice with it, create alignment between the perspectives, and minimize resistance" (2001:371). She identifies two variations of the counseling pattern. In the first, the counselor asks questions to topicalize or to elicit the student's opinion. Then the student responds by confirming or displaying the elicited opinion. The sequence is completed by the counselor who gives advice that is grounded in the view established in the prior turns. The second variation starts with an activation of a problem by the counselor who thus elicits the student's plans regarding a particular task. Then the student responds by describing these plans, ideas and intentions. Finally, the counselor gives advice by commenting on and evaluating the student's response. Vehviläinen (2001: 394) points out that "[i]n practices in which it is considered important that professionals' advice is accepted by the clients, it is useful to produce an aligning position for the advice to minimize resistance". She further emphasizes that her study "adds to the picture of questioning as the 'home base' interactional format of counseling" (2001: 396) identified by Peräkylä and Silverman (1991) and Silverman (1997). In her 2003 article, Vehviläinen draws on the same data, but discusses how counselors react to problematic requests for advice by the students. Such instances were difficult when they ran counter to the ideological counseling aim of non-directiveness (cf. Sarangi & Clarke 2002). In other words, the students should be the "agents of the activities, planning and decision-making involved in the counselling process" (Vehviläinen 2003: 392). She reports that counselors either withhold advice until later and shape the interaction into a questioning sequence, or they respond to the request but sanction it afterwards.

He (1993, 1994, 1995, 1996a, 1996b; He & Keating 1991) studies academic counseling sessions in an American context. In her 1994 study, she focuses on the clashes of expectations that derive from the students who turn to counselors for advice, while counselors are officially directed not to give personal opinions and to let students make up their own minds (He 1994: 314). Such clashes are similar to the events Vehviläinen (2003) described. In He's (1994: 313) data, counselors avoided answering two types of questions: "those concerning their personal opinions and judgments and those which may not warrant a definite answer". He (1994) also found that

> if questions or issues raised by the students are attended to and directly addressed by the counselor, there are usually visible interactional signs which indicate that both parties have oriented themselves to the sequential demands of questions-answers and have met these demands. These signs include an enthusiastic uptake of the response to the question (e.g., overlapped receipt tokens, receipt tokens indicative of the news value of the counselor's response), eagerness to follow up on the response, and a readiness of both parties to move on to the next topic.
>
> (He 1994: 310)

Both advisees and advisors thus adjust to the advice-giving situation by orienting themselves to the question-answer pattern.

Again, we have seen in these case studies that advising is a complicated interactional achievement – especially if the advisors care about the outcome of their advising, i.e., about whether or not the advisees follow the advice given, and if there are institutional constraints on advice-giving as seen in the ideal of non-directiveness. Arriving at an alignment of the students with the counselors augments the likelihood that the advice given is adopted. In these specific contexts, the question-answer format seems to promise more success.

3.3 Radio advice programs: The public dimension

Advice in the public context of radio programs has been discussed by several researchers. Here I will comment on Hutchby (1995), DeCapua and Dunham (1993), Gaik (1992) and Hudson (1990) because they all focus on different aspects of advice in this public setting.

Hutchby (1995) analyses how the expert on a radio phone-in show manages the tension between the 'personal' and 'public' dimension of advice-giving. This tension was already shown in the introduction to be important in such a public context. The data of this study consists of approximately three hours of talk broadcast on the Robbie Vincent Show, Radio London, in summer 1985. There are four parties involved in this particular program: "the advice-seeking caller, the advice-giving expert, the nonexpert host, and the overhearing audience" (Hutchby 1995:220). Hutchby investigated how advice was designed to be relevant for a range of participants, "not just the individual advice-seeker (the caller), but the many potential constituencies represented by the overhearing audience" (Hutchby 1995:222). He thus detects a "'tension' between the personal concerns of the caller-at-hand, whose advice request represents the focus of the call, and the public nature of the call as spate of broadcast talk" (Hutchby 1995:222) and sets out to investigate how the interactants deal with this tension. Hutchby identified two ways in which the interactants modulated their answers. The first concerns the expert who displayed "a tendency to answer more than the question and to package advice as a general prescription" (1995:236). Hutchby thus identified a two-part format, consisting of an answer to the caller's question and "an *auxiliary* response in which subsidiary information or advice is conveyed" (1995:223). The expert is thus "both exhibiting his knowledgeability and 'doing expertise', while at the same time exhibiting his sensitivity to the public context in which he is deploying that expertise" (Hutchby 1995:228). The second way to modulate an answer concerns the host, who, "although not himself a ratified advice-giver, nonetheless can become involved in the provision of advice by working to convey auxiliary advice through the strategy of proxy questioning. This technique allows the host to propose lines of advice without actually encroaching on the specialist territory of the expert" (1995:236). These proxy questions are labeled as "nonnaive" because they are meant to point to another aspect of the problem and elicit a relevant response to benefit the audience. In that sense they can represent advice in themselves as well (1995:232). Finally, Hutchby observes that both host and expert try to return to the caller's particular problem at the end of a call. In this way "a recognition of the personal dimension represented by the caller at hand either remains in play or at some stage is brought back into play" (1995:234).

Like Hutchby, DeCapua and Dunham (1993) emphasize the public context of the two American radio advice programs they investigated. While experts clearly try to support their callers, they also try to reach "the wider listening audience who may have similar problems" (1993:529). DeCapua and Dunham (1993) also point out that in their particular radio shows "the interactions taking place are not occurring solely for the benefit of the interlocutors themselves, but are instead functioning as entertainment and sources of information for a wider listening audience". DeCapua and Huber (1995) take up this tension between public and personal advice and discuss it in the light of how authority and expertise are established. They maintain that in public contexts such as radio shows "authority is assumed and granted through public assent. This authority does not include any presumption of caring or intimacy for an individual advice-seeker" (DeCapua & Huber 1995:121). DeCapua and Dunham (1993:519) found that the principal strategies of the advice-seekers seem to be explanation, elaboration, and narration, while the advice-givers appear to have three major goals: "to help callers clarify their problems, to help them explore their options, and to offer direction, usually regarding some action to be taken in the future".

Gaik (1992), focusing on radio talk-show therapy and working with American data, is interested in psychotherapy and therapeutic discourse with its classical ideals of non-directiveness and facilitating self-knowledge. Counseling, conversely, is seen as a more directive mode of interaction and is described as "a process designed to help a person answer the question 'What shall I do?' (Tyler 1961)" (Gaik 1992:276). In this context, 'counseling' is thus not defined as non-directive, as was the case in the other studies previously mentioned. Gaik asks how radio talk-shows with their goal of "discussion, introspection, and advice" (1992:273) manage the contrast between the practices of counseling and those of psychotherapy. In doing so, he concentrates on the use of "irrealis, non-factive modality, and references to possible worlds in the conversations, demonstrating how they orient patients and doctors to the goals of the phone call" (1992:273). Irrealis refers to such verbs as *could, would, might, can* and *may* that point toward "possibility, epistemic necessity (tentative inference), prediction, and which do not typically involve human judgement about what is or is not likely to happen" (Quirk et al. 1972; as quoted in Gaik 1992:277). As irrealis is used to describe non-factive matters, the interactants can use it to mitigate the illocutionary force of an utterance. Gaik (1992:277) argues that, in addition, its pragmatic character needs to be studied. Gaik finds that the therapeutic and the counseling mode are both part of the radio talk-shows. He summarizes the pragmatics of irrealis as follows:

> [I]n the talk-show conversations whose mode is primarily therapeutic, irrealis serves a crucial and necessary function to help the caller and doctor search for possible unique sources of the caller's anxiety and to promote introspection. When introspection becomes counterproductive, however, the therapist can **deem** (Grice 1982:242) irrealis to be irrelevant and can turn instead to making norma-

tive statements about what seems to be the unchanging nature of the social world.

(Gaik 1992:284–285, emphasis in original)

Gaik also points out that talk-show therapy has a public and commercial quality. The audience expects to hear a competent doctor who is therefore under constant pressure to perform adequately. In Gaik's radio talk-show data, there is a severe time constraint (of usually only five minutes per caller). In addition, radio does not tolerate so-called "dead air", i.e., silence. This is in sharp contrast to therapy sessions, where silence is often considered significant and productive (Gaik 1992:275).

Hudson (1990) looks at gardening advice in one Californian radio broadcast called "The Garden Show". The interactions of 23 different callers with the expert and authority named 'the Garden Lady' during their two-hour broadcast were analyzed. Hudson looked at how advice is realized, whether it occurs in its "prototypical grammatical form for directive advice" which is "the non-agent imperative of the form 'Go ahead and do it' or perhaps just 'Do it'" (1990:285), or whether it is softened by "interpersonal markers" (1990:286). Hudson also argues that in this context, recommendations and knowledge presentation can be regarded as advice. He thus refrains from any analytic distinction between advice and directives (1990:286).

Hudson (1990:288–289) found that there were two text structures in a call: the first he calls a diagnosis text, in which the problem is explained and discussed, the second is termed a how-to text, in which the action that is to be done is explained. Mitigation was found predominantly in the how-to texts. Hudson identified several strategies that de-emphasized agency. These are pseudo-cleft sentences, conditionals, and sentences in the form *I would do X* (1990:288). He also points out that several strategies can be combined to form the directive. While the agent is often "de-focused", this does not mean that "the hearer does not recognize him/herself as the potential agent" (1990:289). Hudson carries out a detailed analysis of the structure of advice in his data. He looks at:

> non-subject imperative,
> the agent imperative with 'you' subject present,
> pseudo-cleft constructions,
> the *I would* projection,
> *Other as Agent* constructions, and
> conditionals.   (Hudson 1990:290)

The first and second categories consist of the pattern '*V + O*' and '*you + modality + V*'. Hudson (1990:290) argues that imperatives that appear together with a modal verb are not presented as agentful – or at least to a lesser degree than imperatives that follow the pattern '*V + O*'. Examples are (3.1) and (3.2):

(3.1) ... and then you'*ll* start working from the outside.   (1990:290, example 11)

(3.2) Keep it in a room that stays cool.   (1990:293, example 17)

A combination of a pseudo-cleft and an *I would* construction is represented in example (3.3):

(3.3) What I would do is wait until they drop all their ro ... all their leaves this
        winter ...   (1990:293, example 18)

Hudson (1990:293) maintains that "the use of the pseudo-cleft apparently de-emphasizes the agent of the action and focuses on the action or state itself". It is thus used as a mitigator.

Others as Agents-strategies include the *I would*-constructions as well as 'I + V', and can be summarized as 'speaker as agent'-strategy. Of the 29 occurrences in Hudson's corpus, 26 took the form of *I would*. Again it is clear that the "advisee is the intended agent" (1990:294). Another alternative is that the advisor "posits some third person who is neither the speaker nor the listener as agent" (1990:293). This occurred seven times in the corpus. Example (3.4) is a case in point:

(3.4) It [the plant] wants a nice bright location indoors.   (1990:294, example 25)

The final category that Hudson investigates in more detail is conditionals. The agency of the directives in conditionals was expressed in the forms discussed above, i.e., through imperative, pseudo-cleft and *Others as Agents* structures. *If*-clauses preceding the main clause were found eighteen times, while *if*-clauses following the main clauses only occurred four times (1990:294). *If*-clauses were combined with imperatives in ten cases, with *I would* in four, with *other as agent* in seven, and with a pseudo-cleft in one case (1990:295). In his conclusion, Hudson (1990:296) summarizes that the 'Garden Lady' generally avoids explicit commands which mention the caller as agent when issuing directives. She prefers to couch the projected agent of the directive with the help of interpersonal moderation, i.e., mitigation.

The discussion of the case studies on radio talk-shows dealing with advice has shown that the public dimension is of the utmost importance. Ultimately, the wider audience is targeted. At the same time, the advisors try to cater to the needs of their particular callers. The advisors are granted authority by public assent. Furthermore, Hudson's detailed linguistic analysis has given us several examples of realizations of advice that will be worth investigating in other data, especially with respect to mitigation.

3.4 Advice in therapeutic contexts

Gaik's (1992) study of therapeutic and counseling discourse in a radio show has already been mentioned. He argues that counseling or giving advice is fundamentally different from therapeutic discourse. The latter aims at non-directiveness, while counseling is a more directive mode of interaction (1992:276). This distinction explains why Labov and Fanshel's (1977) classic study of the therapeutic interview is not so much concerned with advice itself, but with showing in a turn-by-turn analysis how a particular patient and her therapist interact and work on achieving the patient's introspection which should lead to change or transformation. We have seen, however, that other studies have mentioned an ideal of non-directiveness for contexts that are also categorized as 'counseling'. It is therefore important to investigate the propagated ideals for every individual context.

Issues that are dealt with in a therapeutic, face-to-face context can also emerge in other frameworks such as Internet forums where advice is likely to play a greater role. Lebow (1998) investigates the usefulness of Internet resources for patients. He comes to the conclusion that, while there are many mutual support and information sharing groups in the Internet, "chat groups and newsgroups are not a substitute for therapy" (Lebow 1998:204). The usefulness and effectiveness of such forms of interaction, however, still need to be scientifically evaluated. Suffice it to say here that the Internet provides an opportunity for topics to be publicly discussed that would otherwise be restricted to therapy groups or individual treatments. The boundary between advice-giving, counseling and therapy are thus blurred in many instances on the Internet.

One particular study of Internet interaction by Miller and Gergen (1998) should be introduced in the literature review on advice because their coding method is important for my later investigations. Miller and Gergen (1998) are interested in what ways computer networking practices are comparable to face-to-face therapy. They investigated posts on an AOL electronic bulletin board devoted to the topic of suicide, collected over an eleven-month period (232 posts by 98 contributors). These posts were coded with respect to discursive moves, the "kind of contribution that the entry made to the ongoing interchange" (1998:192), and classified into five broad categories of discourse: help-seeking, informative, supportive, growth-promoting and punitive interchanges (1998:193). Several discursive moves could occur per post, which resulted in 564 coded actions and an average of 2.43 moves per post (1998:194). (Note, however, that the study makes no mention of the sequence of discursive moves, i.e., of how they follow each other.) The discursive moves assigned to every category are presented in the following list together with their number and frequency of occurrence taken from the results section (1998:194–198):

1. **Help-seeking interchange** includes the coding categories:
    - *request for help* with a personal problem (n = 17);
    - *problem disclosure* (reveals a personal problem, complains of short-comings, stresses, worries, etc.) (17,9%).

2. **Informative interchange** includes the coding categories:
    - *request for information* on the problem situation (n = 54, 10%);
    - *advice offered* or suggestion made for actions to alleviate the suffering or problem situation (n = 66, 11%);
    - *prediction* for the future (n = 11, 2%).

3. **Supportive interchange** includes the coding categories:
    - *empathy* (identifying the problem as one which is also shared by the respondent, or with which the respondent is personally familiar) (n = 101, 18%);
    - *support* of another through agreement, congratulations, boosting of esteem, etc. (e.g., "you sound like a bright person", "you give good advice") (n = 97, 17%);
    - *gratitude* for something said or implied (n = 33, 6%);
    - *normalization* of a stated problem (indicating its commonly shared features) (n = 14, 2%);
    - *humor* giving a positive or light touch to the problem statement (n = 7, 1%);
    - *attraction*, warmth, or love directly expressed (none).

4. **Growth-promoting interchange** includes the coding categories:
    - *interpretation* of the psychological, social, ideological, or material roots of the problem in question (n = 3);
    - *reframing* of the problem or complaint (offering alternative means of constructing the events or actions in question) (n = 4);
    - *metacommentary* on the individual's relationships or the interchange itself (how the network conversation is proceeding, or might otherwise be directed) (n = 2);
    - *challenges to authority* (e.g., therapists, parents, societal values) designed to help the individual challenge existing structures, demands, or expectations (n = 13, 2%).

5. **Punitive interchange** includes the coding categories:
    - *refutation* (doubt in the individual's description or account of the problem) (n = 18, 3%);
    - *critique* or condemnation of the individual or his or her actions (n = 14, 2%).

(The categories are directly quoted from Miller & Gergen 1998:194; the results are taken from pages 194–198.)

Miller and Gergen's (1998) results for help-seeking interchanges (category 1) show that direct requests for help were rare on this bulletin board. Interactants preferred to use self-disclosure to elicit help. The informative interchanges of category 2 were characterized by quick responses and the range of advice or solutions offered. Predictions were rare. Supportive interchanges (category 3) made up 44 percent of all discursive moves and were thus the largest discourse category. Within this category, empathy and support ranged higher than gratitude, normalization or humor. Growth-promoting interchanges (category 4) were rare indeed and punitive interchanges (category 5) made up only 5 percent of all discursive moves. Overall, Miller and Gergen (1998:198) observe for their data that "[t]he vast preponderance of network interchange is in the areas of self-revelation (or help-seeking) on the one hand, and empathic and encouraging responses on the other". The posts were thus "more sustaining than transforming" (1998:198).

The speech act of advice has been shown to often correlate with information giving in previously introduced studies. In this section, advising and counseling were compared to more therapeutic frameworks, in which patients are encouraged to use self-inspection. The specific environment of interaction in the Internet was touched upon because Miller and Gergen's (1998) study introduces a range of discursive moves to our discussion of advice.

3.5 Everyday advising

I will now move from studies of institutionalized or public advice situations to studies of private, everyday advising. DeCapua and Huber (1995) investigate both public and personal advice. Their data for personal advice exchanges between speakers of American English consists of interviews, questionnaires and direct observations. They are interested in the social norms concerning authority, expertise and intimacy that are manifested in these exchanges. DeCapua and Huber (1995:119) formulate three sets of questions that need to be considered in any advice exchange and that address very different dimensions of advice:

1. How are the roles of authority and expertise allocated by interlocutors? In other words, who is asked for advice, and who grants or assumes the authority to give advice? Furthermore, perceptions of authority and expertise can be asserted, assumed, denied, accepted, challenged, and changed as the interaction proceeds.

2. How accurately is the problem presented by interlocutors? All advice, at least ostensibly, is directed toward solving some perceived concern. Factors such as the apparent gravity of the problem . . . , context or setting of the speech event . . . , type of advice (solicited vs. unsolicited), and espe-

cially intimacy between interlocutors show the importance of congruence in interlocutors' definitions of what is to be 'solved'.

3.   What are the linguistic means available to interlocutors as advice is being sought and/or given? Factors of gravity, intimacy, authority, expertise and setting can influence the semantic, syntactic and stylistic choices here, too.   (DeCapua & Huber 1995: 119)

In their study, DeCapua and Huber focus on the first complex of questions. In general, they found that the notion of authority and perceived expertise is present in all advice events they investigated (1995: 120). This asymmetry between interactants in an advice exchange was already mentioned in the introduction. In unsolicited advice, the advisor presumes authority; in solicited advice, authority is granted to the advisor by the advisee.

Intimacy is a further important factor. DeCapua and Huber (1995: 120) maintain that "[i]n order for advice-givers to know what is helpful or beneficial for another person, there must be some assumption of either intimacy or shared background between advice-givers and -receivers". Intimacy or shared background will thus make advice interpretable and appropriate. Public advice-givers often need to ask questions to establish common background, but they are not expected to know anything personal about the advisee. Their authority is granted to them through public assent and lacks the quality of intimacy. In less public and especially in unsolicited advice situations where interactants have negotiable roles there is much room for misunderstandings and for the possibility of redefining relationships (1995: 121). DeCapua and Huber (1995: 121–122) give the authentic example of a female faculty member who was harassed by an older male student. This person collected the pieces of unsolicited advice which ranged from action to inaction. It is important, however, that the advice which she felt appropriate "was precisely that advice which matched her own personal feelings" (1995: 122). Uncomfortable feelings can therefore arise if the advice given does not match the advisee's own perception of the problem.

DeCapua and Huber (1995: 123) designed a questionnaire to find out whether advice-seekers turn for advice to people they perceive as more knowledgeable than themselves. They presented 26 respondents with ten different problems and offered four possible sources to turn to (intimates, non-intimate professionals, professional published/written advice, and no one). As the authors expected, advice-seekers said they would turn to people they think know more than they themselves do. The majority turned to intimates for advice (148 instances out of 266[1]), 77 to professionals and 41 to no one. DeCapua and Huber (1995: 124) remark that "in the course of daily conversation, advice-giving, receiving, and requesting occurs frequently, often informally, and unremarkably". They assume that in such cases, "advice-seeking may be a rapport-building mechanism" in that it can establish

shared values and intimacy (1995:124). This may be the reason respondents turn
to people they know more often than to professionals.

With respect to directives, DeCapua and Huber (1995:125) note that in American society being seen as ordering someone is "perilous to social harmony". They
detected a preference for mitigation by the advice-givers (also in solicited advice)
in order to avoid the appearance of unwarranted bossiness, badly asserted authority or presumption. Prefaces to advice in naturally occurring conversations could
take the following forms:

> 'When something similar happened to me ...'
> 'I knew someone/I had a friend who ...'
> 'If I were you, I'd ...'
> 'Given what you've told me, I'd suggest ...'
> 'Knowing how you love/hate/feel, I'd think about ...'
> 'I think it might be a good idea if ...'   (DeCapua & Huber 1995:125)

In written sources such as advice columns, a preference for imperatives and imperatives with *should* or *need* was found. DeCapua and Huber (1995:126) offer
the following explanation for this result:

> In these situations and others where there is an openly acknowledged differ-
> ence in status and/or expertise, advice-givers are more direct and explicit. This
> may be due to the fact that the authority role is already clearly defined; the po-
> sition of authority on the part of the advice-giver is not in dispute or being
> negotiated, and neither is intimacy at stake.   (DeCapua & Huber 1995:126)

It will be interesting to see whether this finding is also true for 'Lucy Answers'.

Finally, DeCapua and Huber look at unsolicited advice. It is here where assumed authority and expertise are most likely to be challenged. Nevertheless, in
everyday situations unsolicited advice seems to be acceptable in many situations.
DeCapua and Huber (1995:127) offer as an explanation that advisors will use mitigating strategies to avoid appearing face-threatening in case their roles are not
defined as superior from the outset. DeCapua and Huber (1995:128) conclude
that "[a]dvice serves to establish or maintain rapport, to flatter, to help, to repri-
mand, distance and dominate. However, regardless of the ostensible role of advice
in a particular situation, there are inescapable messages of authority, expertise and
intimacy in advice. In advice events, advice-givers either assume these roles (such
as in unsolicited advice) or are granted them (solicited advice)".

Jefferson and Lee (1992) investigate 'troubles telling' in ordinary daily interaction and in institutional settings. They found a potential for dispute if the telling of
a trouble was followed by advice, and argue that this is because of an asynchronous
alignment between troubles teller and troubles recipient (Jefferson & Lee 1992:
528). More precisely, the troubles teller, as the active participant, is put into the

position of a recipient by advice-giving. Accepting advice "may bring with it re-moval from the category troubles teller", which may not be what the troubles teller intended by his or her sharing of a problem (1992:534). Affiliation, rather than advice, as a response to a troubles telling, however, may not always be welcome either. In the context of institutional talk, Jefferson and Lee (1992:543) found a practitioner to mismatch his responses, offering too much sympathy rather than advice. Jefferson and Lee (1992:546) conclude that "it is from *appropriate* troubles recipients, in the environment of a troubles telling, that a troubles teller properly receives and accepts emotional reciprocity, and from *appropriate* advice givers, in the environment of a service encounter, that an advice-seeker properly receives and accepts advice" (emphasis added).

We can make use of several issues raised in the studies reported on in this sec-tion. The first are the concepts of authority and expertise. Advice from a perceived authority will be more credible than advice from an uninformed interactant. In-teractants will thus turn for advice to somebody they perceive as an expert, or someone they see as having, at least, more knowledge about the issue at hand than they themselves have. The level of intimacy between the interactants will also in-fluence how advice is realized as well as how it is interpreted. There seems to be a preference for turning to more intimate resources if there is a choice. Finally, the level of mitigation was found to be context-sensitive, and, if advice is to be received well, it needs to be rendered in an appropriate way, i.e., in the way developed and subsequently expected in the discursive practice in question.

3.6 Previous research on advice columns

I will now turn to the specific focus of this study and present previous research on advice columns. They constitute a very particular advice event as each exchange is a *written* one, consisting of an advice-seeker presenting a problem to an expert, who then publishes this together with a response in a letter format. According to Hendley (1977), the traces of the first English advice columns go back to the be-ginnings of newspaper culture. In 1691 John Dunton published an advice column with immediate success in *The Athenian Mercury*, which was later followed by *The Athenian Oracle* (1703) and others (Hendley 1977:348).[2] The next important pub-lisher to use an advice column to answer reader questions was Daniel Defoe whose publication was entitled *Review* (1704), and later *The Little Review*. This endeavor was followed by *The British Apollo* in 1716. Hendley (1977:345, 351) maintains that these first advice columns were immediately successful because this format is "naturally appealing" for two reasons: people need advice and are curious and nosy by nature.

Several researchers have dedicated their research efforts to present-day advice columns. Some investigate the societal norms and values that are propagated by means of advice columns (e.g., Currie 2001; Gough & Talbot 1996; Mutongi 2000). Others study the linguistic realization of advice in newspaper advice columns (e.g., Franke 1996; Gough & Talbot 1996; Thibault 1988; Thibault 2002), or focus on the question rather than the advice given (Kreuz & Graesser 1993). In what follows, I will first show some characteristics of advice columns. Then, I will review the research about norms and values conveyed in this text type and conclude with a report on some tendencies in the realization of advice.

3.6.1 Advice columns as a specific text type: Some characteristics

Kreuz and Graesser (1993), who analyze questions in printed advice columns, point out that, in addition to the advice-seeker and expert, there are other participants in the question-answer exchange (antagonists of the letter writer, the readers of the media, the editor of the media, etc.). They identify at least three levels of dialogue in the exchange (1993:66–67):

Level 1: Dialogue between the letter writer and the expert via the 'question and answer' exchange.
Level 2: Dialogue between the expert and the reader via the level 1 dialogue.
Level 3: Dialogue between the editor and the expert about the quality of the level 2 dialogue.   (Kreuz & Graesser 1993:66–67)

Kreuz and Graesser (1993:67) thus stress Bakhtin's (1981) "observation that a text houses multiple dialogues among multiple agents that have multiple goals". These multiple agents impose constraints on the construction of the question-answer exchange (1993:86).

Thibault (2002:91), offering an analysis of one letter to an agony aunt and the corresponding response taken from the Australian magazine *Cleo*, also points out that "a simple distinction between addresser ('I') and addressee ('you') is not adequate" to describe the exchange in advice columns. In his own analysis, Thibault (2002:91) distinguishes between

– the transmitter ("the actual writer of letter(s)"),
– the sponsor ("who makes the publication ... possible"),
– the formulator ("e.g. an editor"),
– the source (the "implicit ideationalized expert discourses and their intertexts"),
– the recipient (the 'you'),
– the wider audience (the readership) and
– the target (an indirectly addressed recipient, "e.g. 'a loving sensitive male'").   (taken from Thibault 2002:91)

Franke (1996, 1997) investigates 'advice-giving informative texts' ('ratgebende Aufklärungstexte') in the German print mass media and the radio. His data ranges from 'tips' in monologue form through advice columns in dialogue form to radio phone-ins. Although his data comprises much more than advice columns, I will report on his findings here, because Franke (1997:148) argues that advice columns are merely a variant of advice-giving informative texts, rather than a category of their own. Franke distinguishes advisory texts from instructing texts. Advisory texts should give an answer to what a recipient can or should do to achieve a desired state, while instructing texts merely impart knowledge on action sequences (Franke 1996:252). Instructing texts thus impart binding knowledge, while advisory texts impart non-binding knowledge about what to do to achieve a certain aim (1997:375). In his study, Franke (1997:199–200) addresses the following set of topics, which he claims to be central to a linguistic analysis of advisory texts:

  – Who is the 'acting subject' ['Handlungssubjekt']? Who can or should carry out an action that will lead to the desired state?
  – What is the 'desired state' ['Handlungsziel'] that will be achieved by this action?
  – How is the message conveyed that the action or the omission of this action is possible or advisable if the desired state is to be achieved?
  – What 'action or action sequences' ['Handlung/Handlungsabfolge'] are possible or reasonable means to achieve the desired state?
                    (Franke 1997:199–200; my translation and reformulation)

In a summarized form advisory texts can thus be described as follows:

  If an acting subject wants to achieve a certain desired state, then he or she should carry out this action (sequence).   (Franke 1997:194; my translation[3])

In his analysis, Franke (1997:247) found two major categories for the aims of actions: 'productive' actions and 'preventive' actions. Productive actions are subcategorized into actions that lead to a state that has not been previously present and actions that remove an already existing state. Preventive actions aim at maintaining an already existing state, or at keeping a non-existing state from arising.

One of Franke's (1997:9) main points is that the public dimension of advice-giving informative texts in the mass media has been neglected. He stresses that the anonymous, dispersed, and heterogeneous audience is the target of the published texts because otherwise they would not have been published in the first place. For the case of a dialogic advisory text as represented in advice columns, he quotes Fleischhacker (1987), who stresses that the questioner's letter and the expert's answer should be interpreted as a single unit, the content of which is aimed at the general public. Otherwise, a personal letter to the questioner would have sufficed. In his own analysis, Franke accounts for the character of the mass media by using the verb 'enlighten' to indicate the primary aim of the published material (1997:374). Franke (1997:14, 1996:251) further characterizes advisory texts as a one-way interaction since the advice-seekers usually have no possibility of reacting, nor can advisors check whether their advice will be followed.[4]

Advisory texts are also characterized by their assumption that there is a deficit in knowledge in the anonymous audience that the text aims to fill (Franke 1996:268). This leads us to the issue of power. Thibault (1988:219, 221) argues that the formal asymmetry between question and reply in advice columns mirrors interactional control in that the response text redefines and interprets the questioner's text. This is because the advice-giver can direct the addressee to some form of social action and because "[t]he basic asymmetry of the writing/publishing situation does not permit this power asymmetry to be reversed" (1988:221).

In his analysis of various advisory texts, Franke (1996:268) found that characteristics such as an expert, a mediator, special motives, or even a specified addressee are not required for this text type and may be part of other types as well. For example, there are advisory texts that merely consist of a piece of advice with a heading and lack a personalized addressee, an identified expert or mediator (e.g., category 'tips for readers'/'Lesertip'). According to Franke (1996:259), to present advice in a monologue or dialogue form is merely a variant of the advisory text and does not represent a distinguishing feature. The only central characteristic point for advisory texts that Franke (1996:268) identifies is content as explained above. However, to choose an (at times fictitious) dialogue form to present advice as in advice columns can serve several functions. Researchers agree that such advisory texts aim at giving an additional incentive for the reader to identify with the acting subject and that they offer the reader the opportunity to take on the role of advisee (Franke 1997:226). General knowledge about action sequences is thus imparted with the help of a concrete and individualized problem case (Franke 1997:230).

Franke (1997:377) also investigated the headings of his advisory texts. He found four functions present in his corpus:

- a brief account of the problem for which the co-text promises a solution
- the announcement of a solution of a problem, without the mention of actions
- the summary of the solution in the form of a headline
- triggering the interest of the reader with cryptic formulations or the use of typographical means   (Franke 1997:377; my translation)

In all cases the headlines were found to represent the first means of contact with the reader (Franke 1997:370) and thus they merit special attention.

To summarize, we have seen that, in addition to their dialogic character, advice columns involve a multilevel interaction and not merely a straightforward question-answer relationship. There are publishers, editors, (teams of) advisors,

the direct addressee and the wider readership involved, as well as the expert discourses of which the advice column is a part (Thibault 2002:91). All of these
elements combined add up to a "web of voices", as Mininni (1991:75) puts it. The
role of the targeted readership is especially crucial and characterizes the tension
between the personal and public dimension in advice columns (cf. Hutchby 1995;
DeCapua & Huber 1995). Advice in advice columns is also solicited by definition.
The advice-seeker thus acknowledges a deficit in knowledge and publicly assigns
the role of expert to the advice-giver. In addition, there is a power asymmetry between the advice-seeker and the team that is responsible for the advice column
since the latter has the control of the text production and publication.

3.6.2 Norms and values

Many researchers are interested in defining the ideological undercurrent, the
norms and values, that are part of the advice columns or the magazines in which
they appear (e.g., Alexander 2003; Duke & Kreshel 1998; McRobbie 1978, 1991;
Talbot 1992, 1995; van Roosmalen 2000). Studies on ideologies are a classical field
for many different research disciplines such as sociology, cultural criticism, popular culture, media studies, feminism or critical discourse analysis. In this brief
review, I shall report on some studies which deal explicitly with advice columns.

Based on his data from the magazine *Cleo*, Thibault (1988:205) maintains
that these texts, which usually treat the sexual experience of young women, "are
a distinct sub-genre which both invites women to confess their 'inner' feelings
and sexual problems in this way as well as co-opting this genre in the service of
a normative matching of the positions of social agents with dominant schemas of
action, knowledge and belief about gender-differentiated heterosexual relations".
The norms of a society or its subgroups will thus be implicitly discussed in these
texts. However, "[v]alues are neither fixed nor given in linguistic forms but are
constituted and reconstituted in the processes of discourse negotiation between
agents" (Thibault 2002:82). Thibault (2002:87) points out that "the expectation
on the part of the client that her fears and doubts can be allayed by the agony aunt
leads to a relation of trust or confidence between the two". He calls this a relation of
'fiduciary expectation' (see also Franke 1997:173). This observation concurs with
the comments made earlier on interactional control and power. The situation in
advice columns is thus "marked both by a climate of confidence and by expressly
asymmetrical relationships" (Mininni 1991:75).

Gough and Talbot (1996) examine one question-answer exchange of Marjorie
Proops' problem page in the *Sunday Mirror*. The authors are interested in coherence and cohesion and present a close reading of this text. They take up Thibault
(1988) in their examination of clause complexes and their functions in interaction and confirm that "[p]roblem page letters and replies contain conventional

activity-structures such as the Request – Reason for Request", "constitute a generic activity-type" and "offer specific kinds of social identity and relationship to writers and readers" (Gough & Talbot 1996:224). These specific identities are shaped by a society's norms and values. The authors demonstrate in their close reading how the questioner's worries about being homosexual are countered by the advice-giver who constructs him as unambiguously heterosexual by using a range of ideological assumptions that actually conflict with each other at times.

Mutongi (2000) analyses an advice column called *Dear Dolly* that was published in *Drum*, an influential and popular magazine in South Africa and other African countries, from 1960–1980. The column's topic is courtship and sexuality. *Dolly* is a pseudonym and was created by a group of editors, most of them male. Mutongi's interest is rather historical and societal than linguistic. Mutongi (2000:2) observes that the column's aim was to "entertain as well as instruct". The responses were seriously didactic and moralistic. Gender was "crucial to the ways in which questions and answers about heterosexual courtship were generated, framed and conveyed" (2000:9–10), with women being advised to enjoy fewer liberties and be more cautious than men. Homosexuality was condemned by the editors. The published questions and responses thus mirror the norms and values that were propagated in this newspaper between 1960 and 1980. Reading the columns itself was a highly gendered process: men enjoyed them as a social public event, while women read them in secret (2000:20).[5] The public image that *Dolly* was given by her editor creators is especially important. They clearly tried to feminize the column, but at the same time, *Dolly* was given a very heterogeneous identity. She was constructed as an older female relative, an aunt or older sister, but also as someone having a sensational and intriguing personality who could flirt with her male advice-seekers (2000:4). Mutongi (2000:4) cautions against taking the exchanges as true experiences by African youth, instead, "the letters are perhaps better read simply as representations of the changing sexual mores in the 1960s and '70s Anglophone Africa."

Currie (2001:259) discusses advice columns in adolescent magazines with a special focus on how "the accomplishment of 'individuality' – as a culturally and historically-specific task of adolescence – is mediated by advice texts". The magazines are *Teen*, *Seventeen*, and *YM*. Forty-eight girls between thirteen and seventeen years of age participated in this study. Currie (2001:261) found that "the question-and-answer format of advice columns" was the favorite reading of this group of girls, because they were searching for practical information and guidance. The advice texts mainly concern "romantic relationships, the female body and the pursuit of beauty", which are the same topics that can be found in women's magazines (2001:264). Interestingly, Currie (2001:265) points out that "[t]he ability of the text to construct the bounds of 'normal' adolescence is illustrated by reader interest in the questions rather than answers". Currie (2001:266) also maintains that the question-answer format of advice "encourages girls to claim that advice texts are 'realistic', in that they address actual problems that girls might encounter". However, "both the content and the format of advice columns are the deliberate choice of magazine editors" (Currie 2001:266). Currie (2001:267) analyses two question-answer sequences in detail and comes to the conclusion that

> [n]o matter how specific an individual reader's question may be, it will not be represented in terms of the peculiarity of her individual existence, but rather her membership in the social world of adolescence. This membership is not constructed through use of the first person plural, 'we'. In fact, the use of the signifier 'we' – which would imply a self-conscious connectedness among women – is conspicuously absent in magazine texts. Rather, the discursive opening which is created for the reader occurs through the use of the first person singular, 'I'. As an 'eye' created for the reader to view the social world of adolescence, this positioning has the paradoxical effect of transforming questions about social relations into questions about personal identity.   (Currie 2001:267)

Textual analysis further illustrates "how 'scientific' authority overrides the readers' everyday knowledge about sexual encounters, the inadequacy of which gives rise to the need for professional intervention" (Currie 2001:271). Advice columns thus establish boundaries of 'normal' behavior. Many girls accorded truth value to the magazine constructions. If they relied on their own experience instead, they would "place themselves outside the normalcy constructed by the text" (2001:277).

Stoll (1998) investigates the relation established by the writer with the readers through text in a women's magazine (*Cosmopolitan*). She maintains that "[a]dvice columns in women's magazines are related to an ideology of femininity which assigns 'private' issues to women, and are described as promoting pro-social behaviour through answers that express either agreement or conflict with the reader" (1998:547). She thus points out that the mass media develop and confirm a "framework of beliefs which will be shared by the public in their interpretation of social reality" (1998:546).

Heritage and Lindström (1998) argued that their data of nurses' visits to mothers is "drenched with implicit moral judgments, claims and obligations" (1998:398). The same can be said of advice columns. Furthermore, these values and norms can also change over time, as Lumby (1976) and Hays (1984) point out in a comparison of Ann Landers' advice columns over several decades, and Smith and Levin (1974) confirm this in their examination of the way "blame was attributed in cross-sexual relations" in advice columns (quoted from McLelland 2001:107). While Franke (1997:46) maintains that studies about such norms and values are better left to psychologists and sociologists rather than linguists, it is nevertheless important to state that norms and values are an inherent and crucial part of advice columns and that they are to a large part transmitted by the use of language. Indeed, critical discourse analysts would maintain that it is exactly these underlying norms and values that are of major interest as well: "Discourse should be studied not only as form, meaning and mental process, but also as complex structures and hierarchies of interaction and social practice and their functions in context, society and culture" (van Dijk 1997:6). Every advice column may be different in the way it views the world and implicitly or explicitly imparts its norms and values to the readership. Different advice columns will thus appeal to and target different readerships.

3.6.3 Linguistic realizations in advice columns

Kreuz and Graesser (1993) focus on the *question* in advice columns appearing in American books and magazines. As their theoretical framework, they use van der Meij's (1987) eleven assumptions behind sincere, information-seeking questions. Examples of such assumptions are "The questioner does not know the information he asks for with the question", "The questioner believes that the respondent knows the answer", or "The questioner desires to know the answer" (1993:70). Their corpus of 432 letters consists of only those that contain just one question identified with a question mark. They found that three out of four letters met all of van der Meij's assumptions, while 26 percent violated at least one of them. Furthermore, Kreuz and Graesser (1993:66) point out that some letters do not adhere to a simple information-seeking frame: "The questions of these letter writers may be functionally described as complaints, indirect requests, rhetorical questions, or pleas for the expert to agree with the letter writer on some issue." In other words, a letter writer may pursue different goals with a question: "to get a problem solved, to draw the readers' attention to an issue, to solicit agreement on an argument, to get into print, and so on" (1993:66). Multiple goals can also be claimed to be characteristic of the answer given by the expert because of the public context of advice columns.

Mininni's (1991) data consists of two Italian (*Gioia* and *Bella*) and two British (*Woman's* and *Woman's Own*) women magazines collected over six months in 1988. Mininni (1991:79) reports the following elements for the advice-seeker to compose the problem letter:

(a) volunteering *identity markers*, such as age, social status, profession (e.g. "I'm 16 and met my 18-year-old boyfriend three months ago");
(b) stating the *core question*, usually introduced by a rationalizing metacommunicative formula such as "I ask myself…", "I'm writing about…", "My problem is…" and so on;
(c) making room for *emotions*, as if the questions should gain relevance by means of emotional evaluations (e.g. "I feel so upset" …);

(d) a *summarizing formulation* aimed at requesting (either directly or indirectly) some modalities of help and advice (e.g. "How shall I handle the
problem now?" and so on).   (Mininni 1991:79, emphasis in original)

The advisors' answers were characterized by

(a) text organization oriented towards *"colloquial"* communicative practice,
concerning the syntactic dimension;
(b) text organization oriented towards the *"given"*, concerning the semantic
dimension; in fact, the answers are full of idiomatic phrases (e.g. "crying
over spilt milk", "to manage to have it both ways", and so on);
(c) text organization focused on the *"other person"*, concerning the pragmatic
dimension: in an attempt to anticipate the reader's doubts, the coun-
sellor aims to give the impression that she shares the same world view.
                                    (Mininni 1991:79–80, emphasis in original)

Further, he found two macro-styles of answering which he called "generalization
of the agreement" or "declarations of conflict" (1991:80). Advisors used these to
make their position towards the letter writer clear in their responses. Mininni reports differences in the presentation of advice columns for his British and Italian
data. In the British magazines, the advisors were introduced with a picture and a
caption listing their credentials. The readers are thus encouraged to believe that
their problems can only be solved by addressing an expert. In the Italian data, this
asymmetry between expert and advice-seeker was not stressed. On the contrary,
solidarity with the advice-seekers was emphasized by showing "how similar the
adviser's experience is to that of writer in search of help" (Mininni 1991:78). A
further difference was found in the use of headlines: in the British magazines the
headlines are "drawn from the letter itself, sometimes even in quotation form",
while the Italian letters reflect the answer rather then the tenor of the question
(e.g., "*She is wrong not to believe in love*"; Mininni 1991:79).

3.7 Summary

While the literature on advice has mainly concentrated on spoken, face-to-face or
radio settings, advice columns constitute a specific type of *written* exchange with a
clear question-answer pattern. The exchanges are usually presented as dyadic with
only one turn for each participant. Answers, and therefore advice, are given as if
they were directed to one particular person. While this exchange is superficially
presented as private and personal, it has an important public function, because
the advice is intended to reach a larger readership. Previous research has shown
that advice columns are bound to convey a particular view of the world and are

thus closely connected to ideologies, norms and values. Linguistic realizations of both the questions and responses have proven to be varied.

In this chapter I have presented a literature review of previous work on advice columns as well as research carried out in other contexts such as face-to-face interactions in everyday advising and institutional settings, radio broadcasts, and the Internet. These studies on advice-giving are relevant to 'Lucy Answers' because they deal with public contexts, the characteristics of advice in institutional health care settings, and expert advice, as well as with the delicacy of giving advice and counseling about sensitive issues. It is now time to return to the results presented in this overview, reflect on them, and formulate research questions for the study of 'Lucy Answers'.

CHAPTER 4

Research questions

After the literature review of studies which investigated advice in different contexts, it is now time to pull the strands together and formulate research questions for my study of the Internet advice column 'Lucy Answers'. I have grouped these questions into five sections, which also reflect the organization of this book as outlined in the introduction: (1) the content structure and linguistic realization of advice, (2) relational work and advice, (3) the tension between the personal and public dimension of advice, (4) *Lucy*'s voice, and (5) the problem letters.

4.1 The content structure of the responses and the linguistic realization of advice

In the literature review, we have seen that there is great variation in the actual linguistic realization of advice and that this advice may occur at different positions within the development of a particular speech event. It is now of interest to see how advice is realized in the letter-exchange format typical of the advice column genre in 'Lucy Answers' – both in the linguistic realization of advice itself and in the sequence of discursive moves, i.e., the 'content structure' of the responses.

I will comment on the content structure first. I am interested in how language is used to perform the social practice of advice-giving, and in particular in how advice is embedded in the entire text of the response letter. To study this, the notion of *discursive move*, defined as the "kind of contribution that the entry made to the ongoing interchange" (Miller & Gergen 1998:192), is helpful. The term 'content structure' is used as a technical term to refer to the organization of the texts into these discursive moves. I will thus try to find sequences of discursive moves – or patterns – of how advice is given in 'Lucy Answers'. One of the questions I will investigate is whether there are different patterns in the seven topic categories. These results can then be compared to the findings of the previous research done in other contexts.

Once the discursive moves of advice have been established in *Lucy*'s answer, the advice can be analyzed linguistically. As we have seen, many researchers have reported on how advice is linguistically realized in their data, and their findings show that it manifests itself in many different linguistic forms and is by no means limited to the performative verb 'advise'. In general, three of the four simple sentence types occur in realizations of advice: imperatives, interrogatives, and declaratives (Quirk et al. 1985:803; the fourth type is exclamatives). Consider (4.1) to (4.3) which are all taken from 'Lucy Answers':

(4.1) Discuss this with your health care provider ... (an imperative as directive, LA 581)

(4.2) Why not crank "Under The Table And Dreaming" the next time your boyfriend is over? (an interrogative inviting a future action, LA 1556)

(4.3) You might try the "Stop-Start" method. (a declarative sentence realizing a suggestion, LA 783)

As all three sentence types can be used to express other contents than advice, an analysis needs to take into account the function of a sentence within the context of the speech event and not merely look at its syntactic form in isolation. Ultimately, this means that a qualitative method is needed and that one cannot merely count, for example, all the imperatives or all the conditional clauses followed by the personal pronoun *you* and the modal *should* and automatically categorize them as advice. There is thus no direct and simple link between the syntactic form and the function of a sentence. This leads to the following set of questions:

− What are the typical content structures of discursive moves in the answers?
− What are the typical syntactic realizations of advice in the answers?
− Do the syntactic realizations and the sequences of discursive moves in the answers vary in the different topic categories?

4.2 Relational work and advice: The face-threatening character of advice

The questions raised in this section are closely related to those in the previous section as they also deal with the linguistic realization of advice and rely on qualitative interpretation. Here the focus is on relational work and, in particular, on the various forms that are used to mitigate or emphasize advice. The process of defining relationships in interaction is called *facework* or *relational work*. Relational work is of interest when dealing with the subject of giving and receiving advice because, as many researchers have pointed out, advice can be very face-threatening in an Anglo-Western context (cf. Hinkel 1994, 1997; Goldsmith & MacGeorge 2000). In cultures where advice is perceived as face-threatening, mitigation of advice will not be a rare phenomenon. Face-saving relational work (work in which the advisor somehow tries to account for the fact that he or she is committing a face-threatening act by counseling the advisee) may explain why the imperative, as the prototypical grammatical form for directive advice (Hudson 1990:285), is not the only sentence type which is used. In what linguistic way relational work manifests itself will be of analytic interest in 'Lucy Answers'. Furthermore, the sequence of discursive moves within the answer of the advice column will also be important in determining whether advice is mitigated or not. In some instances the actual advice will be mitigated, while in others advice will be rendered in a straightforward manner with mitigation occurring in other parts of the answer (e.g., in a section where the problem is acknowledged or in a farewell section). The following questions therefore arise:

– What kind of relational work is used?
– Where does relational work manifest itself in the response letters?
– If mitigation is used, does it occur at the same time as the actual advice or together with other elements of the answer?

4.3 The Internet as a medium of the mass media: The personal versus the public dimension of advice

In their studies of advice in print media, several researchers have argued that advice columns in which an advice-seeker's letter is published together with the response by an expert advisor should primarily be seen as directed at a larger audience, and only marginally as a personal exchange (cf., e.g., Franke 1997; Fleischhacker 1987).[1] Because of this anonymous and large audience, Fleischhacker (1987) maintains that the published question and answer should be treated as a 'unit' because the publishers decide which of the many letters to answer in public. The reason for such decisions may not be primarily the wish to be helpful to the particular individual letter writers, but to cater to the needs of the targeted audience by providing relevant information and/or entertainment. Since the exchanges are published, the people responsible for the advice column will not only decide which questions to answer, but they are also likely to alter the letter writer's questions to adjust them to the standards and forms of propriety of their particular column. At times, they may even write the questions themselves or merge several letters on the same topic into one letter. 'Lucy Answers', however, claims that all the questions are genuine. Be this as it may, Mininni (1991:74) argues that the *actual* transmitter and receiver are marginal in the light of the overall public function of the text. 'Question + Answer' should therefore be studied as a particular form of advisory text targeted at a larger audience. These observations about the print media are most certainly also relevant for Internet advice columns run by professional advisors. In the case of 'Lucy Answers', the problem and response letters are even stored in an Internet archive where they are regularly updated and it is clearly stated that they remain available for the public readership. The following questions can be asked:

- How does 'Lucy Answers' deal with its public dimension?
- How is the private and personal dimension accounted for in the 'question-answer' exchange?

4.4 *Lucy's* voice

Relational work, the process of defining relationships in interaction, is integrally linked to the concept of 'identity'. Identity is a challenging concept to work with because it is "neither categorical nor fixed" (Schiffrin 1996:199) and "people adhere to multiple and shifting identities" which "are displayed in and negotiated through interaction" (Adelswärd & Nilholm 2000:545). In the case of advice columns, we may deal with the identity of a known advice-giver, as is the case for Ann Landers, who also signed as *Ann Landers*, or Pauline Philips and later her daughter Jeanne Philips, who represent *Abby* from 'Dear Abby'. It may also be the case, however, that the advice-giver in question is purely constituted through what can be read on the web site, as is the case for *Lucy*, who is the creation of a team of people. While *Lucy* does not exist as a person, her identity or voice as a health expert still emerges through the repeated exchanges of questions and answers and is reinforced for readers who use the site frequently. We are thus looking at a particular written channel of possible identity construction.

An important aspect of advice is not only the transfer of information, but also the creation of an atmosphere in which the addressee feels that he or she has been taken seriously. This atmosphere will be of great importance for a professional site representing an institutional health service, since it will certainly aim at being true to its standards and mission as well as being attractive, so that as many readers from the target group as possible will turn to it for advice and wish to return to it time and again. From these issues, the following three questions emerge:

- How is the advisor's voice linguistically created in 'Lucy Answers'?
- What role does expertise play in this voice?
- In what way does the advisor's voice contribute to the attractiveness of the site for the target audience?

4.5 The problem letters posted by the anonymous readership

While the response letters in 'Lucy Answers' are written by a team of people that is made up of a finite number of individuals who all adhere to the site's guidelines, the same cannot be said for the authorship of the problem letters. The exact number of *individual* advice-seekers who write to 'Lucy Answers' is unknown because their computer submission information is destroyed as soon as their query reaches the team. They thus remain entirely anonymous. In theory, they could be recruited from members of the entire English speaking Internet community who share an interest in the problems discussed. It is to be expected that such a variety in advice-seekers will also result in a variety of different letter types. In this chapter I will ask questions analogous to the ones I formulated for the response letters:

–   Is there a typical content structure of discursive moves in the problem letters?
–   Does this content structure vary in the different topic categories?
–   What kind of relational work is used?
–   Where does relational work manifest itself in the questions?

4.6 List of research questions

After reflection on 'Lucy Answers' as an Internet advice column and on the results reported in the literature review, a set of questions has been developed. They are summarized here in the form of a list and demonstrate the issues that this study wants to address. They are meant to serve as guiding questions which will structure the study of 'Lucy Answers', the particular social practice under investigation. These questions will be addressed in the chapters indicated:

Chapter 5: The content structure of the responses and the realization of advice

– What are the typical content structures of discursive moves in the answers?
– What are the typical syntactic realizations of advice in the answers?
– Do the syntactic realizations and the sequences of discursive moves in the answers vary in the different topic categories?

Chapter 6: Aspects of relational work and advice

– What kind of relational work is used?
– Where does relational work manifest itself in the response letters?
– If mitigation is used, does it occur at the same time as the actual advice or together with other elements of the answer?

Chapter 7: The personal and public dimension of advice-giving

– How does 'Lucy Answers' deal with its public dimension?
– How is the private and personal dimension accounted for in the 'question-answer' exchange?

Chapter 8: *Lucy*'s voice

- How is the advisor's voice linguistically created in 'Lucy Answers'?
- What role does expertise play in this voice?
- In what way does the advisor's voice contribute to the attractiveness of the site for the target audience?

Chapter 9: The problem letters

- Is there a typical content structure of discursive moves in the problem letters?
- Does this content structure vary in the different topic categories?
- What kind of relational work is used?
- Where does relational work manifest itself in the questions?

The general aim of this study is to identify the strategies of advice-giving used in the particular social practice established in 'Lucy Answers' by analyzing its question-answer units in depth. It is hoped that such a detailed study of a specific discursive practice can improve our understanding both of advice-giving in the context of professional Internet health sites in particular and of advice-giving in general.

PART III

CHAPTER 5

The content structure of the response letters and the realization of advice

5.1 Introduction and methodology

In the literature review we have seen that different discursive practices also use different patterns of offering and accepting advice. For example, Heritage and Sefi (1992) established a stepwise entry into advice for the health visitors and first time mothers of their study; Silverman et al. (1992b) report on an Interview Format or an Information-Delivery Format in the context of AIDS counseling; and Hutchby (1995), in the context of a radio broadcast, found, for instance, that the expert tended to answer more than the question by the caller. To establish how the discursive practice of 'Lucy Answers' produces advice, I will analyze the way in which the responses are composed by looking at the sequence of the *discursive moves* within these letters (Section 5.2). In Section 5.3, I will study the linguistic realization of the advice and the other discursive moves that together make up the responses in 'Lucy Answers'.

I will now proceed to explain the methodology employed. As mentioned before, the subcorpus for the qualitative analysis of 'Lucy Answers' consists of 280 pairs of problem and response letters (see Table 2.3). Each topic category is represented by 40 records. The procedure for selection is explained in detail in Section 2.2. The subcorpus with 119,866 words, representing twelve percent of the entire corpus, is intended to adequately reflect typical language usage in 'Lucy Answers'.

Knowing that advice can take a multitude of realizations, we need an analysis that allows us to separate the actual advice from other elements in the reply to the advice-seeker. This analysis is by necessity qualitative since 'advice' cannot be extracted from the corpus automatically by a program. Every response letter has to be read individually in order to establish how the answer is composed and how the elements identified interact with and influence each other. At the same time, we would like to be able to compare the analyses of the individual records. In order to arrive at such comparability, I have worked with different levels of analysis, as can be seen in Table 5.1. 'Level 0' indicates the topic category of advice. 'Level 1' shows the Question[1] text followed by the Answer. It thus categorizes the interchange in the most general terms as an exchange of the problem letter and response letter.

Table 5.1 The content structure in 'Lucy Answers' (levels 0–3)

Level 0	Level 1	Level 2	Level 3
Topic category	Content Structure Level		
drugs emotional health fitness/nutrition general health relationships sexual health sexuality			
	Question	address	
		unit (one or more)	apology comment on previous record compliment explanation metacomment narrative problem statement question request advice thanks
		pseudonym	
	Answer	address	
		unit (one or more)	advice assessment disclaimer explanation farewell general information metacomment open category own experience referral
		signature	

Level 2 describes the general content organization of the problem and response letters. At the moment I will focus only on the response letter, as the problem letter will be discussed in Chapter 9. The three elements that always occur in the responses are 'address', 'unit(s)' and 'signature'. As already described, the questioner is addressed either as *Dear Reader*, if no pseudonym has been chosen, or as *Dear 'Pseudonym'*. At the end of the answer, *Lucy*'s name appears as a hyperlink. In between these forms of greeting, which act as brackets to the answer, one or more units of discursive moves can occur.

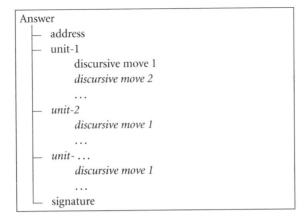

```
Answer
   ├── address
   ├── unit-1
   │       discursive move 1
   │       discursive move 2
   │
   │       . . .
   │
   ├── unit-2
   │       discursive move 1
   │
   │       . . .
   │
   ├── unit-...
   │       discursive move 1
   │
   │       . . .
   │
   └── signature
```

Figure 5.1 The structure of a response in 'Lucy Answers' (italics = optionality)

A 'unit' stands roughly for an idea and its discussion and consists of at least one discursive move, but can also contain a cluster of different moves (see level 3). A unit may also contain multiple occurrences of the same move, while others may not appear at all. The decision as to whether there are one or more units in an answer is thus based on a qualitative content analysis. In the majority of cases the number of units corresponds to the number of paragraphs in the response as it appears on the screen. The unit is thus a category that is largely determined by the original authors' choices when they structured the text. However, in all cases the concept of paragraph-unit correspondence was cross-checked in the ensuing analysis of discursive moves. Only in rare cases was any adjustment necessary. The simplified structure of such an answer can be presented in a tree such as in Figure 5.1, in which italics indicate optionality. (For an illustration with an example see Figure 5.2 below.)

Level 3 contains the categories of discursive moves that make up a unit. Inspired by the studies that investigate phases of advice-giving in different speech events and Miller and Gergen's (1998) study on discursive moves (cf. Section 3.4), I developed a catalogue of the discursive moves which are characteristic of 'Lucy Answers' based on the data itself. The categories allow me to identify the core informational structure of the answer. Initially, an earlier catalogue of discursive moves was used in a pilot study (Locher & Hoffmann 2003). They were revised and further developed at a later stage. The final categories were tested for clarity and usefulness by six researchers at the English Department of the University of Berne, who gave valuable feedback.

Table 5.2 lists and explains the discursive moves that can be found in a unit. Linguistic examples illustrating them will follow in detail after this initial presentation and the presentation of further theoretical considerations. While the level 2

Table 5.2 Discursive moves in the response letters, level 3 (ordered alphabetically)

Discursive moves	Explanation

advice	three different syntactic types of advice are distinguished with type-tags:
	– declaratives ('decl')
	– interrogatives ('int-a': inviting an action)
	                          ('int-i': inviting introspection)
	– imperatives ('imp-a': inviting an action)
	                          ('imp-i': inviting introspection)

list	if there is more than one piece of 'advice' of the same syntactic form, this is indicated by adding the attribute 'list' (e.g., advice=decl list)
assessment	assessment and/or evaluation of the questioner's situation; an uptake of the questioner's narrative; support of the reader
disclaimer	a special kind of assessment, in which it is pointed out that the information given is incomplete or cannot match expectations due to the site's limitations
explanation	an explanation of a point just made; a type-tag indicates which element is being further explained, namely 'advice', 'assessment', 'disclaimer', 'farewell', 'general information', 'metacomment', 'open category', 'own experience', 'referral'
farewell	farewell, good-bye
general information	general information (however, if there is a personal link to the questioner's situation, then it should be labeled as 'assessment')
metacomment	text-structuring comments (e.g., *as to your second question*)
open category	a category for moves that do not fit any other category
own experience	*Lucy* offers a 'personal' anecdote, despite the fact that *Lucy* is no real person
referral	'referral' can be considered a special kind of advice, in that it refers the questioner to professional, personal help as well as phone numbers, addresses, books, etc.; as for 'advice', three different syntactic types are distinguished and the list option is available (cf. 'advice')

categories in Table 5.1 are easily assigned in the cases of 'address' and 'signature', the label 'unit' and the level 3 discursive moves in Table 5.2 call for more interpretation. It is in the nature of qualitative discourse analysis that multiple categorization or different interpretations are possible at times. To secure as much consistency as possible, my interpretations have been regularly checked by the six researchers of the English Department of Berne who had already been involved in the development of the categories themselves.

In Table 5.2 the categories of discursive moves are presented alphabetically for ease of reference. For clarification, I will now proceed to a detailed discussion. For this I have grouped them more thematically. I will start with 'assessment' and 'disclaimer', move to the advice categories 'advice' and 'referral', and continue with 'general information', 'own experience', 'explanation', 'metacomment', 'farewell', and 'open category'. After this, I will demonstrate how entire answers can be analyzed by using these categories.

Assessment and disclaimer. The discursive move 'assessment' refers to a passage in which the questioner's particular situation is mentioned and evaluated (by, for example, voicing support). It is directly related to the questioner's situation and is thus an adoption of the questioner's text. Both assessments in (5.1), taken from "Troubled by attraction to tall women", and (5.2), taken from "Family death five years ago", appear right at the beginning of *Lucy*'s answer:

(5.1) **assessment** If you're 6'3" or 6'4" (approximately 192 or 195 centimeters), then your pool of possible mates will be a bit shallow. But, assuming that you stand somewhere under that mark, the news is good. There are plenty of "tall" women in the world – and at least a portion of them either get a rise out of "shorter" guys, or don't care at all about the heights of their mates. (LA 1659, relationships, "Troubled by attraction to tall women")

(5.2) **assessment** You actually seem to have quite a good grip on your problem, at least in the way you presented it to Lucy. Yes, Lucy thinks that there is a connection between the death in your family, your drinking in college, and your distress now with your boyfriend. (LA, 95, emotional health, "Family death five years ago")

However, assessment does not only appear at the beginning of the answers. As examples three and four, I have chosen occurrences at the very end of a response, where a personal link to the questioner's situation is made. These final assessment moves often act as summaries. (5.3) is taken from "Bad dreams cause bad moods", and (5.4) from "Thinks about killing others and self":

(5.3) **assessment** Pleasant dreams, or not, they're a part of you, and may be another road to better health. (LA 1482, emotional health, "Bad dreams cause bad moods")

(5.4) **assessment** As unsettling, painful, and destructive as the recent, highly-publicized, violent events have been, they've brought greater attention and discussion to very real feelings like yours, which in turn have pushed us to find more effective ways to get assistance. No doubt, your expression of your concerns here will make it easier for others out there to say, "I need help, too." (LA 1574, emotional health, "Thinks about killing others and self")

There is a special kind of assessment which is categorized as 'disclaimer'. In it, there is a clear link to the questioner's particular concern, but the content of the assessment is special in so far as it is pointed out that the answer will be incomplete or cannot match expectations due to the site's limitations or to insufficient knowledge of the questioner's situation. Examples are:

(5.5) **disclaimer** Lucy definitely can't diagnose your friend's illness through your letter, but his symptoms do not appear to match mono. (LA 23, general health, "Mono?")

(5.6) **disclaimer** No one can diagnose without examining your symptoms in person, and because of this, the Internet is not the best resource for getting diagnoses for specific symptoms. (LA 2596, general health, "Red spots on roof of mouth – Oral herpes?")

(5.7) **disclaimer** However, Lucy cannot make a definitive statement about how pot might influence your sexual relations, or those of anyone else, because of the interplay of the above mentioned individual expectations and differences. (LA 860, drugs, "Marijuana and sex")

Advice and referral. Since the focus of this study is on advice, this discursive move is also studied in more detail. Three different syntactic types are distinguished for analysis. They are declarative sentences, interrogatives and imperatives. These categories are to be understood in a purely technical, syntactic sense and not as speech act types. In other words, they are meant to describe how the discursive moves 'advice' and 'referral' are linguistically realized.

Lucy's use of declarative sentences to realize advice can best be described as functioning as suggestions. Often they appear with the verb *suggest* itself, as in (5.8). They may appear in combination with modals, as in (5.9) and (5.10), or as impersonalized formulations, exemplified by (5.11):

(5.8) **advice type=decl** So, Lucy suggests a good cleaning at the dentist and a few extra vitamin C. (LA 424, general health "Bleeding nose and gums")

(5.9) **advice type=decl** In the meantime, you can learn ways to be his friend without enabling his drinking. (LA 7, drugs, "Cocaine versus tequila")

(5.10) **advice type=decl list** You might look at other stress outlets. Exercise might make a difference physically. Psychologically, there might be something you could do to become more available or more receptive to a potential partner. (LA 20, sexuality, "Okay to masturbate five or six times a day?")

(5.11) **advice type=decl** Lucy knows you want this boy and future boys to like you, but it's also important for them to respect you, and for you to respect yourself. (LA 1371, relationships, "Older guy went too far")

Notice that example (5.10) has a further attribute: list. This means that there is more than just one sentence containing advice of the same category. The attribute 'list' can be attached to all types of advice or referral, and allows us to account for the fact that within the same discursive move there are several sentences realizing advice in the same linguistic manner.

Lucy also uses questions to realize advice. This category is further classified into interrogatives which function as suggestions for future *action* ('advice type=int-a') and interrogatives that invite *consideration and introspection* ('advice type=int-i'). The first type can be seen in (5.12) to (5.14):

(5.12)   **advice type=int-a** In the meantime, why not work on staying straight for awhile and rationally looking at the positive and negative effects of your tripping. (LA, 600, drugs, "LSD: Nirvana or burnt out?")

(5.13)   **advice type=int-a** On the behavior modification front, how about seeking the comfort and privacy of a stall instead of a urinal (for urinating, that is)? (LA 873, emotional health, "Bashful bladder")

(5.14)   **advice type=int-a list** Can you cut something out until the class is over? Can you drop the class? (LA 1502, emotional health, "Anxiety ruining family and intimate relationships")

In all of these instances, the reader is invited to *act* according to the suggestion proposed in the question. The second category of advisory interrogatives ('advice type=int-i') encourages the reader to consider a problem first from different angles so as to make attempts at active change only in a second step. Examples are (5.15) and (5.16):

(5.15)   **advice type=int-i list** What makes your particular attraction a problem? Is it due to the fact that we almost always see men romantically involved with women who are shorter than they are? Or, is it because it can seem strange to come upon the opposite? (LA 1659, relationships, "Troubled by attraction to tall women")

(5.16)   **advice type=int-i list** is it possible that the reason why your parents told you that you shouldn't be kissing is because of religious or cultural reasons, or is it based on the belief that kissing will lead to sexual activity? (LA 1714, sexuality, "Can you get any diseases from kissing?")

Imperatives are the last syntactic realization of advice under investigation. Again, we can also make a distinction between the use of imperatives to invite future action, as in (5.17), and those used to invite consideration and introspection, as exemplified in (5.18) and (5.19):

(5.17)   **advice type=imp-a list** – Realize and recognize your loss. – Take time for nature's slow, sure, stuttering process of healing. – Give yourself doses of relaxation and routine busyness. – Know that the powerful, overwhelming feelings will lessen with time. – Be vulnerable, share your pain, and be humble enough to accept support. – Surround yourself with life – plants, animals, and friends. – Use memories to help your mourning and not live in the past. – Avoid rebound relationships, big decisions, and anything addictive. – Recognize that forgiveness (of ourselves and others) is a vital part of the healing process. – Know that holidays and anniversaries – sometimes for decades after a loss – can bring up the painful feelings that you thought you had successfully worked through. (LA 191, emotional health, "Father died")

(5.18)   **advice type=imp-i** Remember, sex is not inherent – it's learned. (LA 14, sexuality, "Women's orgasms")

(5.19)   **advice type=imp-i** Think about the pros and cons of your religion. (LA 190, emotional health, "Falling from faith?")

One particular content of advice is especially prominent in 'Lucy Answers' – to such an extent that it deserves its own category name. This is 'referral' in which the reader is encouraged to seek personal and professional help elsewhere, and/or is given addresses, phone numbers or Internet links to find more information about the topic at hand. The same syntactic types (decl, int-a, int-i, imp-a, imp-i, and list) as for the more general category 'advice' were also analyzed in 'referral'. The category 'referral' thus gives us additional information about the content of the advice given. Examples are (5.20) to (5.22):

(5.20)   **referral type=decl** Lucy would wholeheartedly recommend that you talk to someone about this grief you're having in more detail, so as to help you get through the crisis and be able to continue a healthy life. **referral type=imp-a** Make an appointment at Counseling and Psychological Services (CPS) at xx-xxxx. (LA 31, emotional health, "Divorce pain")

(5.21)   **referral type=imp-a** For more information on hallucinogens and other drugs, search through Lucy's Alcohol, Nicotine, and Other Drugs archives. **referral type=decl** Another good resource is the book, Buzzed: The Straight Facts about the Most Used and Abused Drugs from Alcohol to Ecstasy, by Cynthia Kuhn, Scott Swartzwelder, and Wilkie Wilson. (LA 1357, drugs, "Psilocybin ('Magic') mushrooms")

(5.22)   **referral type=int-a list** Do you have a health care provider who is helping you with your reduction plan and general wellness? Can you consult with a nutritionist about changing what you eat... and how and when you eat it? (LA 1633, sexuality, "Will losing weight lead to a larger penis?")

General information. The category 'general information' designates neutral reporting of facts and delivering of information. There is no personal link to the questioner's individual situation other than that the topic is relevant to the problem at hand. To exemplify this category, I have chosen examples from the topic category 'general health':

(5.23)   **general information** Eye drops or ointment are usually prescribed, mostly to treat a secondary bacterial infection. Conjunctivitis usually clears up in a few days to a week. Of course, viral conjunctivitis will clear up by itself. (LA 1166, general health, "Eye mucus")

(5.24)   **general information** As a result of a severe shortage of non-living donors (most people needing a kidney transplant will be on a waiting list for one to three years), living donors are also used for about one-third of kidney donations. Because people can live a normal life with only one kidney, healthy adults may choose to donate one of their two kidneys to a family member or friend. (LA 2114, general health, "Friend considers organ donation")

(5.25)   **general information** Nausea is the sensation that accompanies the urge to vomit, though it doesn't necessarily have to lead to that in every case. (LA 1870, general health, "Nausea: Causes and treatments")

Own experience. In some cases *Lucy* offers a 'personal' experience. Since *Lucy* is a fictional advisor persona and represents the opinion of a group of advisors, this move is of particular interest and is accounted for in a separate category of discursive moves. Examples are given in (5.26) to (5.28):

(5.26)   **own experience** In this respect, Lucy, too, went to a large Ivy League, and was unused to the large classes, competition, and lack of attention that went along with it. (LA 113, emotional health, "Uncomfortable with college stresses")

(5.27)   **own experience** Lucy loves celebrating special times and accomplishments. (LA 1527, relationships, "Happy Anniversary ideas")

(5.28)   **own experience** Everyone will not agree with Lucy, but Lucy pumps up her vitamins, taking a stress-B formula. (LA 24, general health, "Can't sleep")

Explanation. 'Explanation' is a category that refers by definition to another category, usually the one that directly precedes it. It is, more precisely, an explanation of a point just made. The type-tag indicates which element is being further explained. The explanation in (5.29) thus refers to advice, in (5.30) to referral and in (5.31) to assessment:

(5.29)   **advice type=decl** Hopefully you can start to find friends who are abstainers, or "healthy drinkers" **explanation type=advice** – people who drink to have fun, but not to escape, and people who drink slowly and casually, not people who drink to get drunk. (LA 383, drugs, "Percentage of drinking college students?")

(5.30)   **referral type=decl** If it is at all possible, the best suggestion Lucy can give you is to spend some time with a counselor who will help you identify the areas you need to work on and how to go about doing so. **explanation type=referral** Counselors also provide an objective point of view, as well as lots of support and encouragement – these are things you may not get from other family members who are as entrenched in the situation as you are. (LA 1306, drugs, "Dealing with a brother addicted to heroin")

(5.31)   **assessment** As a parent, it's not unusual to want to do everything you can to make sure your child is successful in her efforts to address her drinking problem – even if this child is herself an adult. This is a commendable desire, but it's also important to recognize that your daughter has to do this work for herself. **explanation type=assessment** As a family, you can be supportive and encouraging, but she will ultimately be responsible for her own actions and behavior. (LA 1736, drugs "Daughter's in AA – What are our responsibilities as her family?")

Metacomment. As some of the answers are quite long, *Lucy* uses text-structuring remarks ('metacomments') to structure her response. This facilitates comprehension for the reader especially in those cases in which the questioner touched upon more than one problem – thus necessitating an answer to more than one issue –, or where a problem needs to be looked at from various angles. In (5.32) and (5.33) *Lucy* takes up a point made by the questioner. Both metacomments occur in the middle of a response at the beginning of a new unit and announce that *Lucy* now proceeds to the next issue:

(5.32)   **metacomment** You said that you felt sick and irritable if you don't smoke up. (LA 1579, drugs, "Wants to stop smoking pot")

(5.33)   **metacomment** Now, back to your question about carbohydrates and diabetes, (LA 1950, fitness and nutrition, "Is it true that eating too many carbohydrates can cause diabetes?")

In (5.34) a further point of view is announced, and, in (5.35) to (5.37) *Lucy* prefaces the next move – in all three cases this happens to be advice – with something similar to a heading:

(5.34)   **metacomment** One last, but certainly not least, thought: (LA 1532, drugs, "Friends say, 'Smoke!'")

(5.35)   **metacomment** So, what's a teen to do? (LA 2106, fitness and nutrition, "Weight loss tricks for big and chunky teens?")

(5.36)   **metacomment** Here are some basic things you can do to decrease allergy symptoms: (LA 2199, general health, "Allergies appear after relocation")

(5.37)   **metacomment** Here are some suggestions for creating healthful sleeping habits for yourself: (LA 99, emotional health, "Can't wake up in the winter")

Farewell. The category 'farewell' has the function of a farewell note and refers to the very last move that *Lucy* may insert before the signature:

(5.38) **farewell** Keep pondering and posing, (LA 1205, drugs, "Hungry for heroin information")

(5.39) **farewell** Good luck with your investigation, (LA 1665, drugs, "Mysterious meds arrive in the mail")

(5.40) **farewell** Enjoy your exploring! (LA 200, sexuality, "New heterosexual sex")

(5.41) **farewell** Please take care of yourself through this traumatic time. (LA 191, emotional health, "Father died")

Open category. This category was used for the small number of discursive moves that could not be clearly assigned to one of the other categories in the list. Examples will be given later in Section 5.3.2.

Presentation of entire answers. I have now introduced each of the discursive moves in the content structure of the responses in 'Lucy Answers' in isolation (level 1–3). I should stress, however, that the meaning of each of *Lucy*'s individual answers is created through the interplay of the different discursive moves, their sequence and internal composition. This interplay helped the process of categorizing. The function of some of the discursive moves tagged as 'advice' became especially clear because they, for example, occurred after an 'assessment' or a 'general information' section, or because they were followed by an 'explanation'. I have selected three examples to demonstrate what entire 'Lucy Answers' responses look like when they are analyzed according to their discursive moves.

The first example is taken from the topic category 'relationships' and is the answer to an advice-seeker who is "Troubled by attraction to tall women":

> *Lucy, I'm a seventeen-year-old man and my problem is that I only like tall girls and I don't feel anything about shorter beautiful girls. It's something that troubleshoots me and I would like to take an advice. Thanks!*

The discursive moves present in the answer to this text can be drawn in the form of a tree to make the hierarchical relationships visible (Figure 5.2). It consists of the address form, two units and the signature. Unit 1 contains an assessment of the advice-seeker's situation in general and does not yet offer any advice as such. Unit 2 is then made up of two different kinds of advice: questions inviting introspection (int-i) and a suggestion in the form of a declarative sentence (decl). This is then followed by the signature *Lucy*.

I argue that the questions, together with the suggestion following them, constitute the core piece of advice in this record. They act as an invitation to the reader

```
Answer
   ├── address
   │      └── Dear reader
   ├── unit 1
   │      └── assessment
   │             If you're 6'3" or 6'4" (approximately 192 or 195 centimeters), then your pool of
   │             possible mates will be a bit shallow. But, assuming that you stand somewhere
   │             under that mark, the news is good. There are plenty of "tall" women in the world –
   │             and at least a portion of them either get a rise out of "shorter" guys, or don't care
   │             at all about the heights of their mates.
   ├── unit 2
   │      ├── advice type=int-i list
   │      │      What makes your particular attraction a problem? Is it due to the fact that we
   │      │      almost always see men romantically involved with women who are shorter than
   │      │      they are? Or, is it because it can seem strange to come upon the opposite?
   │      │
   │      └── advice type=decl
   │             Taller boy with shorter girl may be the norm, but this doesn't mean that anything
   │             is wrong with you, or that you shouldn't enjoy and pursue your higher interests.
   └── signature
          └── Lucy
```

Figure 5.2 The response in "Troubled by attraction to tall women" (LA 1659, relationships)

to reconsider the problem, to look at it from a different angle, and suggest that the solution to the problem – the advice – lies in this change of view.

Figure 5.3 shows the next example which is taken from the category 'fitness and nutrition'. The problem letter for this record is entitled "Gluten Allergy" and reads as follows:

> *Dear Lucy, We have a case in our family where our sister has bone fractures at age 30 due to low bone density. At age 34 she was diagnosed as having a gluten allergy. It seems like that was the root cause of poor calcium absorption, which led to the bone fractures. It is difficult to get a hold of good information on food allergies. Can you provide any that is at your disposal? – Sis living without wheat*

The answer to this question begins with the address form *Dear Sis living without wheat*. The body of the text consists of five units, which reflect the original paragraph structure as it appears on the screen. In unit 1, general information is given about what food allergies are and what they are not. Unit 2 defines food allergies once more and explains possible symptoms. In unit 3, the text concentrates on the advice-seeker's particular concern about gluten and explains where it can be found and what its relation to allergies is. Unit 4 focuses on an illness that can be due to gluten intake. All four units are mainly composed of general information but focus

Answer
— address
     └─ Dear Sis living without wheat,
— unit 1
     └─ **general information** Although about one-third of Americans believe they have
        food allergies, only 1% of adults and 3% of children have true (immunological)
        food allergies, according to the National Institute of Allergy and Infectious
        Diseases. Other reactions to food that do not involve the immune systems (and
        thus are not food allergies) are: – food intolerances – a lack of digestive chemicals,
        such as an inability to digest milk sugar (lactose intolerance); – reactions to food
        additives – such as sulfites and MSG; – reactions to substances naturally in food –
        caffeine in coffee, phenylethylamine in chocolate, tyramine in cheese, etc.; – food
        poisoning – which is caused by microorganisms in the food, not the food itself; –
        unknown reactions – adverse symptoms from a food that actually go away when
        the food is avoided, but manifesting no evidence of a physiological basis for the
        reaction.
— unit 2
     ├─ **general information** Food allergies,
     ├─ **metacomment** as distinguished from the above list,
     └─ **general information** are caused by an immune reaction to a protein that for other
        people is usually harmless. This immune reaction causes some of the body's cells
        to release histamine and other substances that cause the allergic symptoms. Many
        different organ systems can be affected, producing symptoms such as hives,
        itching, rashes, swelling of the face, hands, or feet, abdominal pain, nausea,
        vomiting, diarrhea, and asthma. Severe cases can involve anaphylaxis shock –
        extreme difficulty in breathing, heart irregularities, a drop in blood pressure, and,
        if untreated, death.
— unit 3
     ├─ **metacomment** As far as gluten specifically,
     └─ **general information** it is a protein found in wheat, oats, barley, and rye. Wheat is a
        food that has been documented as causing "allergies," as defined above, whereas
        oats, barley, and rye are much less common allergens. It is rare for a person to have
        an "allergic reaction" to ALL gluten-containing foods.
— unit 4
     └─ **general information** As defined separately from allergies, there is an intestinal
        disease that is affected by gluten intake. It is called "Celiac Sprue" or
        "Gluten-Sensitive Enteropathy," and is characterized by damage to the small
        intestines that leads to malabsorption of virtually all nutrients, including calcium.
        Symptoms become apparent when gluten-containing foods are consumed and
        include: bloated abdomen; flatulence (gas); stools that are abnormal in
        appearance, odor, and quantity; and, growth failure in children. Celiac Sprue
        symptoms can range from being life-threatening to manifesting as anemia or low
        bone density from malabsorption. The disease may first become apparent when an
        infant begins eating gluten-containing foods, or it may not be diagnosed until
        middle- age (usually a milder form of the disease). Treatment includes a diet free
        of wheat, oats, barley, and rye.

Figure 5.3 The response in "Gluten allergy" (LA 462, fitness and nutrition)

```
┌─ unit 5
│      ┌─ assessment It sounds like your sister may have been diagnosed with Celiac Sprue,
│      ├─ advice type=decl and, if so, would need to work with her physician to determine
│      │   an appropriate diet and course of action to minimize the effects of her low
│      │   bone density.
│      ├─ assessment It is not unusual for a doctor to overlook the possibility of Celiac
│      │   Sprue, as it is a fairly rare disease.
│      └─ advice type=decl She simply has to take the time now to see what changes she can
│          make to improve her health for the future.
└─ signature
       └─ Lucy
```

Figure 5.3 (*continuous*)

clearly on different topics. It is only in unit 5 that we can find advice (decl), which is made relevant to the advice-seeker's sister by preceding it with an assessment.

The last example which I will present in this method section comes from the topic category 'emotional health'. The question is from a reader who signs with the pseudonym 'Worried':

> *Dear Lucy, The last week or so I've been having anxiety attacks or at least that's what I think they are. I've been tossing and turning at night. We have just moved, which isn't unusual. My husband's job moves us around a lot. I've never had this problem before and I'm starting to get worried. Should I see a doctor? Worried*

Figure 5.4 presents the tree structure of *Lucy*'s answer to this problem letter. As a form of address *Lucy* uses the pseudonym chosen by the advice-seeker, *Worried*. The body of the answer is structured into two units. Unit 1 contains four discursive moves that belong together. The first is an assessment of the questioner's situation, followed by advice in the form of a referral (decl). This referral is followed by an explanation as to why it may be useful to seek professional help. The last discursive move in unit 1 consists again of a referral piece of advice (imp-a), which directly refers back to the first discursive move in unit 1. In unit 2, the reader is referred to and invited to make use of specific sources of information on anxiety. This is realized by means of imperatives (imp-a). Unit 2 thus offers details of how to access more general advisory information, while unit 1 offers a more personalized response.

The three examples just given have shown how discursive moves are bundled into units which then together with the form of address and signature make up the answer. This kind of analysis was carried out on all 280 records that are in the subcorpus of 'Lucy Answers' applying the categories introduced in this section. An XML editor was used with a schema to ensure that no mistakes could be made when entering the categories. Such a schema also made it possible to check

```
Answer
  ├─ address
  │    └─ Dear Worried,
  ├─ unit 1
  │    ├─ assessment
  │    │   It's not at all uncommon to experience some degree of anxiety when you move,
  │    │   change jobs, graduate, get married, etc. – even if these big life events are
  │    │   positive ones.
  │    ├─ referral type=decl
  │    │   If change-related angst continues well after you've settled into your new situation,
  │    │   then you might consider a visit to your doctor or a counselor.
  │    ├─ explanation type=referral
  │    │   Your poor sleep may be a normal stress-related symptom, not anxiety attacks
  │    │   which are usually characterized by heart palpitations, difficulty breathing, fear, a
  │    │   need to escape, and feelings of impending doom. Health care providers can be
  │    │   very helpful if or when concerns and worries (including frequent moves) impair
  │    │   your regular routine: sleep; work;  studying;  etc.
  │    └─ referral type=imp-a
  │        But, if a trip to the doctor now would help rest your mind and body, then make
  │        that appointment.
  ├─ unit 2
  │    └─ referral type=imp-a
  │        For more info about anxiety, browse these websites and/or call these hotlines:
  │        Anxiety-Panic Internet Resource – National Mental Health Association – Anxiety
  │        Disorders Association of America – The National Institute of Mental Health
  │        (NIMH) – NIMH Anxiety Information Line – (xxx)-x-ANXIETY / -xxx-xxxx –
  │        NIMH Panic Information Line – (xxx)-xx-PANIC / -xxx-xxxx
  └─ signature
       └─ Lucy
```

Figure 5.4 The response in "Anxiety attacks from moving ... again" (LA 1245, emotional health)

the structural correctness of the answer. It was therefore not possible to mix up hierarchies, e.g., to have a category from level 2 appear on level 3, because each category can only be inserted on the level assigned to it by the programmer. For an example of such an XML file, see the Appendix.

5.2 Results: The composition of the response letters

I will now proceed to the discussion of the results of the analysis of the content structure of the responses. First I will report on the number of words and number of units per answer (Section 5.2.1). Then I will look at the number and type of discursive moves overall (Section 5.2.2) and at how many discursive moves can be typically found in a unit (Section 5.2.3). Finally, I will report on the sequence of discursive moves within units (Section 5.2.4). These sections are by necessity rather technical and involve an approach to the response letters which dissects them into fragments expressed by numbers (words, units, discursive moves). All queries, however, are necessary to gain a picture of the recurring patterns found in the composition of the response letters. The results of this analysis, summarized in Section 5.2.5, form the backbone for discussion in the ensuing chapters.

5.2.1 Number of words and number of units in a response letter

Table 2.3 shows that the average length of a response in 'Lucy Answers' ranges from 262 words ('sexuality') to 426 words ('fitness and nutrition'), with great variance within the topic categories. The next step to take in describing the responses is to establish how many units there are in an answer (level 2). Table 5.3 shows that the answers contained between one and thirteen units (column headers). Answers with three or four units were most frequent (19% each, 53/54 answers). Answers containing one (10%), two (16%) or five (11%) units were also fairly common. There were 23 answers with six and 22 with seven units, while answers with more than eight units were rare. Figure 5.5 illustrates this general finding.

If we look at the distribution of answers within the topic categories, a more varied picture emerges. In Table 5.3 I have highlighted in dark gray where the highest number of answers for each topic category occur. In the category 'relationships', 35 percent of the 40 answers contain three units. This category is remarkable because the difference between the highest number (14 answers, 3 units) and the adjacent numbers of answers (5 answers, 2 units; 8 answers, 4 units) is greater than in any of the other categories. In addition, there are no answers that contain only one unit. The categories 'sexual health' and 'sexuality' prefer two and four units

Table 5.3 The number of answers according to the number of units (by topic category; subcorpus)

no. of units per answer → categories ↓	1	2	3	4	5	6	7	8	9	10	11	12	13	total
drugs	4	4	9	8	2	5	7			1				40
emot. health	3	7	6	9	3	4	4	1	2				1	40
fitn./nutrition	3	6	3	7	6	5	6	1	1	1		1		40
general health	5	6	8	5	6	3	4	2	1					40
relationships		5	14	8	6	1	1	2	1	1	1			40
sexual health	6	7	6	7	5	3		1	2	3				40
sexuality	7	9	7	10	4	2				1				40
total	28	44	53	54	32	23	22	7	7	7	1	1	1	280
%	10	16	19	19	11	8	8	3	3	3				100

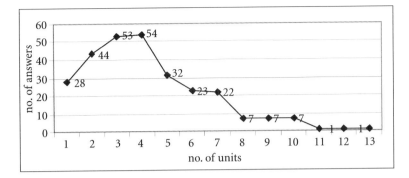

Figure 5.5 The number of answers according to number of units (subcorpus; N = 280)

in an answer. The category 'fitness and nutrition' has almost an equal number of answers containing 2, 4, 5, 6, or 7 units. Overall, the number of units in all the answers adds up to 1,168. The importance of the 'unit' for the response letters lies in its text-structuring function. The information gained about the number of units in an answer will thus help us to find the typical response pattern for every category at a later stage.

5.2.2 Number and type of level 3 discursive moves overall

Table 5.4 shows that, overall, there are 2,705 discursive moves in all the answers; advice and referral moves together add up to 47 percent (n = 1,286), followed by general information (19%, n = 502) and assessment (15%, n = 400). These discursive moves will therefore also be the main players later when we look at possible sequence combinations in Section 5.2.4. (Notice also that the subcategories of advice, referral and explanation (cf. Table 5.2) have been merged into 'ADVICE', 'REFERRAL' and 'EXPLANATION' for this analysis.)

To facilitate comparison I have compiled Table 5.5, which displays the percentages of the different numbers of discursive moves in each topic category. The discursive moves I will comment on are advice/referral, assessment and general information. I have highlighted those percentages in dark gray that correspond to a category's most frequent discursive moves and those that correspond to its second preference in light gray. Table 5.5 tells us that the answers in the different topic categories are indeed constituted differently and fall into two groups. Group 1 contains the categories 'drugs', 'fitness and nutrition', 'general health' and 'sexual health', which all have more advice/referral than general information. Group 2 contains the categories 'emotional health', 'relationships' and 'sexuality', which use advice most, followed by assessments. The reason for this may be that the latter categories deal with topics that are more personal and do not call for actual 'in-

Table 5.4 The number of discursive moves in each topic category according to type (subcorpus)

discursive moves → topic categories ↓	ADVICE*	REFERRAL*	gen. information	assessment	EXPL*	metacomment	farewell	disclaimer	open category	own experience	total
drugs	79	49	100	53	27	26	5	1	2		342
emotional health	193	68	54	75	64	27	6	3		1	491
fitness/nutrition	186	38	107	45	43	32	4	1		1	457
general health	125	39	87	44	42	16	9	6	2	6	376
relationships	202	19	7	82	56	27	12	1	3	2	411
sexual health	82	51	98	43	24	16	8	1	4		327
sexuality	109	46	49	58	22	12	3		1	1	301
total	976	310	502	400	278	156	47	13	12	11	2,705
%	36	11	19	15	10	6	2				100

* The categories advice, referral and explanation contain subcategories.

Table 5.5 The percentage of discursive moves in each topic category (subcorpus)

discursive moves → topic categories ↓	no. of dm† : 100% =	ADV+REF*	gen. information	assessment	EXPL*	metacomment	farewell	disclaimer	open category	own experience	total
drugs	342	37	29	15	8	8	1		1		99‡
emotional health	491	53	11	15	13	5	1	1			99
fitness/nutrition	457	49	23	10	9	7	1				99
general health	376	43	23	12	11	4	2	2	1	2	100
relationships	411	54	2	20	14	7	3		1		101
sexual health	327	41	30	13	7	5	2		1		99
sexuality	301	51	16	19	7	4	1				98
total	2,705	47	19	15	10	6	2				99

* The categories advice, referral and explanation contain subcategories; † dm = discursive move;
‡ Due to rounding, percentages may not add up to 100 in this and in other tables.

formation giving' to the same degree as the former categories. It is also striking that the category 'relationships' is further distinguished from the two categories of its group: it has only five percent of discursive moves containing referral (the others have 14% and 15%) and prefers to use explanations over general information in third position. In fact, there is hardly any general information (2%) in this category, which may again be explained by the topic of this category.

5.2.3 Number of level 3 discursive moves in a unit

Altogether there are 1,168 units in all the answers, and they are composed of 2,705 discursive moves in total. The next question to answer is how many level 3 discursive moves can typically be found in a unit. Table 5.6 summarizes the relevant information. The number of discursive moves in a unit ranged from one to twelve, which shows that the composition of a unit can range from simple to quite complex. It is striking, however, that almost all categories clearly prefer one discursive move per unit (40%, 469 units). Only in the category 'sexuality' are units that contain one or two discursive moves equally represented. As the number of discursive moves per unit grows larger, the percentage grows smaller. There are 293 with two discursive moves per unit (25%), 186 with three discursive moves per unit (16%), etc.

5.2.4 The sequence of level 3 discursive moves

Having established the number of units and the number of discursive moves per unit in the composition of the answer, we can now move to a discussion of how the sequence of discursive moves contributes to the composition of the response letters. The aim is to find the patterns of advice-giving typical for the topic categories in order to compare them at a later stage in Section 5.4 with those discussed in the literature on advice. First, I will look at which moves typically start and end a response letter. The positions of these discursive moves are illustrated in Figure 5.6. (Italics indicate optional components of the response letter.) By means of illustration, I refer back to the example of "Troubled by attraction to tall women", in which the very first discursive move in the response letter is an assessment and the very last is advice (see Figure 5.2).

Table 5.6 The number of units according to the number of discursive moves (subcorpus; N units = 1,168)

no. of dm* per unit → categories ↓	1	2	3	4	5	6	7	8	9	12	total	%
drugs	81	44	22	10	11	2					170	15
emotional health	56	37	34	20	17	6	1	3	3		177	15
fitness/nutrition	80	42	32	21	8	3	5	1		1	193	17
general health	62	43	27	13	14		1		2		162	14
relationships	65	42	30	21	9	3		2	1		173	15
sexual health	86	43	14	12	3	3	2		2		165	14
sexuality	39	42	27	11	5	2	1		1		128	11
total	469	293	186	108	67	19	10	6	9	1	1,168	
%	40	25	16	9	6	2	1	1	1			

* dm = discursive move.

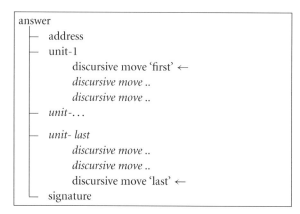

Figure 5.6 The first and last position for discursive moves in an answer (italics = optionality)

Table 5.7 shows that, overall, assessments occur 145 times at the very beginning of a response. This corresponds to 52 percent of all answers. Alternatively, in 85 cases (30%) the answer is initiated by giving general information. Advice (n = 18), metacomments (n = 12) and referral (n = 10) are much rarer in the very first position, and the number of occurrences of the remaining discursive moves is negligible. It therefore seems that 'Lucy Answers' prefers to start the answers by either commenting on the questioner's situation (assessment) to create a personal link at the very beginning, or to begin by giving information.

Table 5.7 also allows us to study whether this general picture of the first position in an answer is reflected in the distribution across topic categories. We can see that this general pattern is the same for five of the seven topic categories. The exceptions are 'emotional health' and 'relationships' (highlighted). Both categories use a strikingly smaller number of 'general information' as starters. In the case of 'relationships', there is only one single case of its use. Instead, both categories make more use of 'advice' in the first position. As previously discussed, this avoidance of general information may be due to the fact that the topics treated in the categories 'relationships' and 'emotional health' do not require information giving as such but instead to a larger degree call for personalizing the answers. This is because in these topic categories giving information alone usually cannot solve the problem.

If we concentrate on the very last discursive move in the answer (cf. Table 5.8 and Figure 5.6), we find that three categories are prominent overall: referral (n = 93), advice (n = 82) and farewell (n = 46). This means that in 62 percent of all answers, the final discursive move before the signature is advice/referral, and in sixteen percent farewell. To end an answer with an assessment (n = 27, 10%) or an explanation of a previous move (n = 17, 6%) is also a recurrent possibility. A look at each individual topic category in Table 5.8 reveals that all categories finish

Table 5.7 The very first discursive move in a response letter (subcorpus)

discursive move → topic category ↓	assessment	gen. information	ADVICE*	metacomment	REFERRAL*	disclaimer	open category	own experience	EXPLAN.*	farewell	total
drugs	22	16	1		1						40
emotional health	21	7	5	4	2	1					40
fitness/nutrition	19	17	1	1	1	1					40
general health	16	17	1		3	2	1				40
relationships	28	1	7	1		1	1	1			40
sexual health	20	14	1	2	1		2				40
sexuality	19	13	2	4	2						40
total	145	85	18	12	10	5	3	2			280
%	52	30	6	4	4	2	1	1			100

* The categories advice, referral and explanation contain subcategories.

Table 5.8 The very last discursive move in a response letter (subcorpus)

discursive move → topic category ↓	REFERRAL*	ADVICE*	farewell	assessment	EXPLAN*	gen. information	open category	metacomment	disclaimer	own experience	total
drugs	19	6	5	1	4	3	1	1			40
emotional health	10	13	6	10	1						40
fitness/nutrition	15	14	4	4	1	2					40
general health	11	14	8	2	2		2	1			40
relationships	4	16	12	3	5						40
sexual health	20	5	8	1	2	3	1				40
sexuality	14	14	3	6	2		1				40
total	93	82	46	27	17	8	5	2			280
%	33	29	16	10	6	3	2	1			100

* The categories advice, referral and explanation contain subcategories.

with either advice or referral in at least 50 percent of all cases. In the categories 'drugs' and 'sexual health', it is striking that referral dominates over other kinds of advice-giving, while 'relationships' prefers advice over referral.

We noticed that 'emotional health' and 'relationships' form a group because of the way they use the first position in response letters. In this examination of the use of moves which occur in the last position, their third preference again set them apart from the other categories. In 'emotional health' there are ten cases that end with assessment, while there are twelve cases that end with farewell in

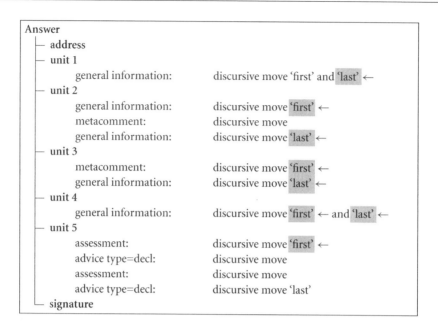

Figure 5.7 First and last position for discursive moves in units, excluding first and last position in answers ("Gluten allergy", cf. Figure 5.3)

the category 'relationships'. Both types of ending an answer ensure that a link is (re-)established with the questioner – an important aspect since the content of the answers in these two categories deals with personal problems that very often call for explicit recognition of a questioner's predicament.

Now that it is clear which discursive move is likely to take the very first or the very last position in an answer, it is time to move the examination to the unit level again. We have seen that 65 percent of the 1,168 units are composed of only one or two discursive moves (Section 5.2.3). This means that a discussion of the first and last discursive moves in units will allow us to treat the composition of 65 percent of all units. Figure 5.7 illustrates these first and last positions in units, excluding the first and last position in the overall answer. To illustrate these positions better, Figure 5.7 makes use of the discursive moves in "Gluten allergy", previously quoted in Figure 5.3. In unit 1, general information is not only the first but also the last discursive move in this unit. This is the reason I have decided to include such moves for study. In unit 2 we find general information in first and last position. In unit 3 metacomment is in first position and general information in last position. In unit 4 general information occurs in both the first and last position at the same time, while in unit 5 only assessment is focused on.

Table 5.9 gives a summary of the first positions in the units. The total number of units studied is 888. This number is derived from the overall total of 1,168 units

Table 5.9 The most frequent discursive moves in the first position of a unit by topic category in percent (subcorpus; N units = 888†)

discursive moves → topic categories ↓	no. of. units: 100% =	ADVICE*	gen. info	assessment	metacomment	REFERRAL*	farewell	total
drugs	130	20	43	8	16	10	2	99
emotional health	137	40	18	18	12	9	2	99
fitness/nutrition	153	28	37	9	14	10	1	99
general§health	122	26	37	11	11	8	7	100
relationships	133	47		26	11	7	8	99
sexual health	125	20	47	10	7	10	5	99
sexuality	88	30	17	23	8	19	3	100
total	†888	30	29	15	12	10	4	100

† If the 280 start positions are added to the 888 units, we arrive at the total of 1,168 units in all the answers. In this table they have been removed. * The categories advice, referral and explanation contain subcategories.

in all the response letters by subtracting the 280 very first positions in the individual answers, which have already been discussed. The table displays percentages.

We can see that this ranking of discursive moves differs from the one for the very first position in an answer:

– First discursive move in the first unit of an answer (Table 5.7; 100% = 280): assessment (52%), general information (30%), advice (6%).
– First discursive move in the other units (Table 5.9; 100% = 888): advice (30%), general information (29%), assessment (15%), metacomment (12%).

There is more variety in the moves used to begin a second (and any further unit) than there is at the beginning of an answer. Strikingly, advice has increased (from 6% to 30%) and assessment has decreased (from 52% to 15%). Metacomments (12%) help to structure the text, and it makes sense that the majority of these discursive moves appear at the beginning of units.

The topic categories display a similar pattern to that already reported for the overall distribution of discursive moves in Section 5.2.2. In the categories in Group 1 ('drugs', 'fitness and nutrition', 'general health' and 'sexual health'), the percentage of general information is higher than advice. In Group 2 ('emotional health', 'relationships' and 'sexuality') advice is the most frequent choice, and assessment is in second position (see Table 5.9; first preference is highlighted in dark gray, second in light gray). The category 'relationships' again distinguishes itself by the absence of general information in the first position of a unit. We can see that the patterns discussed earlier thus start to become more pronounced.

Table 5.10 The most frequent discursive moves in the last position of a unit by topic category in percent (subcorpus; N units = 888[†])

discursive moves → topic categories ↓	no. of units: 100% =	gen. info	ADVICE*	EXPL*	assessment	REFERRAL*	metacomment	total
drugs	130	54	17	8	11	7	3	100
emotional health	137	23	25	18	15	17	2	100
fitness/nutrition	153	40	35	11	5	5	4	100
general health	122	41	25	14	9	7		96
relationships	133	2	52	14	23	6	1	98
sexual health	125	57	15	7	5	13	2	99
sexuality	88	26	32	13	14	15		100
total	[†]888	35	29	12	11	10	2	100

[†] If the 280 end positions are added to the 888 units, we arrive at the total of 1,168 units in all the answers. In this table they have been removed. * The categories advice, referral and explanation contain subcategories.

Table 5.10 presents the same type of information as Table 5.9, but for the last position in units. If we compare this information with that on the typical discursive moves in the very last position of an answer, the following differences can be seen:

–   Last discursive move in the last unit of an answer (Table 5.8; 100% = 280): referral (33%), advice (29%), farewell (16%), assessment (10%).
–   Last discursive move in the other units (Table 5.10; 100% = 888): general information (35%), advice (29%), explanation (12%), assessment (11%).

We can see that referral and farewell do not appear frequently in the last position of any unit other than the very last one. Since referral does not feature often at the beginning of a unit, either, it can be called a typical closing move (as can the more obvious farewell). A unit within an answer is more likely to be completed with general information or advice. The next most frequent moves are explanation and assessment. Table 5.10 shows the ranking of discursive moves within the topic categories (the first preference is highlighted in dark gray, the second in light gray). The same patterning of topic categories (Group 1 and Group 2) can be observed as before: the categories 'drugs', 'fitness and nutrition', 'general health' and 'sexual health' form a group and prefer general information over advice, while 'emotional health', 'relationships' and 'sexuality' use advice more often than general information as a unit completion move. Once again, the category 'relationships' is shown to use hardly any general information; it tends to use assessments instead.

Table 5.11 The sequence of discursive moves within units (subcorpus; row is first element; column is second element)

2nd discursive move → 1st discursive move ↓	'end of unit'	ADVICE*	assessment	disclaimer	EXPL*	farewell	gen. info	metacomment	open category	own experience	REFERRAL*	total
'start of unit'		288	276	7		35	342	116	4	2	98	1,168
ADVICE*	339	254	43	2	213	1	40	13	4	3	64	976
assessment	129	131		1	28	4	53	11	4	2	37	400
disclaimer	3	3	3		1		1	1			1	13
EXPL*	124	106	12			1	3	5			27	278
farewell	47											47
general info	318	102	33	1	1	2		10		3	32	502
metacomment	19	66	23				44				4	156
open category	9		1		1		1					12
own experience	2	5	1		1		2					11
REFERRAL*	178	21	8	2	33	4	16			1	47	310
total	1,168	976	400	13	278	47	502	156	12	11	310	†3,873

† This total shows the total of all discursive moves plus the 1,168 first/last positions in units, which have been discussed earlier (n = 2,705 + 1,168 = 3,873). *The categories advice, referral and explanation contain subcategories.

Establishing the preferred options for the first and last discursive moves in units means that we have already talked about the types of discursive moves that make up the majority of all units, since in 65 percent a unit does not have more than one or two discursive moves. I will now focus on the combinations of discursive moves that are likely to occur within units. Table 5.11 displays the number of discursive moves that follow each other in individual units. In the row headings the first discursive move of a sequence is listed; the column headings name the second discursive move. (The first row entitled 'start of unit' and the column entitled 'end of unit' are used to denote when the discursive move following or preceding it is in first or last position in a unit, including the very first and last discursive moves in a response letter. These positions are the ones which have just been discussed in the previous paragraphs.)

The highlighted results in Table 5.11 all refer to combinations that occur more than 100 times within units. They are advice-advice (n = 254), advice-explanation (n = 213), assessment-advice (n = 131), explanation-advice (n = 106), and general information-advice (n = 102). While it was only to be expected that advice would be dominant in some combinations due to the frequency of its occurrence, it is striking that it combines with so many different discursive moves. The frequency of the advice-advice combination can be explained by the fact that this discursive

Table 5.12 The percentage of combinations of discursive moves within units with more than 10 occurrences in each topic category (subcorpus)

topic categories → discursive move combinations ↓	all categories	drugs	emot. health	fitn./nutrition	gen. health	relationships	sexual health	sexuality
no. of dm*: 100% =	2,705	342	491	457	376	411	327	301
advice-advice	9	4	11	12	6	14	6	11
advice-explanation	8	6	10	8	8	11	6	6
assessment-advice	5	4	6	3	4	7		7
gen. information-advice	4	3	3	7	6		4	4
explanation-advice	4		4	5	5	6		
metacomment-gen. info	4			2				
advice-referral	2		3		3		3	
assessment-gen. information	2	4					3	3
metacomment-advice	2		2			4		
advice-gen. information	1			3				
assessment-referral	1		2				3	
explanation-referral	1		2					

* dm = discursive move.

move contains subcategories (cf. Table 5.2), which were counted as single instances of advice-giving. In 213 instances, advice is followed by an explanation. Since advice is the core message of a response in 'Lucy Answers', it is to be expected that some of these discursive moves must also be explained. (In comparison, explanations only rarely follow the other discursive moves.) In 106 cases more advice follows after explanatory remarks. Assessment followed by advice (n = 131) or general information followed by advice (n = 102) can be called the preferred version of advice-giving in 'Lucy Answers'. In comparison, the opposite patterns advice-assessment (n = 43) and advice-general information (n = 40) occur much more infrequently (Table 5.11).

Let us now turn to the sequence patterns within units in the individual topic categories. Table 5.12 shows the percentage of combinations of discursive moves containing more than ten occurrences in each topic category. For comparison I have also included the overall percentage scores for these types of combination. All categories have either advice-advice or advice-explanation as their most frequent combinations. The categories 'emotional health', 'relationships' and 'sexuality' also use the sequence assessment-advice often (highlighted in light gray in Table 5.12), while the combination of general information followed by advice (highlighted in dark gray) is more frequent in the categories 'fitness and nutrition' and 'general health'. The category 'drugs' uses very few combinations overall because 47 percent of all units consist of only one single discursive move (cf. Table 5.6).

5.2.5 Summary

In Section 5.2, the focus has been on establishing the content structure of the 280 response letters in the subcorpus of 'Lucy Answers', by assessing the number of units per answer, the number and type of discursive moves making up these units, and the sequence of discursive moves within units. In every subsection, it was also always of interest to see whether patterns existed across topic categories. This analysis has resulted in several interesting findings:

- The number of units per answer varies in the topic categories. Answers consisting of either two, three or four units represent the largest share in each category (Table 5.3).
- In all the categories 65 percent of all units are composed of either only one or two discursive moves. In all categories 81 percent of all units are composed of one to three discursive moves (Table 5.6).
- Advice moves and referral moves together make up 47 percent of all discursive moves, followed by general information (19%) and assessment (15%; Table 5.5). This distribution was different in the individual topic categories. There, two groups appeared: the categories 'drugs', 'fitness and nutrition', 'general health' and 'sexual health' (Group 1) use advice and referral more often than general information. The categories 'emotional health', 'relationships' and 'sexuality' (Group 2) use advice most, followed by assessments. The category 'relationships' uses hardly any general information moves, which then influences all the other results.
- The first discursive move in the first unit of an answer is likely to be either assessment (52%), general information (30%), or advice (6%; Table 5.7). The categories 'emotional health' and 'relationships' avoid general information moves. The first discursive move in the other units is either advice (30%), general information (29%), assessment (15%), or a metacomment (12%; Table 5.9). There is variation across the topic categories, which again split into the same two groups: the categories 'drugs', 'fitness and nutrition', 'general health' and 'sexual health' form one group (Group 1) while the categories 'emotional health', 'relationships' and 'sexuality' form another (Group 2). The latter group has more assessment moves than the former.
- The last discursive move in the last unit of an answer is likely to be either referral (33%), advice (29%), farewell (16%), or assessment (10%; Table 5.8). The distribution of farewell and referral show that they are typical closing moves. The last discursive move in the other units is likely to be either general infor-

mation (35%), advice (29%), explanation (12%), or assessment (11%; Table 5.10). The same grouping of topic categories could be observed again for the last positions in units. Assessment is more frequently used in the last position in 'emotional health', 'sexuality' and 'relationships'. While the category 'relationships' clearly belongs in the same group as 'sexuality' and 'emotional health', it often behaves somewhat differently because there is less general information in this topic category.

–   A typical pattern has emerged in the sequence of discursive moves within units: assessment followed by advice (n = 131) or general information followed by advice (n = 102) occurs more often than advice followed by assessment (n = 43) or advice followed by general information (n = 40) (Table 5.11). It seems therefore that advice-giving in 'Lucy Answers' avoids beginning immediately with an advisory move, and thus advice is usually prefaced with other moves (Table 5.7). This practice of embedding advice and its possible mitigating function will be further discussed in Section 5.4 and Chapter 6.

–   The reason the two groups of topic categories emerged is to be found in their content. The categories 'sexuality', 'emotional health' and 'relationships' (Group 2) have more assessment, advice and fewer general information moves than the other categories because, for their topics, there are generally no solutions that can be backed up with ready-made general information. Instead the issues raised call for personalizing the answers by means of assessments and advice.

The findings from my analysis point to a content sensitivity in the structure of the responses in 'Lucy Answers'. The similar patterns within the topic categories in Group 1 and Group 2 are not contradicted by other systematic patterns in the few cases where I could not confirm similar behavior (number of units, number of discursive moves per unit, range). An overview of the results of the analysis of the content structure, which has just been summarized, can be found in Table 5.13.

5.3   Results: The linguistic realization of discursive moves

After having established the typical content structure of the response letters in the last section, I will now discuss the linguistic realization of the discursive moves. I will start with the advice and referral categories. As they represent the main focus of this study, they will be investigated in detail. After that, the other discursive moves which make up the responses in 'Lucy Answers' will also be briefly analyzed and illustrated.

Table 5.13 Summary of the typical content structures of response letters in 'Lucy Answers' by categories and group (subcorpus)

characteristics → topic categories ↓	typical n. units	typical n dms* per unit and typical range	preferred types of dms* (first two)	typical first dm* in an answer	typical first dm* in a unit	typical last dm* in a unit	typical last dm* in an answer	typical sequence
Group 1								
drugs	3	1; 1–5	advice/referral general info	assessment general info	general info advice	general info advice	referral	advice-expl.
fitness/nutrition	4	1; 1–7	advice/referral general info	assessment general info	general info advice	general info advice	referral advice	advice-advice advice-expl. gen. info-advice
general health	3	1; 1–5	advice/referral general info	general info assessment	general info advice	general info advice	advice referral	advice-expl. advice-advice gen. info-advice
sexual health	2, 4	1; 1–4	advice/referral general info	assessment general info	general info advice	general info advice	referral	advice-advice advice-expl. gen. info-advice
Group 2								
emotional health	4	1; 1–5	advice/referral assessment	assessment	advice assessment general info	advice general info	advice referral assessment	advice-advice advice-expl. assessm.-advice
relationships	3	1; 1–5	advice/referral assessment	assessment	advice assessment	advice assessment	advice farewell	advice-advice advice-expl. assessm.-advice
sexuality	2, 4	1; 1–4	advice/referral assessment	assessment general info	advice assessment	advice general info	advice referral	advice-advice assessm.-advice advice-expl.

*dm = discursive move.

5.3.1 The advice and referral discursive moves

The categorization of the advice and referral moves always contained an analysis of their syntactic type; in other words, it was determined whether the advisory moves were realized as imperatives (imp-a, imp-i), interrogatives (int-a, int-i), or declarative sentences (decl; Table 5.2), and it was noted whether the type of advice occurred on its own or in a cluster (list; Table 5.2). The result of this categorization can be seen in Table 5.14. We can see that advice in the form of declarative sentences (decl) accounts for 52 percent of all advice moves (n = 511). Declaratives are followed by imperatives inviting future action (imp-a; n = 306; 31%). Together these two types of giving advice make up 83 percent. Interrogatives inviting introspection (n = 85, 9%) and future action (n = 23, 2%), and imperatives inviting introspection (n = 51, 5%) are rarer in comparison. If we look at the occurrence of advice in single instances or in list form, we can see from the row percentages in Table 5.14 that one third of the declaratives and imperatives inviting future action occur in clusters. Imperatives inviting introspection (n = 49, 96%) and interrogatives inviting future action (n = 20, 87%) are more likely to occur in single instances, while interrogatives inviting introspection use both equally.

The individual topic categories all prefer suggestions in the form of declarative sentences as well. Table 5.15 shows that there are differences with respect to how pronounced this preference is. The category 'drugs', for example, uses three times more declaratives than imperatives to realize advice. The category 'relationships' uses them still twice as often; and 'general health' and 'sexuality' almost twice as often. Only the categories 'emotional health' and 'fitness and nutrition' use a fairly similar number of imperatives and declaratives. Two categories from Group 2

Table 5.14 'Advice' according to syntactic realization, single instances and occurrence in list form (subcorpus; all categories)

advice types	single	list	total	column %
imperative inviting future action (imp-a)	215	110	306	31
% row	65	35	100	
imperative inviting introspection (imp-i)	49	2	51	5
% row	96	4	100	
interrogative inviting future action (int-a)	20	3	23	2
% row	87	13	100	
interrogative inviting introspection (int-i)	41	44	85	9
% row	48	52	100	
declarative realizing a suggestion (decl)	341	170	511	52
% row	67	33	100	
total	649	327	976	100
% row	66	34	100	

Table 5.15 The percentage of advice types by topic category (subcorpus)

topic category → advice type ↓ (N = 976) 100% =	Group 1				Group 2		
	drugs n = 79	fitn./nutrition n = 186	gen. health n = 125	sexual health n = 82	emot. health n = 193	relationships n = 202	sexuality n = 109
imperative inviting future action (imp-a)	19	41	34	28	35	24	29
imperative inviting introspection (imp-i)	9	4	2	9	4	5	6
interrogative inviting future action (int-a)	3				4	4	3
interrogative inviting introspection (int-i)	9	4		5	15	16	6
declarative realizing a suggestion (decl)	61	50	62	59	42	51	55

('emotional health' and 'relationships'; 19–20%) and 'drugs' from Group 1 (12%) use interrogatives to realize advice far more frequently than the other categories. This grouping does not confirm the influence of thematic links established earlier, nor can it be explained in any other way.

With respect to the occurrence of advice types in clusters or single instances, the individual topic categories again fall into two groups. The categories 'drugs', 'relationships' and 'sexuality' use more imperatives as single instances of advice, while the categories 'emotional health', 'fitness and nutrition', 'general health' and 'sexual health' use more declaratives.

Referral moves use declaratives and imperatives inviting future action in a similar way to the more general advice category. But overall, only twenty percent occur in clusters (Table 5.16). There were no interrogatives inviting future action at all in the referral moves; and interrogatives and imperatives inviting introspection occurred only once each. This can be explained by the content of referral advice, which deals with passing on information about where to find help and who to contact, thus inviting action rather than introspection. Overall, referral advice represents 24 percent of all advisory moves.

The category 'relationships' uses very little referral with only nineteen instances overall (Table 5.17). The topic categories 'drugs', 'emotional health', 'relationships' and 'sexual health' prefer suggestions in declarative form over imperatives. The other three topic categories use more imperatives than declaratives. All categories use more single occurrences of imperatives than single declaratives.

Table 5.16 'Referral' according to syntactic realization, single instances and occurrence in list form (subcorpus; all categories)

referral type	single	list	total	column %
imperative inviting future action (imp-a)	129	17	146	47
% row	88	12	100	
imperative inviting introspection (imp-i)	1		1	
% row				
interrogative inviting introspection (int-i)		1	1	
% row				
declarative realizing a suggestion (decl)	118	44	162	52
% row	73	27	100	
total	248	62	310	99
% row	80	20	100	

Table 5.17 The percentage of referral types by topic category (subcorpus)

		Group 1			Group 2		
	drugs	fitn./nutrition	gen. health	sexual health	emot. health	relationships	sexuality
topic category → referral type ↓ (N = 308) 100% =	n = 49	n = 38	n = 39	n = 51	n = 68	n = 19	n = 44
imperative inviting future action (imp-a)	47	53	56	41	44	32	52
declarative realizing a suggestion (decl)	53	47	44	59	56	68	43

5.3.1.1 *Advice and referral: Suggestions in the form of declarative sentences*

We have just seen in Table 5.14 that there are 511 discursive moves which contain advice realized by declarative sentences. This type can of course take many different linguistic realizations. First the focus is on agency and non-agency, understood as technical terms used to describe whether the declarative sentence has the advice-seeker as its explicitly mentioned active subject (agentive), or whether an impersonal variant is preferred (non-agentive, cf. Hudson 1990). The decision whether a sentence is counted as agentive or non-agentive is therefore based on whether the advice-seeker is explicitly addressed as the acting subject either with a personal pronoun or any other noun/name. Examples of non-agentive usage of declaratives for suggestions are given in (5.42) to (5.44):

(5.42)   These can be constructive issues to discuss with the therapist – assuming that overall the relationship feels safe and supportive. (LA 1669, emotional health, "Help when therapy boundaries are violated")

(5.43) Asking for what you want and need in a relationship can be difficult, but could be worth the risk. (LA 1674, relationships, "Wife is movie star struck")

(5.44) Douching is no longer recommended for a number of reasons. (LA 1657, sexual health, "Douching")

In (5.42) we have an infinitive *to discuss* with an empty subject position, which may or may not be under the control of the advice-seeker, thus any explicit mention of her or him is avoided. In (5.43) the questioner *you* appears as the non-agentive subject of a sentence embedded within the gerundive clausal subject of the verb phrase *can be difficult*, thus the addressee is not necessarily implicated as an active agentive subject of the verb *ask*; and in (5.44), the subjectless gerundive clausal subject of the verb phrase *is no longer recommended, douching*, leaves it to the questioner to make it relevant for him- or herself. While "the agent in the advice giving is de-focused" in all three examples, the context of the sentences makes its relevance to the reader clear (Hudson 1990: 289). The difference of such sentences from explicitly agentive constructions is thus not that sentences such as (5.42) to (5.44) may be ambiguous, but that they are more indirect and offer more optionality. This point will be expanded on later in my discussion of relational work in Chapter 6.

Examples of advice in declarative form which have the questioner as their explicitly mentioned acting subject are given in (5.45) to (5.47):

(5.45) You can, however, make good food choices. (LA 2, fitness and nutrition, "First-year fifteen – can it be avoided?")

(5.46) You could ask your wife to think about how she would feel if you were to post sexy shots of (fill in the blank) all around your desk. (LA 1674, relationships, "Wife is movie star struck")

(5.47) You might also want to[2] talk with a trusted friend or family member about how you've been feeling and your need for his or her support. (LA 1579, drugs, "Wants to stop smoking pot")

In all three examples, the questioner is directly addressed with *you* followed by a modal (*can, could, might*) and the actual advice.

Discursive moves can also contain both agentive and non-agentive advice sentences that follow each other. Consider (5.48), taken from the category 'relationships' and addressed to a person who is worried that her *boyfriend will drink, cheat, and forget*:

(5.48) **It would probably be helpful for you** to take some time to think about each of these issues before talking with your boyfriend about them. **You may** want to explore your feelings with a trusted friend or family member, or even with a counselor, who can help you sort through how you'd like to handle the situation. When you're ready, **talking openly** with your boyfriend about how you feel could give you the reassurance you need and ease some of your anxiety. **You may** want to address each of your concerns separately, rather than bombard him with all of them at the same time, all lumped up together. (LA 1669, relationships, emphasis added, "Afraid that boyfriend will drink, cheat, and forget")

In this passage we can see non-agentive suggestions alternating with agentive realizations (indicated by bold face). This kind of combination occurs in 66 discursive moves in the corpus. Overall, the 511 discursive moves result in 757 advisory declarative sentences, 476 (62%) of which are non-agentive and 281 (38%) are agentive. It seems therefore that the more indirect variant of declaratives is preferred. The same picture emerges in the case of the referrals: there are 193 referral declarative sentences in 162 discursive moves; 117 of these (60%) are non-agentive; and there are also fifteen combinations of agentive and non-agentive referrals in the same discursive move.

Let us now turn to constructions that were used several times to realize advice and referral sentences. Table 5.18 ranks by frequency the most important realizations of referral discursive moves, which are by definition fairly similar in content. In 47 cases the realization begins right away by indicating the helpful item, such as a website or a book, as can be seen in (5.49):

(5.49)   The Planned Parenthood web site is a resource that has more details about what happens during an annual gyn exam. (LA 1968, sexual health, "Needs birth control pills, but fearful about doc's evaluation to get them")

In 66 cases, the reader is directly addressed with *you* and a modal. 41 of these are combinations with *can* that are followed by *call, contact, look at, read, make an appointment* + the relevant source. (5.50) is a case in point.

Table 5.18 The most frequent types of realizing referrals (subcorpus)

n =	realization	agentive / non-agentive
47	X offers/can shed light/provides/is available/is a resource that/has more information/…	non-agentive
41	you can call/contact/look at/read/make an appointment	agentive
15	you may/might want to read/see/consider/check out X	agentive
11	it is essential/important/helpful/appropriate/time/makes sense	non-agentive
8	there are X (e.g., a few books)	non-agentive
6	Lucy recommends/encourages	agentive / non-agentive

(5.50) You can look at their website for more information, and call their hotline number, xxx.xxxx, for meetings in your area. (LA 1736, drugs, "Daughter's in AA – What are our responsibilities as her family?")

In fifteen cases *you may want to* or *you might want to* occur in combination with *check out/read/see/consider X*. Impersonal constructions such as *it is important* or *it makes sense* are found eleven times. (5.51) shows an instance of a *there are* construction which is found eight times in the corpus:

(5.51) There are also many chapters of Marijuana Anonymous, a self-help group modeled after the design of other twelve-step programs. (LA 1579, drugs, "Wants to stop smoking pot")

Finally, in six instances, *Lucy* herself recommends or encourages readers to take steps. One example has already been given in (5.20) above. In (5.52) *Lucy* explicitly encourages the questioner or *someone you know* (because the advice-seeker had asked his or her questions in a way which made it unclear whether he or she had been molested as a child) to get professional help and to read up on the issue:

(5.52) And if child molestation is an issue for you, or for someone you know, Lucy encourages that person to get any assistance s/he might need, such as talking with a professional who has experience in this area, joining a survivors group, or even spending some time in a bookstore or library reading about child molestation. (LA 1081, emotional health, "Molested as a child – promiscuous as an adult?")

The realizations of advice in the discursive moves categorized as advice are more varied than those for referral, because the topics treated cover a wider range than just referring questioners to further sources of advice. I will look at the agentive and non-agentive pieces of advice separately. As can be seen in Table 5.19, the agentive realizations consist mainly of the '2nd person pronoun + modal'. *You can* with 92 occurrences is most frequent, followed by *you may* (n = 38), *you might* (n = 33) *you could* (n = 27), and *you need to* (n = 15). Examples are given in the second column in Table 5.19. In 44 cases, a third person pronoun is used in combinations with modals. These are instances in which advice is directly given for the benefit of either the wider readership by using third person singular, plural pronouns, impersonal nouns such as *person* or *people* or nouns which refer to a particular group of people (*blondes*, cf. Table 5.19). In other cases, questioners asked not for themselves but for persons close to them (e.g., a brother, partner, colleague) and *Lucy* adapts her advice to this individual while still addressing the advice-seeker.

The realizations of the 476 non-agentive suggestions in the form of declarative sentences can be seen in Table 5.20. They are listed in two columns. The first

Table 5.19 Realizations of agentive advice (decl) by frequency (subcorpus; N = 281)

n = type	example
92 you can	You can let him know over the phone, or you can see him one last time.
44 3rd person + modal	Blondes might try a chamomile shampoo, which has mild bleaching properties.
38 you may	You may need some help during those periods of hopelessness.
33 you might	You might look at other stress outlets.
27 you could	Or if you are sure this won't go over well, you could speak with a pastor on your campus.
15 you need to (1 negated)	You need to have a culture done to determine the exact cause and appropriate treatment.
9 you should	You and your girl should go right ahead!
8 you have to (6 negated)	If not shaving is something you're unwilling to give up, then you don't have to.
5 you will	Perhaps you'll share what you learn with your friend, too.
2 you would; negation of a main verb; you must; Lucy recommends + agentive; this doesn't mean + agentive	After receiving treatment, you must have at least two follow-up blood tests (6 months and 1 year later) to insure that the infection has been adequately treated.

Table 5.20 Realizations of non-agentive advice (decl) by frequency (subcorpus; N = 476)

type without modals	n =	type with modals	n =
be + subject predicative	141	can	54
it-constructions	81	may	26
'other structures'	77	should	23
there is / there are	15	might	16
Lucy recommends / ... + non-agentive	13	will	14
		would	6
		could	5
		need	5
total	327		149

column shows constructions without modals (n = 327); the second is reserved for constructions with modals (n = 149).

The category with most occurrences is '*be* + subject predicative' (n = 141). According to Biber et al. (1999: 126), a subject predicative can be a noun phrase, adjective phrase, a prepositional phrase, a finite or a non-finite nominal clause. Examples of each type of subject predicative are given in (5.53) to (5.58):

(5.53)   Sweating is another way that the body gets rid of toxins. (**noun phrase**) (LA 2590, general health, "The health of a couch potato")

(5.54) Maintaining good nutrition is also important if one is a vigorous exerciser. (**adjective phrase**) (LA 2598, fitness and nutrition, "Is it okay to feel light-headed and dizzy after running?")

(5.55) Help, fast, is also in order if the alcohol puts you in such a state that you're not even aware that you're up another building without a lift. (**prepositional phrase**) (LA 1557, drugs, "Gets drunk, climbs buildings")

(5.56) One way to handle peer pressure is to be clear about yourself and your responses. (**infinitive clause**) (LA 1532, drugs, "Friends say, 'Smoke!'")

(5.57) The key here is being clear and yet sensitive. (*ing*-**clause**) (LA 1873, relationships, "How to tell a nosy roommate to step off")

(5.58) – Something else to consider is how much second-hand smoke you'll inhale while hanging out with your smoking peers. (**nominal clause**) (LA 1532, drugs, "Friends say, 'Smoke!'")

In 'Lucy Answers', noun phrases (n = 51) occur most often (e.g., taking heads such as *way, option, key, solution, step*). They are followed by adjective phrases (n = 38; e.g., *important, available, helpful*); prepositional phrases are infrequent (n = 6). Of the non-finite clauses, infinitive clauses are most frequent with 32 instances; *ing*-clauses (n = 7) and nominal clauses (n = 7) occurred more rarely.

A further category entailing use of *to be* are *it*-constructions (subject extrapositions and expletive *it*[3]). They are listed separately because of their pervasiveness: With 81 instances they rank in second position. The most important combinations to be found in this construction are *it is important* (n = 22), *it is a (good) idea* (n = 7), *it is time* (n = 7), *it is better* (n = 5), *it is useful* (n = 5), *it is helpful* (n = 4) and *it is good* (n = 3). Three examples are given in (5.59) to (5.61):

(5.59) If your nausea is combined with vomiting, it's important to consume as much fluid as possible without further aggravating your stomach. (LA 1870, general health, "Nausea: Causes and treatments")

(5.60) It's a good idea to practice taking it in and out a few times before you leave the office. (LA 581, sexual health, "Diaphragm effectiveness")

(5.61) Now that you know what to look for when purchasing condoms, it's time to make your selection. (LA 2047, sexual health, "Let's go condom shopping! Any advice before I 'put the rubber to the road'?")

The choice of complements (*important, helpful, useful, good, better, time*) shows that *Lucy* uses these constructions to highlight and stress a point that she is about to make.

'Other structures' refers to a category which contains 77 occurrences. This is a mixed bag of sentences which, at first sight, might also be taken for general information. In their context, however, they clearly give advice and are thus listed here.

Looking at (5.62) to (5.64), we can thus say that the information about dairy products is an invitation to add them to our diet, we are advised not to leave our drinks unattended, and we are reminded of the importance of *protection and prevention:*

(5.62)   Dairy products, such as milk, yogurt, and cheese, provide most of the calcium in the adult diet. (LA 92, fitness and nutrition, "Women, calcium, and osteoporosis?")

(5.63)   Rohypnol's misuse also makes it advisable not to leave drinks unattended, even in familiar surroundings. (LA 884, drugs, "Rohypnol 'Roofie' and rape")

(5.64)   This points to the importance of protection and prevention. (LA 2049, sexual health, "Another treatment option for genital warts")

In (5.65) we are reminded what thorough tooth brushing does for us, in (5.66) usage of a particular exercise machine is said to lead to a desired result, and in (5.67) a change in a woman's diet is suggested which may be beneficial to her health:

(5.65)   Thorough brushing at least once a day keeps the bacteria from sticking and organizing. (LA 1509, general health, "Tongue brushing")

(5.66)   If you have access to a gym, the low back machine allows you to increase resistance as you become stronger. (LA 1505, fitness and nutrition, "Back-strengthening and stretching exercises")

(5.67)   Also, many women find that cutting down on refined sugars helps lessen the severity of urinary infections, and prevent them from happening in the first place. (LA 473, sexual health, "Urinary tract infection?")

From examples (5.62) to (5.67) we can see that the linguistic realizations of these advisory declarative sentences are indeed varied. They make up sixteen percent of the overall group of non-agentive advice sentences.

Fifteen cases of existential *there* constructions can be found in the corpus as well; once again, it is their force derived from their context which identifies them as advice. The background to (5.68) is that a questioner needs help because he or she cannot swallow pills. *Lucy* reassures the advice-seeker by telling him or her that many people share this problem and then suggests a way out:

(5.68)   There are, however, liquid, powder, and even suppository forms of medications, herbs, and other healers; (LA 1985, emotional health, "Help! I can't swallow pills")

In thirteen cases, *Lucy* introduces her advice with verbs such as *suggest, recommend, encourage* or *caution* followed by non-agentive constructions. Two examples are:

(5.69)   Lucy suggests gradually working up to these levels, under the supervision of your health care provider or other trained health care professional. (LA 1419, drugs, "Smokin' runner")

(5.70) Lucy encourages you to follow through on your work in fighting this depression and your eating disorder. (LA 409, emotional health, "Depression, bulimia, and Zoloft")

All the constructions with modals taken together add up to 149 instances, or 31 percent of the total of the non-agentive pieces of advice. In Table 5.20 they are listed individually so that the frequency of each can be seen: *can* (n = 54), *may* (n = 26), *should* (n = 23), *might* (n = 16), *will* (n = 14), *would* (n = 6), *could* (n = 5), and *need* (n = 5). Examples are given in (5.71) to (5.78):

(5.71) Test-driving different brands with your partner can be fun. (LA 2047, sexual health, "Let's go condom shopping! Any advice before I 'put the rubber to the road'?")

(5.72) The process of self-realization may help you figure what is behind your actions and lowered self-esteem. (LA 2370, emotional health, "My need for sexual attention is getting out of hand")

(5.73) The program's plan should be adaptable to habits and tastes. (LA 331, fitness and nutrition, "Weight loss camps?")

(5.74) For these dilemmas, time management and effective communication skills might work to your advantage. (LA 761, emotional health, "How to reduce stress at work")

(5.75) Obviously an all-around healthy diet will provide even more protection from heart disease, and other maladies, too. (LA 1758, fitness and nutrition, "Health benefits of fish oils")

(5.76) jogging slowly at first before dropping down to a brisk walking pace could do the trick. (LA 2598, fitness and nutrition, "Is it okay to feel lightheaded and dizzy after running?")

(5.77) If you are concerned about your own blackouts, or the memory-challenging episodes of others, cutting back or setting limits on your alcohol intake would be wise and responsible. (LA 887, drugs, "Alcohol use and memory loss")

(5.78) Your first meal of the day needs to be consumed within 2-3 hours of waking. (LA 1137, fitness and nutrition, "Fast all day and feast at night – healthy?")

Within the 757 agentive and non-agentive advice sentences, the particular group of conditional sentences merits an individual examination since they make up nineteen percent (n = 146). (Recall that the use of conditionals is also typical for Hudson's 'Garden Lady' (1990: 294)). Typical examples can be seen in (5.79) and (5.81):

(5.79) If you haven't already, perhaps you and your girlfriend could talk about your concerns and try to reach a mutual decision on what form(s) of contraception you both want to use. (LA 1186, sexual health, "Is pulling out safe?")

(5.80)   If you and she are close, your friendship should be able to weather a conversation about the possibility of becoming more intimate. (LA 1339, relationships, "Close friends – take it to the next level?")

(5.81)   You can use some of the suggestions below to talk with your recent date about your feelings – if you feel okay doing so. (LA 1371, relationships, "Older guy went too far")

In (5.79) and (5.80) the *if*-clause precedes the main clause, while it follows it in (5.81). In all three cases, the questioner is addressed in the *if*-clause to make sure that the advice in the main clause is appropriate and correctly understood. Thus the advice in the main clause is only relevant if the condition applies to the individual reader. In a face-to-face counseling situation, the advisor might in fact enquire about these conditions with a question. In the advice column format, this option of interrogatives is also used, as we shall discuss later. The use of *if*-clauses to ensure that pieces of advice are appropriate for the advice-seekers is another means to achieve this connection. *If*-clauses preceding the main clause are preferred (n = 110), and they were combined with an agentive main clause in 53 percent (n = 78) of all occurrences. Once more a similar picture emerges for the referrals (n = 50). They also have more *if*-clauses in first position (n = 42, 84%) and combine it slightly more with agentive main clauses (n = 28, 56%). It seems therefore that *Lucy* prefers to establish relevance for her readers as soon as possible.

5.3.1.2 *Advice and referral: Imperatives*

With 36 percent overall, the use of imperatives in the advisory discursive moves is clearly part of advice-giving in the discursive practice established in 'Lucy Answers'. After suggestions presented in declarative form, the second most utilized type of advice realization in 'Lucy Answers' is 'imperatives inviting future action'. There are 521 imperatives in the 306 discursive moves. An additional 77 imperatives appear in a somewhat atypical example, which is reproduced in (5.82). It is the answer to *Dear Lucy, Is there a natural way to get high?*

(5.82)   "Natural highs" (LA 1577, drugs)

Dear Reader,		
YES!:		
Laugh	Smell the flowers	Make a new friend
Make someone else	Hug someone	Call an old friend
laugh	Have a baby	Help a friend in need
Run around the block	Go to a Springsteen	Work hard on
Run a marathon	concert	something
Help an old lady across	Listen to a symphony	Complete a project
the street, if she	Take a bath	Vote
wants to cross	Meditate	Clean your house

Be a big brother or big sister	Masturbate	Shop till you drop
Volunteer	Spin around	Grow vegetables and eat them
Watch a sunset	Ride on a rollercoaster	
Write a poem	Have a meal in an unusual location: at the beach, in a park, on the roof of a tall building	Play with your kids, your little brother, or your dog
Kiss		Sing
Fall in love		
Love	Go to the top of the Empire State Building	Make a present for someone
Make love		
Orgasm	Scale or hike to the top of a mountain	Take a deserved day off
Go sailing		
Scuba dive or snorkel	Do yoga	Do something you've always wanted to do but never have
Take a ferry ride	Get well	
Bake a cake	Pamper yourself	
Watch fireworks	Stand up for what you really believe	Be one with nature
Play in the snow		Be in the moment

Oh, did you mean like highs from plants (roots, leaves, stems, twigs, bark, flowers, seeds, pods, nuts, and fruits)? Yes, there are those, too: everything from the less-risky and hallucinogenic Yerba Maté, to the more dangerous and trippy Madrake (Satan's Apple), which can also produce an irregular heartbeat, violent diarrhea, and coma. Two sources of information for this latter brand of natural highs, including effects and risks, are:
Vitamins, Herbs, Minerals, and Supplements: The Complete Guide, by H. Winter Griffith
Professional's Handbook of Complementary and Alternative Medicines, by Charles W. Fetrow and Juan R. Avila

Lucy

After a long list of imperatives suggesting how to get "high" naturally (notice that the very number and range of imperatives in this example introduce an element of optionality since no one is likely to follow all the suggestions mentioned), *Lucy* focuses on what the advice-seeker most probably wanted: information on how to get high from plants. *Lucy* then offers resources for further information. The number of imperatives in this response is clearly atypical. It does, however, give a nice illustration of how *Lucy* also makes use of them in a humorous way.

A closer look at the 521 imperatives in the other records results in the frequency list presented in Table 5.21. The most frequent imperative is *try* (n = 48), which is combined with another verb to complete the advice. *Take* is used 22 times, in very different combinations, from *take action* to *take time*. *Use* appears in such combinations as *use a condom* or *use a lemon based shampoo* (n = 14). The thirteen instances with *keep* were made up of combinations such as *keep weight, choles-*

Table 5.21 The number of imperatives inviting action (imp-a) higher than four in the advice category (subcorpus; n=248 of N=521)

verb	n =	verb	n =	verb	n =
try	48	make X	8	begin	4
take	22	let her/him	7	check	4
don't do	21	look at/for/around/their way	7	eat	4
ask	16	call	6	exhale	4
use	14	choose	6	get	4
keep	13	give up	6	pull	4
be	12	place	6	put	4
avoid	11	repeat	6	remember to	4
make sure	11	add	5	think of	4
tell them	11	start by	5		
talk with/to	10				

Table 5.22 The number of imperatives inviting action (imp-a) higher than three in the referral category by frequency (subcorpus; n = 152 of N = 183)

verb	n =	verb	n =	verb	n =
call	39	make an appointment	13	talk with	4
see	23	contact	11	look at/for/in	3
check	21	try	10	pick up	3
read	15	go to	7	visit	3

terol, and blood pressure at healthy levels, but also *keep an open mind*. Examples of complements for *be* are *active, aware, clear, conscious, patient, sure, willing, yourself*. Further typical verbs are *ask* (n = 16), *tell her/him/them* (n = 11) and *talk to/with* (n = 10). They are evidence that the advice in 'Lucy Answers' is often to talk about and share problems with others. The eleven instances of *make sure* are a way for *Lucy* to highlight a point that is relevant for the advice-seeker. '*Don't* + verb' (n = 21) and *avoid* (n = 11) as imperatives for what *not* to do occur only 32 times. This number constitutes six percent of all imperatives; this small percentage indicates that 'Lucy Answers' avoids this type of advice-giving.

In the category of referrals, the total number of imperatives is 183 in 146 discursive moves. The verbs found there are of a more unified kind in that they tell advice-seekers to turn to sources or to contact further professional help (Table 5.22). *Call* leads the list with 39 instances. *See* (n = 23), as well as *check* (n = 21), and *read* (n = 15) all refer the reader to written material (either online or references for print material). In 38 cases, they are prefaced with *for more information. Make an appointment* (n = 13) and *contact* (n = 11) are used to encourage advice-seekers to get personal professional help either at AEI or elsewhere. Finally, *try* is also used ten times in the referrals.

In the 306 advisory discursive moves that contain imperatives inviting action, 66 conditional sentences are found. In the earlier discussion of declarative advisory sentences, I have distinguished between main clauses which address the reader straightforwardly (agentive), and those which use an impersonal form (non-agentive). In the case of imperatives which occur in the main clause this distinction is not necessary since the reader is directly addressed by definition. This can be seen in (5.83), taken from the category 'fitness and nutrition', in which *Lucy* gives instructions to an advice-seeker who inquired about "Gym manners". This extract deals with what to do if more than one person wants to use the same exercise machine at the same time.

(5.83)   If you're a multi-set kinda gal or guy, glance around to see if someone else is waiting to use the machine or area you currently occupy. Offer to let them work in (alternate) with you, and if you're feeling particularly generous, ask if they'd like you to "spot" them. (LA 111, fitness and nutrition, "Gym Manners")

The imperatives used with the two conditional clauses are *glance around* and *ask*. There is no doubt that the reader him- or herself is meant to carry out these actions. In 56 of the 66 cases, the *if*-clause preceded the main clause. Further examples are given in (5.84) and (5.85):

(5.84)   If you are the "victim" in your sleepy cinema, for example, try to imagine yourself in a new role as "victor." (LA 1482, emotional health, "Bad dreams cause bad moods")

(5.85)   If you do develop bursitis, try the following: – Rest the part of your body that hurts. If you suspect that one activity has caused the pain, stop it for awhile. (LA 205, general health, "Chronic bursitis")

In both examples the quite common *try to* occurs. In the second example, the conditional clause is followed by the imperative *stop*. In 53 cases, conditional sentences also occur in the referral sections. The *if*-clauses precede the main clause in 45 cases. There is thus a preference in 'Lucy Answers' to *first* establish for whom the main clause is relevant by means of the *if*-clause, rather than to do this later. As pointed out before, conditional clauses are a possible way for *Lucy* to qualify her advice and make it suit the particular situation of the advice-seeker. In a face-to-face situation this might have been achieved with a question-answer sequence.

5.3.1.3 *Advice and referral: Questions*

Interrogatives are the third way advice is realized in 'Lucy Answers'. We have seen at the beginning of Section 5.3.1 that the categories 'emotional health', 'relationships' and 'drugs' use them more frequently than the other topic categories. As was the case for conditional clauses, questions are used to engage the reader to an even

Table 5.23 Interrogatives inviting an action (int-a) by type and frequency (subcorpus; N = 25)

n =	type	example
indirect questions (N=14)		
11	why not	Why not incorporate vegetables into other foods?
2	how about	On the behavior modification front, how about seeking the comfort and privacy of a stall instead of a urinal (for urinating, that is)?
1	what if	Speaking of your description, what if you printed out your letter to Lucy, but address it "Dear Dad," instead?
yes no questions (N = 10)		
3	can	Can you fit fifteen to thirty minutes into your day to take a bath or go for a run?
2	be	Or, is there a personal shower you can use instead?
2	have	Have you approached him about your concerns?
1	do	Or, do you know of any counselors in your area with whom you could make an appointment?
1	could	Before you do that, could you use it to shut off the TV in advance of getting intimate?
1	would	Would it be possible for you to let him know of your relationship and sexual interests – not for him, but in general, when you're having one of those deep, late-night conversations?
other types (N = 1)		
1	elliptical	[You said that you spoke with the resident adviser (RA)] – how about the residence hall director (RD) or residence life coordinator (RLC)?

greater extent. The advice lies in encouraging the advice-seeker to ask the questions posed and to draw conclusions from them that may be a part of the solution to the problem. In categorizing interrogatives, a distinction was made between questions inviting introspection and consideration (int-i; n = 190) and questions which encouraged future action (int-a; n = 25). Overall, there are 215 questions in the 108 discursive moves established in 'Lucy Answers'. They were classified according to their type (*wh*-question, *yes/no*-question, alternative, elliptical and indirect questions) and according to the auxiliary verbs realizing them. Table 5.23 summarizes the results and gives examples of the 25 questions that encourage taking action in 'Lucy Answers'. Sentences with *why not* occurred most often (n = 11). All the other types that are listed were found three times or even less than that.

As can be seen in Table 5.24, of the 190 questions inviting introspection, 120 were *yes/no*-questions (63%). Within this group, questions with *be* dominated (n = 51, 42%). In the *wh*-questions, *what* (n = 22) and *how* (n = 18) were most frequent. Alternative, elliptical and indirect questions appeared only rarely.

The examples given in Tables 5.23 and 5.24 neatly show how *Lucy* tries to place the ball in the reader's court. By engaging the reader in this way, i.e., by making him or her think, *Lucy* points to aspects of the problem at hand that are important to

Table 5.24 Interrogatives inviting introspection (int-i) by type and frequency (subcorpus; N = 190)

n =	type	example
yes/no questions (N = 120)		
51	be	Are other things going on that bother or upset you?
35	do	First things first, do you know what you'd like to be doing?
14	have	Has your boyfriend done or said anything to lead you to believe that he is cheating on you?
7	could	Could your boyfriend have an ailment unknown to you?
6	can	can you identify the causes of your angst, stress, and irritability?
4	will	Will your friend be willing to pay for you?
2	would	Would you like her to spend more time with you, or pay more attention in ways that she currently isn't?
1	might	Short of sex, might it be spending some extra time with her, paying her extra attention, looking in her eyes a little longer and more intensely than usual, or touching her on the hand, arm, or shoulder in a way that communicates more than just friendship?
wh-questions (N = 54)		
22	what	What is causing your frustration?
18	how	How exactly do you and he define SEX?
8	why	Why does he use steroids?
3	when	When did you first become aware that you didn't feel as deeply for the person you are with as he does for you?
2	who	Who else and what else is around that may distract you and your audience, and is there enough time for a response and some meaningful dialogue?
1	where	Where do your doubts stem from?
other types of questions (N = 16)		
7	alternative	Will this be short-term or long-term?
5	elliptical	[Who will listen to you?] A close family friend or relative? A counselor or teacher at your brother's school?
4	indirect	Lucy wonders if you've been feeling isolated?

clarify before more advice can be given. In addition, the questions are formulated in such a way that considering them will indeed already be part of the solution. At the same time they ensure that readers can take or leave the advice depending on how they would answer the questions raised. In this way, these questions have a similar function to the *if*-clauses previously discussed. In a face-to-face counseling situation, many of the questions raised in Table 5.24 would be resolved by question-answer sequences or by the joint development of a topic. In an advice column, the advisor does not have these options. The questions, however, give the texts the flavor of interaction despite the fact that they have to remain on a purely rhetorical level.

5.3.1.4 *Records with no advice or referral discursive moves*

Up to now the tacit assumption has been that there are advisory discursive moves which can be identified in every response in 'Lucy Answers'. And indeed, this is the case in 276 records, the advice and referral discursive moves of which I have just analyzed. There are, however, four records that have neither advice nor referral information: One is from the category 'sexuality' and is composed of an assessment and an open category move;[4] one record from the category 'drugs' is composed of an assessment and general information; one answer in the category 'fitness and nutrition' contains two general information moves; and, finally, one response from the category 'sexual health' consists of three general information moves. With the exception of the first record mentioned, all contain general information, which takes over the main message of the answers. A look at the letters which prompted these responses reveals that the three writers do ask questions, but they seek information rather than advice. Overall, with only four responses in the entire subcorpus, answers containing no advice or referral are exceptional (just as problem letters without any question or explicit request for advice are rare as well, as we shall see in Chapter 9).

5.3.2 The linguistic realization of the other level 3 discursive moves

Since the focus of this study is on advice-giving, the realizations of the discursive moves just discussed receive the most attention. In what follows, I will treat the remaining discursive moves in less detail, but still in such a way that an impression of their realizations can be gained. I will start with the discursive moves of general information (n = 502) and assessment (n = 400) since they are among the most frequent in 'Lucy Answers' (compare Table 5.4 above). General information moves were defined as those reporting facts neutrally and as giving the general background that is necessary to understand the advice given in a particular record. Assessments are those parts in a response which comment on the advice-seeker's particular situation by showing, for example, awareness of difficult aspects of a problem or by 'diagnosing' what might be the issue at hand. Apart from their obvious differences in content, these two categories differ in the level of involvement they show with the reader. Since relational work is the subject of the next chapter, I will restrict myself here to giving a few further examples of these realizations.

My previous discussion of sequences of discursive moves has shown that assessments are typical for Group 2 and often occur in the first position of a response (cf. Table 5.13). In (5.86), taken from a record entitled "Disappointed with therapist?", this is in fact the case:

(5.86)   **assessment** Kudos to you for seeking help. It's a shame that your first therapist isn't a good match, but that's not unusual. People say that finding a therapist is like shopping for clothes, the first, second or even third outfit doesn't always fit quite right. That's not a reflection on you or the therapist; you and s/he just aren't a good match. (LA 253, emotional health, "Disappointed with therapist?")

In (5.86) we see praise for the advice-seeker (*kudos to you*), the display of empathy (*it's a shame*), an assessment of the questioner's situation by means of a simile (*finding a therapist is like shopping for clothes*), and a reassurance move (*you and s/he just aren't a good match*). *Lucy* then proceeds to give advice. The only piece of general information in this response has to do with financing a therapy, as can be seen in (5.87), which follows immediately after (5.86):

(5.87) **advice type=imp-a** Discuss with him/her whether you might see someone else in Health Services or whether s/he would be willing to refer you to someone off campus with whom you could do longer term work. **general information** If your Health Services counselor refers you off-campus, your student health insurance will cover it. **advice type=decl** If you don't have student health insurance, or money is not a big issue right now, you can find your own therapist outside of AEI. (LA 253, emotional health, "Disappointed with therapist?")

General information is a discursive move which appears in the first position of a response as well as in any other location. In (5.87) it is placed in between two pieces of advice. In example (5.88) it follows an assessment. This is the beginning of a response to a questioner who is *vomiting and can't keep anything down.*

(5.88) **assessment** This probably means that you have a gastrointestinal virus. **general information** Most "stomach bugs," or gastroenteritis, run their course within 24–36 hours, but not until after they've caused plenty of discomfort, pain, and even misery. While most people recover uneventfully from their bout of vomiting and/or diarrhea, some become seriously dehydrated. Dehydration occurs when the body loses too much fluid. Body chemistry also becomes unbalanced, because along with the fluid, one is losing essential salts and sugars, such as sodium, potassium, glucose, etc. Symptoms of dehydration include: – dry, sticky feeling in the mouth – dry eyes - peeing only tiny amounts of dark yellow urine – sunken eyes – extreme weakness. In the most severe cases of dehydration, an individual may become confused, unconscious, and/or experience seizures. (LA 2609, general health, "I'm vomiting and can't keep anything down – Help!")

After a brief assessment – or in this case diagnosis – *Lucy* proceeds to explain what effects a gastrointestinal virus can have on a human body. This is done in general terms and there are no allusions to the advice-seeker's particular situation. General information moves are particularly frequent in the topic categories 'drugs', 'general

Table 5.25 The number of explanations according to the discursive move they explain by topic category (subcorpus; N = 278)

discursive moves → topic categories ↓	ADVICE*	REFERRAL*	assessment	disclaimer	gen. info	open category	own experience	total
emotional health	48	13	2		1			64
relationships	44	5	6				1	56
fitness/nutrition	36	2	5					43
general health	31	5	5	1				42
drugs	19	4	4					27
sexual health	18	1	4			1		24
sexuality	17	3	2					22
total	213	33	28	1	1	1	1	278
%	77	12	10					100

* The categories advice, and referral contain subcategories.

health', 'fitness and nutrition', and 'sexual health' (Group 1). It was argued that this was the case as these categories not only give advice but also pass on information. They are thus more focused on facts than the topic categories 'relationships', 'emotional health' and 'sexuality' (Group 2), which are more concerned with the particular emotional situation of a particular advice-seeker.

Having discussed the discursive moves of advice, referral, assessment and general information, we have already covered 81 percent of all discursive moves (see Table 5.4 above). The remaining types, explanation (n = 278, 10%), metacomments (n = 156, 6%), and farewell (n = 47, 2%), occur to a much smaller degree. Disclaimers (n = 13), mentions of *Lucy*'s own experience (n = 11) and the open category (n = 12) constitute less than one percent of the moves.

As the overview of discursive moves in Table 5.4 illustrated, we know that explanations appear most often in the categories 'relationships' (n = 56), 'emotional health' (n = 64) and 'general health' (n = 42). From my discussion of sequences of discursive moves, we know that they predominantly follow advice. Table 5.25 offers a more detailed analysis of the explanation moves. We can see that they follow advice in 77 percent of all cases. As pointed out, it is no surprise that advice receives this kind of attention since it is a declared aim of 'Lucy Answers' to be straightforward and clear. The thirteen instances of explanations of referral in the category 'emotional health' are special. Eight of them explain that accepting help from psychologists and counselors may be beneficial. These explanations thus try to counteract the fear that advice-seekers might feel when they move from the anonymity of online counseling to speaking in person to 'real life' counselors. Consider (5.89) as a case in point:

(5.89)   **referral** Please make an appointment at Counseling and Psychological Services (xx-xxxx). **explanation** It may only be a matter of a few sessions, but it could make a great difference in your relationship now and the rest of your life. (LA 95, emotional health, "Family death five years ago")

Metacomments make up six percent of all discursive moves (or 156 instances). In 58 cases an introductory sentence is used as a heading for the next discursive move. Twelve of these contain the construction *here are* as in (5.90). In ten cases, an elliptical heading is used, which introduces the issue (5.91). Questions appear in 37 instances with an introductory function (5.92). Explicit references to the text of the advice-seeker occur in 35 instances (5.93), and, in 26 cases, sequence indicators are used to structure an answer, such as in (5.94). These means of structuring the text may occur in tandem.

(5.90)   Here are some things to keep in mind as you make your decision to smoke or not to smoke: (LA 1532, drugs, "Friends say, 'Smoke!'")

(5.91)   For the obliques (the muscles on either side of the center of your belly): (LA 1716, fitness and nutrition, "Sit-ups")

(5.92)   So how and from whom can you continue to get help? (LA 1574, emotional health, "Thinks about killing others and self")

(5.93)   You also asked if, in particular, Psilocybin Mushrooms are safer than LSD. (LA 1357, drugs, "Psilocybin ('Magic') mushrooms")

(5.94)   Three final thoughts on osteoporosis and calcium: (LA 1036, fitness and nutrition, "Calcium – how much is enough?")

A farewell comment by *Lucy* is most characteristic in the category 'relationships' (n = 12) but is an infrequent move with only 47 occurrences in the entire subcorpus. Fourteen of these moves were realized with *good luck*. In five cases, a structure such as *Hope you feel better soon!* is used. One of the single instances, *keep pondering and posing*, summarizes the mission of 'Lucy Answers' in a poignant way.

Disclaimers – a type of assessments – turn out to be an infrequent discursive move as they occur in only thirteen cases in the entire corpus. Six of these are in the category 'general health'. Their content ensures that the readers understand that *Lucy* cannot diagnose everything over the computer. (5.95) is a typical example:

(5.95)   Lucy couldn't even begin to diagnose this over the computer. (LA 50, general health, "Sharp chest pains?")

There are only eleven examples in the category 'own experience', in which *Lucy* offers a 'personal' anecdote. These instances will be discussed in Chapter 8 when we look at the linguistic strategies that are involved in the construction of *Lucy*'s identity.

Finally, the open category which was reserved for moves that did not fit any of the other categories only had to be used in twelve cases. In four instances *Lucy* reaches out to the readership and the questioner by inviting reactions to the problem; and in three cases *Lucy* thanks the advice-seeker for the question. (5.96) is an example of such a case. The infrequency of these occurrences, however, does not warrant the creation of separate categories.[5]

(5.96)   Thank you for giving 'Lucy Answers' the opportunity to respond. (LA 2150, sexual health, "You need an answer on vulvar cancer!")

5.4 Summary and comparison with other advisory situations

In the last section I have analyzed the linguistic realization of the discursive moves found in 'Lucy Answers'. Advice and referral moves received the most attention since they are the main focus of this study. I distinguished between three syntactic types of advice, 52 percent of which were accounted for by declarative sentences, 36 percent by imperatives and only 11 percent by interrogatives. If we consider the declaratives and interrogatives together (63%), and acknowledge that they are a more indirect way of giving advice than imperatives, we see that 'Lucy Answers' seems to prefer to give options rather than directives. This first impression is confirmed when we look at the 757 declarative advisory sentences in the discursive moves, 476 (62%) of which are non-agentive. At the same time, however, it needs to be stressed that the use of imperatives with 36 percent is clearly part of the norm of advice-giving established in the discursive practice of 'Lucy Answers'.

Referring back to the literature review, we see that similar linguistic strategies are used by Hudson's (1990) 'Garden Lady' (agent de-emphasis, imperatives, conditionals, etc.), who, however, avoids the use of imperatives to a greater extent than *Lucy*. Compared to other contexts in which advice is given 'Lucy Answers' appears to give advice less directly. The strategies used by health visitors in Heritage and Sefi's study (1992: 368–369), i.e., overt recommendations, the imperative mood, modal verbs of obligation, and factual generalization, were all found to be employed in 'Lucy Answers' as well. However, factual generalizations – which correspond to the 476 non-agentive advisory declarative sentences – are reported as less common by Heritage and Sefi, while they are rather frequent in my corpus. In this, 'Lucy Answers' also differs from the district nurses in Leppänen's (1998: 235) study, who "did not form advice as recommendations or factual generalizations"; but there is overlap in the use of the imperative mood and modal verbs of obligation. To a certain degree even advice as *alternatives* or as *descriptions of patients' future actions* found in Leppänen's (1998: 224) data can be argued to be part of *Lucy*'s strategies for advice-giving, if the use of conditional sentences and the description of action sequences is interpreted as such. The use of conditionals in particular also reminds us of the hypothetical advice sequences found in Kinnel and Maynard's (1996:417) data of HIV pretest counseling. These sequences allow the patients to decide themselves whether or not to reject the hypothetical situation and the advice which is embedded in this situation. In 'Lucy Answers' the advisory conditional sentences function in a similar way. DeCapua and Huber's (1995:126) finding that in public contexts in which "there is an openly acknowledged difference in status and/or expertise, advice-givers are more direct and explicit" (i.e., that there is a preference for imperatives and constructions with *should* and *need*) cannot be confirmed by 'Lucy Answers'. The reason for this preference for mitigated advice-giving in 'Lucy Answers' may be the site's orientation to an ideal of non-directive counseling, which is also found in other health care or counseling contexts (cf. He 1994; Sarangi & Clarke 2002; Vehviläinen 2003) and which is explicitly mentioned in the mission statement of 'Lucy Answers'. These points will be further developed in Chapters 6 and 8, in which I will explore the function of the linguistic strategies in greater detail when I look at relational work and *Lucy's* advisor voice.

The studies just mentioned deal with face-to-face settings and explore the interactional sequence of the meetings of advisors and counselors with advice recipients. 'Lucy Answers' belongs to a different type of discursive practice because we are looking at *written* advice that appears on screen in the form of a question letter and a response letter. While *Lucy* cannot ask for clarifications about the concerns raised by the advice-seeker, the advisor team can at least take up and comment on elements of the problem letter. This is not the case for the advice-seekers, who cannot react to the points raised in the response.[6] These constraints are part of the genre of advice columns and result in the typical structures of content which I studied in this chapter.

The studies on interactional sequencing of advice encounters and Miller and Gergen's (1998) catalogue of discursive moves for postings in an Internet electronic bulletin board in particular were used as a starting point to develop a set of discursive moves that is particular to 'Lucy Answers'. These categories were then applied to the 280 records in the subcorpus of 'Lucy Answers'. This method allowed me to find the typical content structure of responses in the seven topic categories and at the same time to isolate the advisory sequences within a response. Section 5.2 contained a detailed description of the composition of an answer into its number of units and discursive moves, as well as a description of the sequence of discursive moves. It became apparent that the seven topic categories in 'Lucy Answers' fall into two groups for many of the points investigated, namely 'drugs', 'general health', 'fitness and nutrition', and 'sexual health' (Group 1), and 'emotional health', 'relationships', and 'sexuality' (Group 2) (cf. Section 5.2.5). I argue that the reason for this grouping is the approach the advisors take to the topics of the categories (content sensitivity). My analysis showed some of the consequences of this division for the composition of the answers. For example, Group 1 contains more general information than Group 2, which uses more assessment and advice. In my analysis, I made a distinction between the discursive move of general information and advice given in the form of non-agentive declarative sentences that might be read as general information out of context (see also Section 3.1). Giving advice in such a way or, as Silverman et al. (1992b) have shown, adopting a strategy of delivering information in a counseling setting may be considered to be less face-threatening. It is certainly interesting to observe that the categories in Group 1 use more general information than the categories in Group 2. Sensitive topics such as those treated in 'sexual health' (Group 1) are thus approached by giving more technical information, while the arguably equally sensitive topics of sexual relations in the category 'sexuality' are treated as the other interpersonal topics of the categories 'relationships' and 'emotional health'. Solutions to problems raised in Group 2 often rely less on giving general information than those raised in Group 1. In Group 1 advice also followed general information more often, while in Group 2, advice followed assessments more frequently.[7]

I have already compared the actual advisory parts of the responses to the results of other studies reported on earlier. Now I offer a few observations on the sequence of the discursive moves, well aware that I am comparing mainly face-to-face interaction with a written exchange that is limited to only one 'turn' for the advice-seeker (i.e., the problem letter) and for the advice-givers (i.e., the response letter). The first point worth mentioning is the role of the assessment sections. In face-to-face interaction or even in a multi-turn Internet communication situation, much of what may be unclear about an advice-seeker's problem can be clarified by asking follow-up questions. Since this is not possible in an advice column, patterns with alternating speaker parts similar to the ones observed by Heritage and Sefi (1992), Kinnel and Maynard (1996), Leppänen (1998), Silverman (1997) and others can obviously not be observed in 'Lucy Answers'. I argue, however, that it is in fact the assessment sections that largely take over the function of creating relevance by acknowledging a problem, i.e., by offering a (sometimes partial) interpretation of what is considered to be the issue at hand. Assessments, for example, resemble in function the diagnosis texts found in Hudson (1990) which are then followed by how-to texts. These assessments thus often fulfill the function of aligning the reader with a view of the problem, which was pointed out to be important in Vehviläinen's (2001: 394) data on advice-giving within labor market training. She observes that "[i]n practices in which it is considered important that professionals' advice is accepted by the clients, it is useful to produce an aligning position for the advice to minimize resistance". While Vehviläinen here refers to eliciting the points of view of the advisees, I argue that the assessments in 'Lucy Answers' fulfill a similar function in that they leave it to the advice-seeker to accept or refuse the interpretation of the problem. If it is refused, 'Lucy Answers' has made sure that the ensuing advice is not mistaken as universally valid. If it is accepted, the advice has reached the persons for whom it is relevant.

It is striking that assessments usually appear either at the beginning or end of a unit und mainly precede advice (cf. Tables 5.7 to 5.10). Advice, on the other hand, hardly ever occurs at the very beginning of a response letter (n = 18; Table 5.7). General information, the other frequent way to open a response letter (especially typical for Group 1), also couches the actual advice-giving in the text and it may be argued to have a similar function to that of assessments because it also confronts the reader with information that may or may not be relevant to him or her. 'Lucy Answers' thus avoids beginning immediately with advice. Kinnel and Maynard (1996:413) also found that 'advice after information' was one of the frequent patterns of advice-giving in their study (see Section 3.1). Despite the fact that the overall frame of 'Lucy Answers' is clearly defined as advice-giving, the pattern observed shows a preference for preceding advice with other discursive moves. The preference for mitigated advice-giving in 'Lucy Answers' which was previously noted is thus reinforced by the overall composition of the answers, and, it could be argued, that this composition constitutes a 'stepwise entry' into advice.

'Lucy Answers' is an advice column run by professional health educators who have declared that they want "to increase access to, and use of, health information by providing factual, in-depth, straight-forward, and nonjudgmental information to assist readers' decision-making" (Lucy Answers 2004). A study of the manner in which this professional team displays expert knowledge, interprets a problem, and finally gives advice will also be crucial in Chapter 6, when we look at the relational work that accompanies the responses given in 'Lucy Answers'.

CHAPTER 6

Aspects of relational work
in the response letters

6.1 Introduction

The analyses in Chapter 5 focused on the content structure of the response letters, the syntactic realization of advice, and on where advice sequences occur within the answers. At this point, we should add yet another level, relational work, to our interpretation. Relational work was described as the process of defining relationships in interaction in Section 4.2. I prefer the term relational work to the more established term *facework* because it highlights the involvement of at least two interactants, in our case the team of advisors, who represent the institution of 'Lucy Answers' by means of their fictional mouthpiece *Lucy*, the advice-seeker, and the general readership. I understand relational work as also including rudeness and impoliteness, thus covering the entire continuum from polite and appropriate to impolite and inappropriate behavior, because impolite behavior also carries meaning with respect to defining relationships (cf. Locher 2004; Locher & Watts 2005).

Relational work is of importance in an advice situation because advice can be very face-threatening in the Anglo-Western context of this study.[1] Goldsmith and MacGeorge (2000: 235) explain this as follows: "By telling a hearer what to do, advice can threaten the hearer's identity as a competent and autonomous social actor". This may even be the case when advice is solicited by the advice-seeker in the first place (as is the case for 'Lucy Answers'). Nevertheless, as Hudson (1990: 285) points out, "adults are generally remarkably adept at negotiating their way through this potentially troublesome situation". In the case of a professional advice column such as 'Lucy Answers', which functions within the frame of health care advice-giving, the advisor team can be expected to pay attention to the way in which they convey the relevant information.

The notion of 'face' is at the heart of relational work. Face may be explained as the public self-image or 'mask' that interactants want to display and have confirmed in interaction. It should be stressed that face is not a static concept, but is discursively negotiated by participants in every interaction. An individual may want to present many different faces, or masks, in the course of interactions, and is not tied to just one single role. The use of this metaphor in linguistics can be traced back to Goffman (1967), who based his understanding on Durkheim (1915), and it received particular attention in the work on politeness by Brown and Levinson ([1978] 1987) and many others (cf. Locher & Watts (2005: 12–13) for a discussion of the term). Brown and Levinson (1987) also introduced the term 'face-threatening act' and identified linguistic strategies that speakers may want to employ to redress the potentially face-threatening character of an inter-action. However, instead of using their distinction between positive and negative face and the corresponding strategies, i.e., strategies that are oriented toward "the positive self-image that the [hearer] claims for himself", or strategies that are "oriented mainly toward partially satisfying (redressing) [the hearer]'s ... basic want to maintain claims of territory and self-determination" (Brown & Levinson 1987: 70), I prefer Scollon and Scollon's (2001: 47) terminology. They speak of the involvement and independence aspect of face and hence of involvement and in-dependence strategies (cf. Locher 2004: 55). I wish to emphasize that I consider such strategies to be part of relational work in general and that they do not nec-essarily constitute politeness, which I argue elsewhere resides in only a small part of appropriate and politic relational work (cf. Locher 2004; Locher & Watts 2005). For the purpose of this study, I will make a distinction between relational work strategies that mitigate a face-threatening act (face-saving; e.g., the use of hedges), strategies that threaten the addressee's face (face-threatening; e.g., criticism) and strategies that aim at increasing involvement (face-enhancing; e.g., bonding with the reader). What I will focus on in Chapter 6 is therefore not a contribution to the discussion of politeness as such, but to the study of how the interpersonal level of the advisory exchange is negotiated in the texts overall.

As mentioned earlier, mitigation of advice will not be a rare phenomenon in cultures where advice is perceived as face-threatening. The form of mitigation may vary. We have seen, for example, that Hudson (1990: 288) found his 'Garden Lady', who prefers mitigated advice over blunt advice, to use forms which de-emphasize agency such as pseudo-cleft sentences, conditionals, and sentences of the form *I would do X*. In the more delicate context of HIV counseling, Silverman et al. (1992b) have shown that giving general information rather than personalized ad-vice was found to be the more frequent and less face-threatening alternative. In 'Lucy Answers', advisory declarative sentences and interrogatives – arguably more indirect in their force than imperatives – make up 63 percent of the advice given. Of the declarative sentences, 62 percent are realized in a non-agentive form, thus also de-emphasizing agency. Apart from this syntactic variation, advice does not simply occur on its own in 'Lucy Answers' either. The analysis of the content struc-ture of the responses has shown that it is surrounded by other discursive moves that together make up the meaning of the text. For example, the discursive moves of general information or assessment are often followed by advice, which means that they give advice its legitimation and relevance. Advice is thus embedded in the overall composition of the response texts, which may be said to have a mitigating effect. In addition, mitigation may also accompany the advisory moves in the form of lexical hedges such as *maybe, perhaps,* or *it would be a good idea to.* The use of humor may also have the effect of toning down the face-threatening character of advice-giving. We cannot generalize and state that these means of mitigation always function in the same way. Just as we have seen that there is no direct link between syntactic form and function, there is no straightforward link between linguistic form and social imposition (Goodwin 1990; Leppänen 1998). Relational work thus requires a careful analysis of the linguistic data in its context.

Mitigation is only one manifestation of relational work. In 'Lucy Answers' there are also involvement strategies to be observed such as bonding, empathizing and praising, but also more face-threatening means such as overt criticism of the advice-seeker. In this chapter I will look at mitigation as well as at the other aspects of relational work in order to establish what role relational work plays in 'Lucy Answers'. I am therefore interested in the types of relational work present as well as in the discursive moves in which they occur. The following questions, proposed in Chapter 4, will now be addressed:

- What kind of relational work is used?
- Where does relational work manifest itself in the response letters?
- If mitigation is used, does it occur at the same time as the actual advice or together with other elements of the answer?

While it is my aim to give as comprehensive a picture of the use of relational work as possible, it should be stressed that this picture will remain incomplete by necessity due to the complex nature of relational work. I am thus dealing with specific *aspects* of relational work and intend to demonstrate how they contribute to the discursive practice found in 'Lucy Answers'.

6.2 Methodology

In order to analyze relational work in 'Lucy Answers' I employed a methodology similar to the one used to analyze the content structure in that I developed a catalogue of relational work categories that was based on the literature on facework, on the one hand, and emerged from my qualitative close readings, on the other hand. I then added this level of analysis to the record files which already contained the content structure analysis. This method allowed me to establish in which discursive moves relational work occurs. However, before I proceed to illustrate the categories employed, I need to make some important methodological points. First, relational work cannot be 'counted' as such. For example, it does not make sense to say that one occurrence of humor corresponds to three usages of *maybe* as a lexical hedge or to one display of empathy.[2] The numbers established will, however, give us an idea of the relational work types which are used in each category of discursive move and each topic category. What I have aimed for in categorizing relational work in my database is thus to give a very broad picture of the *kind* of relational work that manifests itself in 'Lucy Answers' and where it occurs. The numbers resulting from this analysis can therefore only be taken as indicators of tendencies rather than a reflection of the complete picture of the usage of relational work in 'Lucy Answers'. Second, in 'quantifying' relational work strategies, it also should be stressed that small numbers do not necessarily mean that the strategies investigated are not important. At times it is the very fact that there is humor, empathy or criticism *at all* which contributes to the overall effect of the responses. Finally, I wish to highlight that there is no communication without a relational aspect (Watzlawick et al. 1967). In other words, even when a discursive move was found to contain none of the relational work strategies studied in this chapter, relational work is still present – either in the syntactic and lexical choices manifest in the discursive move itself, or with one of the strategies investigated in other discursive moves adjacent to it, or in the composition of the response letter as a whole.

Table 6.1 shows the categories assigned to relational work (level 4) in the responses in 'Lucy Answers' next to the previous levels 0 to 3. In addition to the syntactic information gained about indirectness and mitigation from the discussion of level 3 discursive moves, the types of relational work that were analyzed are *bonding, boosting, criticizing, empathizing, hedging, praising* and *the use of humor*. This means that I will look at very different types of relational work. Bonding, empathizing and praising can be seen as representing involvement strategies for supportive relational work. Hedging is interpreted as a face-saving strategy in the context of 'Lucy Answers'. Mitigating a face-threatening act also pays tribute to the advice-seeker's face needs, but may also be a means to protect the advisors. (The latter is, for example, the case when 'Lucy Answers' makes clear that there may be more than one interpretation of a reader's predicament and thus protects the advisor team from appearing to misrepresent facts.) Boosting and criticizing are face-threatening strategies in our context. Boosting is a means of emphasizing the content of a discursive move and may, for example, stress expertise. This highlights the power difference between the advice-seeker and the advisors. Criticism can be seen as a face-threatening strategy in that the advice-seeker's face is threatened if disagreement with his or her actions, attitudes or points of view is voiced. The use of humor will be explained in more detail below. Suffice it to say here that it can be a means to realize face-threatening, face-saving and involvement strategies.

Every discursive move in level 3 *may*, but does not have to, contain the relational work moves chosen for analysis (Table 6.1). Furthermore, it is possible that

Table 6.1 Categories for the content structure (levels 1–3) and relational work (level 4) in the responses of 'Lucy Answers'

Level 0	Level 1	Level 2	Level 3	Level 4
Topic category	Content structure level			Relational work level
drugs emotional health fitness/nutrition general health relationships sexual health sexuality				
	Answer	address		
		unit (one or more)	advice assessment disclaimer explanation farewell general information metacomment open category own experience referral	bonding boosting criticizing empathizing hedging praising using humor
		signature		

for each level 3 discursive move one or more occurrences of the same or a combination of different level 4 moves are categorized. For example, an assessment might contain several instances of bonding and a criticism; advice might contain only one act of hedging; a general information section might contain no relational work strategy of the kind studied here at all (see comment above), etc.

Not only can a discursive move contain several relational work categories, but the same linguistic expression may at times have more than one relational function. For example, it is possible that a sentence realizes bonding and empathizing with the reader at the same time. In this case, a mixed category was used for tagging: 'empathizing-bonding'. Table 6.2 gives an overview of the relational work categories for the responses in 'Lucy Answers', their combinations, and a brief explanation. Relational work categories that formed combinations are listed in both sections.

It is important to stress that – with the exception of humor – all relational work categories can occur on their own. They are therefore hierarchically on the same level. Humor is different in this respect since this category cannot appear by itself. Instead, it is the other categories that are realized by the use of humor, as will be discussed in more detail below.

Table 6.2 Relational work in the answers, level 4 (ordered alphabetically)

	Level 4 category	Explanation
bonding	bonding	bonding with the questioner or the readership
	bonding-hedging	bonding and hedging occur in combination
	empathizing-bonding	empathizing and bonding occur in combination
	humor-bonding	humor which aims at bonding with the questioner or the readership
boosting	boosting	a word or phrase used to give a point more weight
	criticizing-boosting	criticizing and boosting occur in combination
	empathizing-boosting	empathizing and boosting occur in combination
criticizing	criticizing	criticizing of the questioner's attitudes and actions
	criticizing-boosting	criticizing and boosting occur in combination
	criticizing-empathizing	criticizing and empathizing occur in combination
	criticizing-hedging	criticizing and hedging occur in combination
	humor-criticizing	humor as a means to mitigate criticism of the questioner's attitudes and actions; this is a special type of humor-hedging
empathizing	empathizing	display of understanding of a questioner's situation, reassurance
	empathizing-bonding	empathizing and bonding occur in combination
	empathizing-boosting	empathizing and boosting occur in combination
	empathizing-hedging	empathizing and hedging occur in combination
	empathizing-praising	empathizing and praising occur in combination
	criticizing-empathizing	criticizing and empathizing occur in combination
hedging	hedging	a word or phrase used to downtone the weight of an imposition
	bonding-hedging	bonding and hedging occur in combination
	criticizing-hedging	criticizing and hedging occur in combination
	empathizing-hedging	empathizing and hedging occur in combination
	humor-criticizing	humor as a means to mitigate criticism of the questioner's attitudes and actions; this is a special type of humor-hedging
	humor-hedging	humor which mitigates the content of an imposition
praising	praising	the questioner's attitudes and actions are highlighted as good
	empathizing-praising	empathizing and praising occur in combination
use of humor	humor-bonding	humor which aims at bonding with the questioner or the readership
	humor-criticizing	humor as a means to mitigate criticism of the questioner's attitudes and actions; this is a special type of humor-hedging
	humor-hedging	humor which mitigates the content of an imposition

First I will give a general definition of each of the relational work types that can be combined in alphabetical order, then I will explain the combinations. These introductions will be brief since more information will be given in the discussion sections.

Bonding (involvement strategy). For my purposes here, 'bonding' is defined as an attempt to establish a connection with the advice-seeker and/or the readership. It is therefore a supportive relational work strategy that aims at creating positive rapport. Consider (6.1) in which *Lucy* wishes the questioner *good luck* in the farewell section of the record, or (6.2), in which a foreign student at AEI is welcomed to the United States in an assessment section at the very beginning of the answer. In both cases, the function of these sentences can best be described as creating rapport, or bonding, with the advice-seeker and the wider readership:

(6.1) **farewell** <bonding> Good luck with your investigation, </bonding> (LA 1665, drugs, "Mysterious meds arrive in the mail")

(6.2) **assessment** <bonding> Welcome to the United States! </bonding> (LA 1181, general health, "To shave or not to shave")

Notice that the relational work categories are given with their starting point <bonding> and their end point </bonding>. This is common usage in XML or other hypertext languages. While this notification is used for the actual analysis (see Appendix), it will only be shown in the examples for discussion in this chapter. At times, an entire sentence will be categorized as *containing* the relational work move discussed, rather than pointing at single isolated words.

Boosting (face-threatening strategy). 'Boosting' devices "intensify or emphasise the force" of an utterance (Holmes 1995:76). In the context of advising, boosters were categorized as such when there is emphasis on a certain aspect of advice, or on the importance of a point being made. In (6.3) the advice to go and see a health care provider (referral) is stressed by starting the advice with *It is essential.* In (6.4) the advice-seeker is told not to take full responsibility for a friend's behavior and this is highlighted by *It is important.* In both cases the booster is interpreted as emphasizing the importance of this piece of advice:

(6.3) **referral type=decl** <boosting> It is essential </boosting> to talk with your health care provider and/or pharmacist about your prescription, over-the-counter, and herbal medications, their side effects, their contraindications (including whether or not grapefruit juice is safe to consume when using these drugs), and your history of drinking grapefruit juice, to see if the dosage of your medicine(s) needs to be adjusted accordingly. (LA 2352, drugs, "Grapefruit juice and drug interactions")

(6.4)   **advice type=decl** <boosting> It is important </boosting> for you not to take
responsibility for her behavior and whether or not she will change. (LA 266,
fitness and nutrition, "Friend has a weight complex")

Boosting is a means *Lucy* uses to qualify her advice. By doing this she makes use
of her status as expert, i.e., boosting underlines her expertise. Since it may be perceived as face-threatening to emphasize status differences, boosting is interpreted
as face-threatening in the context of 'Lucy Answers', and for this reason we are
looking at it here with respect to relational work.

Criticizing (face-threatening strategy). Brown and Levinson (1987:66) describe
criticism as face-threatening. This is explained by saying that if criticism of a
person is voiced, then this may indicate to the addressee that "the speaker does
not care about the addressee's feelings, wants, etc." Criticism of the questioners'
attitudes and actions in 'Lucy Answers' will therefore contribute to the negotiation of the relationship between the questioners and the respondents. Once more,
consideration of *Lucy*'s role as expert advisor will be central in this discussion.

In the first example (6.5), a questioner is told in no uncertain terms that he or
she has a bad habit: *It isn't good to smoke no matter what else you do.* In (6.6) *Lucy*
criticizes the questioner for being unhappy about her sexual activity and yet taking
no initiative (*instead of waiting for some magic*):

(6.5)   **assessment** To begin, although what you're suggesting may seem logical, the
positive health effects of exercise will not negate the negative health consequences of smoking. <criticizing> It isn't good to smoke no matter what else
you do. </criticizing> (LA 1419, drugs, "Smokin' runner")

(6.6)   **advice type=imp-a list** Try to take your time and be assertive about your
needs in sex, <criticizing> instead of waiting for some magic </criticizing>
to make the intercourse pleasurable. Be active about your sex life – and see
what happens!! (LA 378, sexuality, "No stimulation from intercourse")

Empathizing (involvement strategy). According to Jessner (1996:89), "[f]rom a
psychological perspective, empathy is described as a cognitive awareness and understanding of the emotions and feelings of another person, i.e. an intellectual or
conceptual grasping of the affect of another". Silverman and Peräkylä (1990:312–
313) point out that empathy should be understood as "the social ability to pick
up behavioural and cultural cues present in what the patient is saying and doing",
and ultimately as an interactional phenomenon. I have categorized comments as
empathetic when they displayed such awareness or understanding of an advice-
seeker's particular (emotional) situation or when they reassured a questioner. In
(6.7), which is taken from the example already introduced in Figure 5.4, the ques-

tioner's worries are qualified as *not at all uncommon*. A similar occurrence can be seen in (6.8), previously shown in Figure 5.2, in which the advisee is reassured that his preference for taller girls is nothing out of the ordinary (*but this doesn't mean that anything is wrong with you*):

(6.7)   **assessment** <**empathizing**> It's not at all uncommon to experience some degree of anxiety when you move, change jobs, graduate, get married, etc. – even if these big life events are positive ones. </**empathizing**> (LA 1245, emotional health, "Anxiety attacks from moving...again")

(6.8)   **advice type=decl** <**empathizing**> Taller boy with shorter girl may be the norm, but this doesn't mean that anything is wrong with you, </**empathizing**> <**humor-hedging**> or that you shouldn't enjoy and pursue your higher interests. </**humor-hedging**> (LA 1659, relationships, "Troubled by attraction to tall women")

Hedging (face-saving strategy). 'Hedging' aims at mitigating a face-threatening act. Mitigation can be achieved in various ways. Examples of lexical hedges are *sort of, maybe, I mean, well.* Aijmer (1986) defines the function of these words or phrases as follows:

> Hedges make it possible to comment on one's message while one is producing it either 'prospectively' or 'retrospectively.' The hedge signals that a word is not treated in the usual sense (as a resource available to form messages with) but that it is inappropriate, insignificant, negatively evaluated or approximate.
>
> (Aijmer 1986: 14)

Aijmer (1986: 14) points out that for oral communication hedges are a means to hesitate before choosing, to comment on what is on one's mind, or to abbreviate or condense information; this can also be achieved by intonation and voice-quality. Tannen (1993: 28) adds that a hedge may "soften the impact of the negative statement"; they can, thus, be a means to express relational work which is geared to protecting the addressee's face. Finally, Brown and Levinson (1987) define a hedge as

> a particle, word, or phrase that modifies the degree of membership of a predicate or noun phrase in a set; it says of that membership that it is *partial*, or true only in certain respects, or that it is *more* true and complete than perhaps might be expected.   (Brown & Levinson 1987: 145; emphasis in original)

In our context of American advice-giving, the hedging of the advice is central. By mitigating, the advisor acknowledges that advice is potentially face-threatening because the advisor is telling the advisee what to do. Mitigation already played a role when we considered the three syntactic realizations of advice/referral analyzed in Chapter 5: declaratives, interrogatives and imperatives. I will discuss the degrees of optionality that are obtained in these three different ways of rendering advice in Section 6.3.1.

As well as looking at suggestions in the form of interrogatives and declarative sentences as hedged, I have also tagged instances of specific lexical hedges and their variants. They were either taken from lists previously used for similar analysis (cf. Locher 2004) and then looked for in 'Lucy Answers', or were directly found in 'Lucy Answers' and then systematically tagged (single instances are not listed here). They are: *a bit, actually, Lucy suggests, anyway, as it were, certainly, difficult, helpful, honestly, Lucy thinks, good idea, in a way, in any case, in fact, it's possible, kind of, let me, little, makes sense, may/might want to, maybe, more or less, of course, perhaps, please, probably, somehow, sort of, suppose, type of, useful, well, what you call, whatever, why not, wise, wonder, sometimes, it sounds like.* The decision to label any of these lexical items and their variants as a hedge was always made on the basis of the context in which they occurred. Examples of hedging can be seen in (6.9) and (6.10):

(6.9)   **advice type=decl** If you decide to break off the relationship, <hedging> it might be useful </hedging> to rehearse what you want to say and how you'll handle his reactions. (LA 2589, relationships, "My partner feels more strongly about me than I do about him")

(6.10)   <hedging> maybe </hedging> saying to them what you've told Lucy will help diffuse present and future strain. (LA 1446, emotional health, "Anxiety ruining family and intimate relationships")

In (6.9), the phrase *it might be useful to* could also have been left out, i.e., the core message of the advice would have remained the same without it. Its addition, however, functions as a hedge to the advice which follows. In (6.10), *maybe* prefaces and mitigates *Lucy's* suggestion that the advice-seeker should talk to her family and boyfriend about her anxiety problem.

Praising (involvement strategy). Lucy does not only criticize a questioner's attitudes and actions, she also praises. Since highlighting something positive about an addressee, i.e., complimenting him or her, also necessarily reflects on the relationship that you have or wish to create and shape, praise is a manifestation of relational work. Self-explanatory examples of praise are given in (6.11) to (6.12):

(6.11)   **assessment** <praising> Kudos to you for seeking help. </praising> (LA 253, emotional health, "Disappointed with therapist?")

(6.12)   **assessment** <praising> How fortunate your girlfriend is to have a companion with the caring and courage to ask such a question. </praising> (LA 1513, sexuality, "What should I do with her breasts?")

The use of humor (face-saving, face-threatening, or involvement strategy). In her study on the functions of humor in the conversation of men and women, Hay (2000:716) maintains that, generally, "every attempt at humor is an attempt to both express solidarity with the audience and construct a position of respect and status within the group". She then goes on to classify instances of humor into the three areas of 'solidarity', 'psychological' (i.e., defend and cope) and 'power'. Hay's (2000:215) method of identifying humor is to "regard humor as being anything the speaker intends to be funny". By analyzing audience reactions and with the help of detailed background knowledge, Hay assesses the effect of the investigated utterances and judges whether they are humorous. In the case of 'Lucy Answers' I cannot rely on audience reactions to establish what is taken to be humorous and what is not. For this reason, I have been conservative when I categorized instances I consider humorous. Since humor itself is multifunctional, as many researchers have pointed out (e.g., Holmes 2000), it does not appear in a category of its own but is always assigned a specification. I have identified three categories in 'Lucy Answers':

– humor which aims at bonding with the questioner or the readership (humor-bonding),
– humor which mitigates the content of an imposition (humor-hedging), and
– humor as a means to hedge criticism of the questioner's attitudes and actions (humor-criticizing; this is a special type of humor-hedging).

One example from each category is given to illustrate these types of humor used in 'Lucy Answers'. Humor-bonding can be seen in (6.13), in which a questioner, who identified him- or herself as *a young adult who can't swallow pills*, is assured that many other people share his or her problem. (6.13) appears in an assessment section at the very beginning of *Lucy's* answer:

(6.13) **assessment** <empathizing> Rest assured </empathizing> that many young adults <**humor-bonding**> and some not-so-young </**humor-bonding**> adults share your problem. (LA 1985, emotional health, "Help! I can't swallow pills")

This reassuring move is interpreted as showing empathy for the questioner's situation. A humorous note enters this sentence with the phrase *and some not-so-young adults* because *Lucy* takes up and plays with the words used for identification by the questioner (i.e., *a young adult*). I argue that this humorous word play functions as a way of bonding with the questioner and the wider readership.

Humor can also be used as a means of mitigation to hedge the content of an imposition. The following example of a questioner who has fallen in love with a banker and wonders how to make the first move is a case in point. After humorous bonding (*See what happens when you leave your computer for some real live human contact!*), *Lucy* proceeds to her first piece of advice which is formulated in the form of an interrogative inviting an action (6.14). The humor in the wordplay on ATM ("automated teller machine" vs. "approach that man") hedges the advice given:

(6.14)   **advice type=int-a <humor-hedging>** Since this fine financier isn't your boss or teacher, why not take the letters A-T-M to stand for Approach That Man. **</humor-hedging>** (LA 1602, relationships, "Should I cash in on hot banker?")

The last humor-category is really a special case of humor in a hedging function since a criticism of the questioner's attitudes or actions is mitigated with humor. In (6.15) a questioner who is concerned about the shape of his genitals is humorously reminded that his worries are unfounded:

(6.15)   **general information** Erection is caused during arousal by more blood flowing into the penis than flows out. **<humor-criticizing>** However, erect does not mean exactly straight as an arrow, hard as nails, perpendicular to your body, and parallel to the floor. **</humor-criticizing>** Each person's erection is unique as well. (LA 21, sexuality, "Curved penis")

The humor lies in showing the worried person that his expectations may be idealistic by giving repeated exaggerated images of his assumed idea.

Combinations. As previously mentioned, the general types of level 4 discursive moves identified in 'Lucy Answers' can be combined (Table 6.2). They can, in other words, be realized by the same linguistic expressions. In addition, relational work strategies may of course appear in discursive moves that are already considered mitigated (advisory interrogatives and advisory declarative sentences). Table 6.3 shows the combinations which occur in 'Lucy Answers'.

Bonding, for example, occurs both on its own ('bonding-bonding' in Table 6.3) and in combination with empathizing and hedging, and is also realized by the use of humor. Hedging, in contrast, occurs with bonding, criticizing and empathizing, appears on its own, and is realized by means of humor. The case of humor has already been discussed because humor needs a further sub-categorization

Table 6.3 The types of relational work combinations in 'Lucy Answers'

	bonding	boosting	criticizing	empathizing	hedging	humor	praising
bonding	x			x	x	x	
boosting		x	x	x			
criticizing		x	x	x	x	x	
empathizing	x	x	x	x	x		x
hedging	x		x	x	x	x	
humor	x		x		x		
praising				x			x

by definition. I have chosen two more examples to illustrate some other possible combinations. In (6.16) we see criticizing combined with hedging. The questioner, who is unhappy about his or her weight, is reminded that the problem may not be weight as such but the attitude of the questioner. This implied criticism is hedged with a sub-clause *Although the way you feel about your body is valid,* and the preamble *sometimes it is helpful to.* Notice also that the criticism, which is already hedged, is followed by praise.

(6.16)   **assessment** **<criticizing-hedging>** Although the way you feel about your body is valid, sometimes it is helpful to remember that we are harder on ourselves than we need to be. **</criticizing-hedging>** **<praising>** You are smart for not wanting to "diet." **</praising>** (LA 384, fitness and nutrition, "Eating poorly, no exercise")

In (6.17) we can observe empathy occurring in combination with a booster. A questioner's wish to control his or her depression and eating disorder is supported:

(6.17)   **advice type=decl** **<empathizing-boosting>** Lucy encourages you to follow through on your work in fighting this depression and your eating disorder. **</empathizing-boosting>** (LA 409, emotional health, "Depression, bulimia, and Zoloft")

I argue that there is empathy because of the metaphor of 'work' and 'fight', which acknowledge the struggle the questioner is going through. The boosting function is seen in the use of the verb *encourage* and the explicit mention of *Lucy,* which gives the sentence more weight (cf. Chapter 8).

6.3 Results and discussion

While the analysis in Chapter 5 aimed at giving a complete picture of the content structure in *Lucy's* response letters, my discussion of relational work is different and aims at showing tendencies of *what kind of* relational work is expressed, and *where* relational work manifests itself within the answers. I have already indicated that relational work is not quantifiable as such. The numbers shown in the tables in this chapter are therefore presented as tendencies, rather than as absolute values. In what follows I will first look at the overall results of my categorization in all the topic categories before I discuss the relational work categories individually.

Table 6.4 shows the results of my categorization of the relational work moves introduced above. Overall, I found 1,351 relational work manifestations. The combinations are listed in both respective categories, which means that the numbers reflect the overall usage of the individual types of relational work. The only exception to this are the instances of hedging which are underrepresented in Table 6.4.

Table 6.4 Relational work moves in 'Lucy Answers' by type and category (including combinations; subcorpus)

topic category → rel. work type ↓	Group 1				Group 2			total	%
	drugs	fitn./nutrition	general health	sexual health	emot. health	relationships	sexuality		
hedging	79	67	64	62	100	135	62	569	42
empathizing	20	16	13	18	64	48	17	196	15
boosting	22	27	24	27	30	22	13	165	12
bonding	13	29	31	18	22	29	14	156	12
humor-hedging	13	11	9	8	6	24	10	81	6
humor-bonding	6	10	15	5	10	13	9	68	5
praising	7	12	7	7	10	11	11	65	5
criticizing	7	4		2	9	20	9	51	4
total	167	176	163	147	251	302	145	1,351	100
%	12	13	12	11	19	22	11		

This is because the knowledge gained about syntactic hedging from my discussion of the discursive moves of advice (i.e., advisory interrogatives and advisory declarative sentences are considered to be more hedged than imperatives) is not included in the numbers.[3] Despite this, hedging is still the most frequent relational work type, which tells us that there is a strong tendency towards mitigation in 'Lucy Answers'. Table 6.4 also shows that, overall, the topic categories 'relationships' (n = 302, 22%) and 'emotional health' (n = 251, 19%) seem to contain more relational work of the types analyzed. All three categories of Group 2 appear to feature empathy more than the other topic categories (see gray highlighting, which marks the first and second preference for every category). Bonding seems to be an important device in the topic categories 'fitness and nutrition' and 'general health', while 'drugs' and 'sexual health' have quite a number of boosters. I will comment on these findings in the discussions of the individual types of relational work.

In what follows, I will first deal with the complex of hedging, which means that I will discuss hedges and combinations that entail mitigation. I will start by dealing with this face-saving aspect of relational work because it is the most prominent type in 'Lucy Answers'. I will then move to empathizing, bonding, praising, boosting, and criticizing. I will, in other words, move from relational work that aims at mitigating a face-threatening act (hedging) to relational work which aims at supporting the advice-seeker (empathizing, bonding, praising), and will end with relational work which may be said to be face-threatening to the reader to a certain degree (boosting and criticizing). As there are many combinations of relational work, my analysis will touch on many of these categories several times in the individual sections.

6.3.1 Hedging

In my analysis of the linguistic realization of advice in Chapter 5, I discovered that in 63 percent of all discursive moves 'Lucy Answers' prefers either advisory interrogatives or declarative sentences over direct and straightforward imperatives. If we look at this finding with respect to relational work and mitigation, we can say that syntactically redressing or hedging the advice occurs more often than unmitigated variants (cf. Section 5.3.1). This is especially relevant, since, in the case of declaratives and interrogatives inviting an action (rather than introspection) the same content could also have been rendered in a more direct way. It is therefore a deliberate choice to use a more indirect form of advice.[4]

This tendency is confirmed even within the advisory declarative sentences, of which 62 percent are non-agentive rather than agentive. These instances could be argued to be yet one more level removed from giving a direct imperative as an instruction for advice (cf. Section 5.3.1.1). Furthermore, there is yet another degree of relational work to be observed in the agentive advisory declaratives which are combinations of 'pronoun + modal'. While the largest single category is *you can* with 92 instances, the variants which indicate even more optionality (*could, may, might*[5]) add another 98 occurrences (N = 281). 'Lucy Answers' thus plays with the degree of optionality. It is indicated to the advice-seeker that he or she *may* adopt the advice given, but that, in the end, this decision is up to him or her.

As a case in point, consider (6.18), an advisory declarative sentence in which *Lucy* proposes that *maybe* the questioner *could* have the meetings with her friends (which caused the problems discussed in this response) at her house rather than elsewhere to accommodate the needs of the questioner's mother:

(6.18)   **advice type=decl** <hedging> Maybe your friends could meet you at your house, so that your mother, who seems to like your friends, knows that you are all together and safe. <hedging> (LA 451, relationships, "Curfews on break")

In addition to the syntactic choice, the usage of *maybe* and the modal *could* mitigate the content of the advice in (6.18). The same can be observed in (6.19) in which the interrogative that contains the advice proposes an action which could also have been rendered without the introductory *Would it be possible for you to:*

(6.19)   **advice type=int-a** <hedging> Would it be possible for you to let him know of your relationship and sexual interests – not for him, but in general, when you're having one of those deep, late-night conversations? <hedging> (LA 1623, relationships, "Should I tell my friend that I'm attracted to him?")

In addition to the mitigating role of the question, the introductory words hedge the advice because they acknowledge the fact that it is the advisee who has to decide whether the action proposed is feasible for him.

Even the category of advisory and referral sentences realized by imperatives may contain mitigation. The most frequent verb is *try* (n = 48 for advice and n = 10 for referral), which can be argued to constitute a hedge. Another possibility of mitigation was demonstrated in example (5.82), in which 77 imperatives are listed to 'get naturally high'. These imperatives clearly function as suggestions (rather than as instructions for a given sequence of actions), because the large number of activities proposed indicates that the reader is invited to make a selection. This means that the force of the imperatives is mitigated.

Along with this syntactic analysis, it is of interest to find lexical instances of hedging as outlined in the methodology section, and as just observed in (6.18) and (6.19). In particular, it is of interest to see in which topic category hedging is used, in which discursive moves the hedges chosen for analysis can be found and with what other types of relational work they combine. Table 6.5 answers the first two questions. It shows the number of occurrences of relational work moves in the discursive moves for each category. I have not normalized these numbers because neither the number of words, nor the units, nor the discursive moves can serve as a straightforward point of reference.[6] I have, however, added the number of discursive moves in the last column to indicate in how many of them relational work moves could have been displayed. But, since more than one relational work move can occur per discursive move, even this point of reference remains an approximation. I will thus examine the overall occurrence of a particular type of relational work in all 40 response letters of a topic category.

Table 6.5 shows that, in the 40 records analyzed for each topic category, the categories 'relationships' (n = 135) and 'emotional health' (n = 100) use lexical hedges such as *maybe, perhaps, please*, but also *it's not a bad idea to* or *it makes sense to* most often. The third category from Group 2 ('sexuality') uses this kind of hedging in the same way as the categories from Group 1 (n = 62–79), all of which use hedging as their most frequent type of relational work. Furthermore, we can see that lexical hedges mainly occur within the advice moves already discussed. Within these the majority are used to mitigate advisory declarative sentences (n = 188). Imperatives combine with lexical hedges in only 33 instances. This seems to indicate that it is acceptable in 'Lucy Answers' to use imperatives in an unmitigated way within the advisory moves. Hedges, however, are also quite frequent in assessments and explanations. Within explanations they occur most often in those which explain advice (n = 47). Hedging thus centers around advising and assessing.

Assessing can, of course, also be quite face-threatening to the advisee since *Lucy* might misunderstand or misrepresent the problem stated in the problem letter. Thibault (1988:219, 221) referred to this difficulty by highlighting that advice

Table 6.5 Hedging in the discursive moves in 'Lucy Answers' by topic category, ranked by overall frequency (including combinations; subcorpus)

topic category → discursive move ↓	Group 1				Group 2					
	drugs	fitn./nutrition	gen. health	sexual health	emot. health	relationships	sexuality	total	%	in n dm*
advice	29	32	26	22	47	75	31	†262	46	976
assessment	21	13	16	9	24	34	18	135	24	400
explanation	7	4	4	4	15	22	3	59	10	278
gen. information	11	9	8	12	2	2	4	48	8	502
referral	5	4	4	12	8	1	2	36	6	310
metacomment	5	4	1	2	2		3	17	3	156
disclaimer	1	1	2	1	1	1		7	1	13
farewell					1			1		47
open category			1				1	2		12
own experience			2					2		11
total	79	67	64	62	100	135	62	569	98	2,705
%	14	12	11	11	18	24	11			

† The total for hedging in advice is considerably higher if syntactic information were included;
* dm = discursive move.

columns mirror interactional control because the advisors redefine and interpret the questioner's text, and these actions stress the asymmetry between advisee and advisor. Assessments are thus delicate. To avoid giving an impression of misrepresentation, which might lead to an *a priori* rejection of the ensuing advice, *Lucy* is thus careful not to be too assertive about her judgments and to provide the reader with the possibility of distancing him- or herself from the interpretation offered in case the problem was not clearly presented. At the same time, it is also in *Lucy*'s interest to cover *her* tracks, so to speak, since bluntly misrepresenting a questioner's case might be interpreted by the readership as "face-loss" on the part of the advisor and might result in a loss of *Lucy*'s credibility. Consider (6.20), in which *Lucy* responds to a reader who is troubled because her boyfriend suspects her of faking orgasms:

(6.20)   **assessment** <hedging> *Lucy bets* that something has *probably* happened to make him question his skill as a lover, or his belief in your honesty. *Maybe* he is getting older and feels less secure, *or perhaps* he has read something in a magazine that has made him question you. </**hedging**> (LA 1141, sexuality, "I'm NOT Faking orgasm", italics added)

In this assessment, *Lucy* offers her point of view, but takes care to state that this interpretation is one of several readings by writing *Lucy bets*, *probably*, *maybe* and *or perhaps.* In (6.21) *Lucy* hedges her assessment of the problem of a questioner's sister with *it sounds like:*

> (6.21)   **assessment** <hedging> *It sounds like* your sister may have been diagnosed with Celiac Sprue. </hedging> (LA 462, fitness and nutrition, "Gluten allergy", italics added)

Hedging appears in the following combinations: humor-hedging (n = 75), empathizing-hedging (n = 33), criticizing-hedging (n = 7), humor-criticizing (n = 6) and bonding-hedging (n = 1). While bonding occurs only once in combination with hedging, humor is used 81 times to mitigate a face-threatening act (six of those are criticism). Fifty-one of these are hedging advisory moves. With 24 instances, the category 'relationships' makes most use of humor as a means for mitigation. The other categories all have less than thirteen occurrences. It therefore seems that this type of humor is more typical for the category 'relationships'. In addition, there are seven further cases of criticism that are mitigated. Hedging and empathy also appear together in 33 cases. Of these, eighteen are to be found in assessments and ten in advice. (As we shall see later, empathy is typically to be found in assessments.) In (6.22) *Lucy* acknowledges to a person who is unhappy about his job situation that finding a new position is difficult, but also implies that an effort has to be made (hence the hedging aspect) if he or she wants to succeed:

> (6.22)   **assessment** <empathizing-hedging> Searching for a new job *can take some time and a lot of effort*, but finding a job that meets your goals and excites you *is worth it.* </empathizing-hedging> (LA 1684, emotional health, "I want a better job!", italics added)

(6.23) is an example in which empathy occurs in combination with hedging in an advisory declarative sentence. Here *Lucy* suggests that a person who is worried that schizophrenia may be genetic and might hence affect her/his children *may want to* consult professional help (hedge). Empathy is to be found in the fact that *Lucy* acknowledges that the advice-seeker has *concerns*:

> (6.23)   **advice type=decl** <empathizing-hedging> The slightly increased risk need not unduly affect any decisions you make about your having children in the future, but you *may want to* explore *your concerns* with a psychotherapist. </empathizing-hedging> (LA 2422, emotional health, "Schizophrenia – Are genes involved?", italics added)

To illustrate hedging once more I have chosen an example from the category 'relationships'. The question for Figure 6.1 is asked by somebody who is attracted to 'older' women and is worried about this fact:

Dear Lucy, I cannot stop fantasizing about having sex with very old women. I recently picked up a 65-year-old in a bar and had the best orgasm of my life with her. I am 40 and now can't stop thinking of geriatric sex – is there something wrong with me and if not, where can I meet more likeminded pensioners?

```
Answer
├── address
│   └── Dear Reader,
├── unit 1
│   ├── assessment
│   │   <empathizing> There's certainly nothing wrong </empathizing> with forty- and
│   │   sixtysomethings, or GenX'ers and octogenarians, getting it on as long as all
│   │   involved are caring and consenting. Big age differences between partners,
│   │   especially if one is a lot older than the other, raise eyebrows because it's not the
│   │   "norm." Many people don't want to imagine or accept that older people are sexual
│   │   and sexually desired, or suspect that the younger halfs are in it for the money or
│   │   impending inheritance.
│   └── advice type=decl
│       <hedging> You, and hopefully your partner, enjoyed your time together, so it
│       sounds like hanging around at your local senior center would be a good idea.
│       </hedging>
├── unit 2
│   ├── advice type=decl list
│   │   On- and off-line dating services are available where you can search for older
│   │   women who fancy youngsters like yourself, and vice-versa. <humor-hedging>
│   │   And, if you place a personal ad in the Miami Herald or the Scottsdale Tribune,
│   │   your phone would probably ring off the hook. </humor-hedging>
│   ├── metacomment
│   │   Where else?
│   └── advice type=imp-a
│       Try continuing ed classes, bookstores, libraries, the supermarket, health clubs,
│       town meetings, political events, and definitely at the polls on Election Day.
├── unit 3
│   ├── metacomment
│   │   One more piece of advice:
│   ├── advice type=decl
│   │   <criticizing-hedging> you might avoid the words "very old women" in your quest
│   │   for senior sex. (Besides, 65-years-young would be considered mature or older, not
│   │   very old.) </criticizing-hedging>
│   └── explanation type=advice
│       <criticizing-hedging> Some of these women you lust after might take offense to
│       this description, especially those who can outperform you in more ways than one.
│       </criticizing-hedging>
└── signature
    └── Lucy
```

Figure 6.1 The response in "Younger man hot for senior citizens" (LA 1853, relationships)

In the first unit of the response, *Lucy* reassures the advice-seeker first in an assessment section and then gives him the advice that they should enjoy their time together, hedged with *hopefully, it sounds like* and *would be a good idea*. In the second unit, the matter-of-fact advice to try dating services is followed up by a suggestion to place an ad in a newspaper which is hedged with humor. Rather than being linked to an individual lexical hedge, the humor is here derived from the evocation of associations: *Lucy* mentions two newspapers which, for an American audience, are linked with places where many people move when they retire. This suggestion is followed up with further advice. In the last unit *Lucy* voices criticism addressed at the advice-seeker, both in an advisory and an explanatory discursive move. While the message is clear – namely that the questioner should be careful in his wording when talking about 'older women' – *Lucy* nevertheless uses lexical hedges to mitigate her criticism to a certain extent: *might, some, might*. Notice also that *Lucy* prefaces her criticism in the metacomment section by specifically mentioning *One more piece of advice*. She thus sets the frame for the way in which the criticism that follows should be understood.

Hedges are clearly the most dominant aspect of the relational work moves analyzed in 'Lucy Answers', both in their syntactic as well as in their lexical realizations. It has also been shown that hedging is not only restricted to the mitigation of advice, but also appears in other discursive moves. Hedging is used especially in assessments to indicate that *Lucy*'s interpretations of the advice-seeker's dilemma may be only one of several. As a consequence, a reader who distances him- or herself from such an assessment can consider the ensuing advice irrelevant, too. The hedges used in this way in the assessments thus fulfill a similar function to the conditional clauses in the advisory moves previously discussed, because they offer the advisee the option of accepting or refusing the advice.

In Section 5.4, I compared *Lucy*'s tendency to prefer mitigated advice with the findings on face-to-face or radio interaction. I would like once more to stress that 'Lucy Answers' displays a considerable sensitivity to the face-threatening character of advice in that there is a preference for using mitigation rather than straightforward directives in the imperative mood. The site's declared orientation towards facilitating decision processes is therefore also in evidence in the linguistic realization of advice and the composition of the answer. A similar orientation was observed for the student counselors in He's (1994) data, the experts in Sarangi and Clarke's (2002) data of genetics risk communication, and the career counselors in Vehviläinen's (2003) study. However, for all of these experts the counseling ideal caused a dilemma between directiveness and non-directiveness. This was the case because the clients expected advice in many instances, while the counselors were held to remain non-directive. In the case of 'Lucy Answers' this dilemma is less pronounced since the advice-seekers can only express their concerns once. After that, the advisor team is free to formulate its response carefully within the given framework. They do not need to react to any immediate demands made by the advisees.

6.3.2 Empathizing

Showing awareness of another person's feelings, expressing understanding or solidarity, can be a powerful strategy to create a positive rapport between interactants. The display of empathy is therefore clearly an important component of supportive relational work. Miller and Gergen (1998: 198) found that empathy and support were important parts of the response postings found on the electronic bulletin board, and that these created a discourse that was "more sustaining than transforming". Empathy also plays an important role in 'Lucy Answers'. It is, however, not without its risks, as Jefferson and Lee (1992: 543) point out in their example of an advisor who offered too much sympathy rather than advice and was consequently perceived as mismatching his reaction. If a person's dilemma is acknowledged, the vulnerability of this person is also stressed. Thus, in some cases, showing empathy may not be appreciated or may even be perceived as patronizing or condescending. This may be the reason why the 196 occurrences of empathy in 'Lucy Answers' are all of a subtle kind (Table 6.6). They show a sense of awareness for the questioners' troubles, but do not expand into a display of intimacy which might not be appreciated by the readership.

Table 6.6 shows that empathizing occurs predominantly in the discursive moves of assessment and advice. Since a questioner's situation is discussed by

Table 6.6 Empathy in the discursive moves in 'Lucy Answers' by topic category, ranked by overall frequency (including combinations; subcorpus)

| topic category →
discursive move ↓ | Group 1 | | | | Group 2 | | | | | |
	drugs	fitn./nutrition	gen. health	sexual health	emot. health	relationships	sexuality	total	%	.in n dm*
assessment	11	11	4	9	38	27	12	112	57	400
advice	9	3	3	3	14	13	2	47	24	976
explanation		1	1		8	5	2	17	9	278
gen. information		1	1	2	2		1	7	4	502
farewell			4		1	1		6	3	47
referral				3	1	1		5	3	310
metacomment				1		1		2	1	156
total	20	16	13	18	64	48	17	196	101	

* dm = discursive move.

Lucy in the assessment moves, it is not surprising that the majority of displays of empathy appear in this category (n = 112). Two examples have been chosen to demonstrate this usage. In (6.24) a person who is feeling insecure because of his wife's adoration of a movie star is offered reassurance:

(6.24)   **assessment** <empathizing> Feelings are not silly; they are feelings after all. It's not unusual for people to be hurt, jealous, troubled, angry, or confused if their spouses or partners pay special attention to someone else, even if that person were to pose no real threat to their marriage or relationship. </empathizing> (LA 1674, relationships, "Wife is movie star struck")

By stressing that the advice-seeker's feelings are not *silly* and in fact not *unusual*, *Lucy* first shows that she understands his dilemma, and then that she is also able to offer reassurance. By evaluating the advice-seeker's situation in such a way, *Lucy* 'normalizes' or 'naturalizes' the situation. The significance of such a move is pointed out by Currie (2001:274), who writes that advice columns "establish boundaries of normal behaviour" and may thus be influential in shaping ideologies about what is considered to be appropriate in a given society (see also Talbot 1995; Gough & Talbot 1996; Thibault 1988, 2002).

In the next example *Lucy* answers a person who is frustrated with a long and unsuccessful psychotherapy which is already in its twelfth year. *Lucy* explicitly acknowledges the questioner's difficult situation in (6.25), when she refers to the description of the advisee's experience and shows that she has taken note of the fact that he or she feels *worse now* and that none of the *problems have been resolved:*

(6.25)   **assessment** And what you consider to be non-productive therapy need not be a reason to give up entirely, <empathizing> especially if none of your problems have been resolved, or if you even feel worse now. </empathizing> (LA 2360, emotional health, "For how long should I be in therapy?")

In 47 cases, empathy occurs in the advisory moves in order to acknowledge how difficult it may be to carry out a piece of advice, or to admit that concerns are legitimate, or to reassure a questioner that he or she will be on the right track. One such example is given in (6.26) in which a college student who is unhappy with her living situation is advised to look for housing elsewhere if all the other pieces of advice given in *Lucy*'s response fail:

(6.26)   **advice type=decl** In the future, <empathizing> or if you find your current situation unbearable </empathizing>, you <hedging> may want to </hedging> investigate some of the different housing options available. (LA 1410, relationships, "No one cares about drunken, messy hallmates, or do they?")

It is of interest here that the advisee is told that alternative housing should already be considered an option if the *current situation* proves to be *unbearable*. *Lucy* thus clearly acknowledges that the problem might be rather urgent for the advisee and shows her understanding.

Empathizing occurs in the following combinations: empathizing-hedging (n = 33, eighteen in assessment), empathizing-bonding (n = 14; six in assessment, five in farewell), empathizing-boosting (n = 7; two in assessment, two in advice), empathizing-praising (n = 3, all in assessment), and criticizing-empathizing (n = 1, in advice). Only empathizing-hedging, which has already been discussed, and empathizing-bonding occur in fourteen or more cases. Bonding is yet another strategy of supportive relational work in that it represents an attempt to establish a connection with the questioner and/or the readership. Once more the largest number of occurrences appears in assessments (n = 6), but there are also five instances in the farewell discursive moves, which is one of the typical locations for bonding, as we shall see in the next section. (6.27) is taken from such a farewell remark. *Lucy* wishes a reader a good recovery from a bothersome congestion and itchy eyes:

(6.27) **farewell** <**empathizing-bonding**> Hope you feel better soon! </**empathizing-bonding**> (LA 2199, general health, "Allergies appear after relocation")

Here, *Lucy* not only shows empathy, but she also reaches out and adds this comment which is, strictly speaking, not necessary to complete the response.

Table 6.6 shows that two topic categories in Group 2 use empathy most often: 'emotional health' with 64 instances and 'relationships' with 48. Together they account for 57 percent of all empathy moves. The category 'sexuality', however, uses empathy much less often and this time it finds itself more like the topics in Group 1. In theory, all problems could evoke displays of empathy. In 'Lucy Answers', however, relationship or emotional problems are favored with such displays. The more factually oriented topics of Group 1, as well as the more intimate topics treated in the category 'sexuality' do not trigger empathy to the same degree. This may be explained, hypothetically, by suggesting that problems in Group 1 give less motivation to display empathy, while problems in the category 'sexuality' may be too charged to risk the use of empathy. As mentioned before, the display of empathy is a sensitive issue and it is important to strike the right balance.

6.3.3 Bonding

Establishing a connection with the questioner and the reader is categorized as 'bonding' in the responses by *Lucy*. This strategy to reach out to the reader(ship) is considered to constitute supportive relational work. Overall, there are 158 instances of bonding; 75 of these appear on their own, while the combinations are as follows: humor-bonding (n = 68), empathizing-bonding (n = 14), and bonding-hedging (n = 1). Bonding in combination with either humor or empathy thus

Table 6.7 Bonding in the discursive moves in 'Lucy Answers' by topic category, ranked by overall frequency (including combinations; subcorpus)

topic category → discursive move ↓	drugs	fitn./nutrition	general health	sexual health	emot. health	relationships	sexuality	total	%	...in n dm*
	Group 1				**Group 2**					
assessment	4	8	13	7	8	11	6	57	36	400
farewell	4	4	9	8	5	11	3	44	28	47
advice		7	3	1	3	4	1	19	12	976
general info	4	5	2	1	2		2	16	10	502
metacomment	2	2	1	1	1	2		9	6	156
explanation		3			2	1	1	7	4	278
open category			2			1		3	2	12
own experience			1		1			2	1	11
referral							1	1	1	310
total	14	29	31	18	22	30	14	158	100	

* dm = discursive move.

accounts for 51 percent of the total of 158. Table 6.7 shows that bonding appears mainly in assessments (n = 57) and farewell (n = 44), followed by advice (n = 19) and general information (n = 16).

As is the case with displays of empathy, bonding can be found in assessments because the advisee's situation is discussed there. This allows a direct way to establish a connection with the advice-seeker. Examples of bonding in this discursive move are given in (6.28) and (6.29):

(6.28) **assessment** <**bonding**> Like you, Lucy is continually learning more about Severe Acute Respiratory Syndrome (SARS), which was first recognized only in February 2003, in Vietnam. <**/bonding**> (LA 2400, general health, "Severe acute respiratory syndrome (SARS)")

(6.29) **assessment** You may be referring to a drug called Rohypnol (flunitrazepam), street-named "roofies," "roachies," "rophies," "ruffies," "roofenol," "roche," "La Rocha," "rope," and "the forget pill." (Rohypnol is manufactured by the pharmaceutical company F. Hoffmann-La Roche.) <**bonding**> But as we know, drug street names change all the time. <**/bonding**> (LA 884, drugs, "Rohypnol 'Roofie' and rape")

In (6.28) *Lucy* addresses the reader directly (*like you*) and stresses that both the reader and *Lucy* are engaged in a continual learning process. In (6.29), *Lucy* does not simply inform the reader that *drug street names change all the time*, but she states that this is knowledge that the reader and *Lucy* share (*but as we know*). In both examples connectedness is thus stressed. In Section 5.4, I pointed out that one function of the assessments is to align the advice-seeker and reader with a certain interpretation of the problem at hand (cf. Vehviläinen 2003). Since bonding most frequently occurs within assessments, we can say that it is used to reinforce the attempt at creating a common point of view in this discursive move.

There are only 47 farewell sections in the entire corpus, as discussed in Section 5.3.2. Of these, 44 entail bonding (the remaining three entail praise in two cases and empathy combined with hedging in one instance). The reader may recall that *good luck* occurs in fourteen of the 47 farewell moves and that variants of *Hope you feel better soon!* are used in five cases. The remaining instances are unique occurrences. As the name of this discursive move already suggests, the farewell sections clearly have the function of establishing a final connection with the reader before *Lucy* completes the response with her signature. The fact that all instances of farewell can be assigned the relational work moves of bonding, empathizing or praising shows that this discursive move serves primarily as a means for supportive relational work.

The advice sections contain only nineteen cases of bonding, nine of which are instances of humor-bonding. I have chosen two examples to illustrate this usage. In (6.30) a bonding remark is inserted within a list of suggestions for the correct execution of sit-ups (*This can get really tough!*). This implies that *Lucy* has experience with this type of exercise and thus has a common interest with the advice-seeker:

(6.30)   **advice type=decl list** Beginners may start with 10–15 repetitions. As you become stronger, you may perform more repetitions, or hold each contraction for five seconds, or longer. **<bonding>** This can get really tough! **</bonding>** Since your stomach muscles are comprised of different sections, you can work each separately. (LA 1716, fitness and nutrition, "Sit-ups")

The advice-seeker for (6.31) wonders what to *do after sex?* (*Should I just lay there? Should I talk about it?*). *Lucy* gives a couple of suggestions, among them *have a cigarette*:

(6.31)   **advice type=decl list** You could also go to sleep, take a shower, hold your partner, get ready for work, watch TV, brush your teeth, have a snack, do the laundry, return to your seats, call your grandmother, do it again, **<humor-bonding>** have a cigarette – oops, strike that last one. One way to know is … altogether now… to talk with your partner(s) about it. **</humor-bonding>** (LA 1863, relationships, "What should I do after sex?")

To *have a cigarette* is of course not in line with the general task of the health educators working for 'Lucy Answers', who ought to represent the opinion that smoking is a health risk. This is clear to the readership and also to the team of advisors. *Lucy*'s comments directly following the "faux-pas" (– *oops, strike that last one* and

… *altogether now…*) therefore function as means to create rapport between the reader and the advisor by alluding to exactly this shared knowledge.

Bonding also occurs sparingly in general information sections (n = 16). Consider (6.32) in which information is passed on about the topic of mineral absorption by the body. This is an extensive passage (shortened here), which, towards the end, contains a brief summary to involve the reader once more (*as you can see*):

(6.32)   **general information** [several sentences on the topic of mineral absorption by the body omitted] Heme iron, the form of iron found in animals or animal sources, is more readily absorbed than non-heme iron, which is of plant origin. Phytates, a substance in some plants, bind iron, reducing its availability in our digestive tract. Vitamin C, however, increases our absorption of non-heme iron. <bonding> As you can see, many factors come into play with nutrient absorption, whether a mineral has a positive or a negative charge. </bonding> (LA 1984, fitness and nutrition, "What's the difference between ionic and colloidal minerals?")

The background to (6.33) is that a young woman, who uses the signature *nervy in North Carolina,* is worried about her wedding day and wonders whether she could get medicine prescribed to calm her down for this event. *Lucy,* among other things, describes a breathing exercise that may help (the actual instructions of how to do this exercise follow afterwards):

(6.33)   **general information** <bonding> There's a deep-breathing exercise that works wonders to calm the nerves of students, professionals, performers, *and of course, the wedding-bound,* when faced with sudden and stressful situations. </bonding> This technique pronounces the movement of your diaphragm (a muscle in the center of your chest cavity) which in turn, sends chemical signals to your heart (via the vagus nerve) to slow down. This results in a decreased breathing rate, reduced muscle tension, clearer thinking, less sweating, and a calmer stomach. (LA 995, emotional health, "Wedding bell butterflies", italics added)

I argue that the bonding within this discursive move lies in the *and of course*. It creates a link between praising the benefits of this exercise for several types of people (*students, professionals, performers*) and then leading over to *the wedding-bound,* which is the position of the advice-seeker. The *of course* highlights that *Lucy* has not lost sight of the advisee and thus constitutes supportive relational work.

Interestingly, it is in the categories 'fitness and nutrition' (n = 29), 'general health' (n = 31) and 'relationships' (n = 30) where most of the bonding occurs. Its presence in the category 'relationships' is not exceptional since this category also uses empathy frequently. The categories 'fitness and nutrition' and 'general health', however, use empathy much more sparingly than bonding. It should be remembered that Table 6.4 revealed bonding as the second most frequent type of relational work for both categories. This shows that involvement strategies are important in 'Lucy Answers', since, if empathy is not called for, bonding may still be used as a means to create rapport between *Lucy* and the readership.

6.3.4 Praising

In her study on the ways men and women use compliments in New Zealand English, Holmes (1995) defines a compliment as follows:

> A compliment is a speech act which explicitly or implicitly attributes credit to someone other than the speaker, usually the person addressed, for some 'good' (possession, characteristic, skill, etc.) which is positively valued by the speaker and the hearer.   (Holmes 1995: 117)

In addition, in her literature review of the findings on complimenting (cf. Pomerantz 1978; Wolfson 1983; Wierzbicka 1987; Brown & Levinson 1987; Lewandowska-Tomaszczyk 1989; Herbert 1990; Tannen 1990; Johnson & Roen 1992; Kissling 1991), Holmes (1995: 121) points out that, in different contexts, compliments may not only function (1) as expressions of solidarity, but also (2) as expressions of "positive evaluation, admiration, appreciation or praise", (3) as expressions of "envy or desire for hearer's possessions" or even (4) "as verbal harassment". Of special relevance for 'Lucy Answers' are compliments with function (2), i.e., compliments as a means to "provide a positive critical evaluation of a selected aspect of the addressee's behaviour or appearance, or whatever, which in some contexts may carry some communicative weight" (Holmes 1995: 118). The expert *Lucy* points out that an advice-seeker's attitude or action is positive and thus highlights this behavior not only for the advisee him- or herself, but also for the benefit of the wider readership. The compliments used in 'Lucy Answers' are thus best described as praise of behavior which fits the institutional goals of 'Lucy Answers'. Taking up a position, i.e., evaluating the advice-seeker's attitudes and actions, was also reported by Mininni (1991) for British and Italian advice columns.

Two examples of praise have been chosen from the category 'fitness and nutrition'. In the question for (6.34), an advice-seeker is worried whether the amount of sodium and other electrolytes in sports drinks affects children negatively. *Lucy* starts her response with praise (*You bring up a good point*), before moving on to general information:

(6.34)   **assessment** <praising> You bring up a good point. </praising> **general information** The main idea behind sports beverages is to help keep people hydrated and supplied with energy throughout extended bouts of exercise.

[…] (LA 2482, fitness and nutrition, "Is it safe for children to drink sports beverages regularly, even when they're not exercising strenuously?")

In the next example, *Lucy* not only compliments the advice-seeker on the choice of topic as in (6.34), but also on a course of action mentioned in the question text (*I refuse to diet. It's such a waste of time and I know it's worse for me than anything else.*):

(6.35)   **assessment** [cf. (6.16)] <**praising**> You are smart for not wanting to "diet." </**praising**> **explanation** Restricting food intake usually backfires because you end up eating more in the long run. This is especially true for college students with late night study schedules. […] (LA 384, fitness and nutrition, "Eating poorly, no exercise")

The complimenting of the questioner's attitude is then followed by an explanation, which clarifies why *Lucy* also believes that dieting is not a good strategy to lose weight. This compliment nicely creates cohesion with the question text, serves as a trigger for the ensuing explanation (which is important from the point of view of the health educators), and creates rapport with the reader.

Table 6.8 shows us that there are 65 instances of praise in the corpus, 59 of which appear in the assessment sections. This means that praising is clearly linked to this type of discursive move. This was to be expected since the praise given refers to the advice-seeker's particular situation and concerns, which are mainly discussed in the assessment moves. All three supportive relational work types of praising, empathizing, and bonding are thus typical in assessment sections. Praise rarely appears in combination with other relational work types; there are only three instances of empathizing-praising to be reported.

Table 6.8 Praise in the discursive moves in 'Lucy Answers' by topic category, ranked by overall frequency (including combinations; subcorpus)

| topic category → discursive move ↓ | Group 1 | | | | Group 2 | | | total | % | .in n dm* |
	drugs	fitn./nutrition	gen. health	sexual health	emot. health	relationships	sexuality			
assessment	6	11	7	6	10	10	9	59	91	400
farewell	1	1				1	1	4	6	47
advice							1	1	2	976
open category				1				1	2	12
total	7	12	7	7	10	11	11	65	101	

* dm = discursive move.

The distribution within the topic categories shows that, with one exception, the categories in Group 1 (n = 7), and Group 2 (n = 10–11) have a similar number of instances of praising. Only the category 'fitness and nutrition' switched group (n = 12) and uses an even greater number than the categories 'emotional health', 'relationships' and 'sexuality'.

6.3.5 Boosting

While hedging aims at mitigating a face-threatening act, it would be wrong to say that boosting is always face-threatening. The nuances of relational work are also subtle in this type of relational work. Holmes (1995: 77) summarizes the characteristics of boosters as follows: "[boosters] intensify the illocutionary force of any utterance in which they are used. Moreover, ... boosters may intensify or boost the effect of utterances with negative as well as positive intentions or 'affect'". In 'Lucy Answers' boosting is a means to qualify advice in that the point being made is highlighted as, for example, *important* or *essential*. Since 'Lucy Answers' belongs to an institution that employs professional health educators to run the site, which has quality health care advice as its aim, the notion of power and expertise will play a role with such boosters. When the 'Lucy Answers' team has the advisor *Lucy* intensify the force of advice, the entire weight of the expert knowledge and the institution are in the boosters. This is not to say that expertise is absent in the other realizations (in fact, the discourse of expertise is always present as the frame within which 'Lucy Answers' operates), but the boosters stress this aspect. Therefore the boosters in 'Lucy Answers' can be interpreted as face-threatening, since they emphasize status differences. The degree of face-threatening, however, can be expected to be moderate since the advice-seekers know that they address experts and may expect boosting of this type. Once again, while the overall number of occurrences (n = 165, Table 6.9) may not be very high, the impact of these boosters on the text and ultimately the readership may be considerable.

Table 6.9 shows that boosters occur most frequently in the advice discursive moves (n = 89) and to a far smaller extent in assessments (n = 23), general information (n = 20) and referrals (n = 18). If the number of boosters in referrals and advice are taken together, then the tendency to mark specific pieces of advice is even more pronounced (n = 107): in 'Lucy Answers' boosters thus function predominantly as a means to highlight particular aspects of advice. Three examples were chosen from three different topic categories to illustrate this:

(6.36)   **advice type=decl </boosting>** *The best way to* deal with morning sickness is
          to never allow the stomach to be empty, and to eat small, easily-digested meals
          frequently, rather than eating larger ones only three times a day. **</boosting>**
          (LA 1870, general health, "Nausea: Causes and treatments", italics added)

Table 6.9 Boosting in the discursive moves in 'Lucy Answers' by topic category, ranked by overall frequency (including combinations; subcorpus)

topic category → discursive move ↓	drugs	fitn./nutrition	gen. health	sexual health	emot. health	relationships	sexuality	total	%	in n dm*
		Group 1				Group 2				
advice	9	14	13	15	16	13	9	89	54	976
assessment	4	2	2	2	6	6	1	23	14	400
gen. information	5	6	2	4	2		1	20	12	502
referral	2	4	3	4	3	1	1	18	11	310
explanation (adv)	1			2	3		1	7	4	278
disclaimer			3					3	2	13
metacomment	1	1				1		3	2	156
own experience			1			1		2	1	11
total	22	27	24	27	30	22	13	165	100	

* dm = discursive move.

(6.37)   **advice type=decl </boosting>** *Again*, if diagnosed, *you need to* use a condom all the time when participating in intercourse. **</boosting>** (LA 47, sexual health, "Pus-filled vaginal sores", italics added)

(6.38)   **advice type=decl list <boosting>** For this reason, *it's important to* consider where and with whom one might try this drug. When experimenting with any drug, *it is essential to* be in a safe environment with people you trust, preferably some who are not using any alcohol or other drugs. **</boosting>** (LA 1357, drugs, "Psilocybin ('Magic') mushrooms", italics added)

In (6.36) the boosting effect is achieved by qualifying the advisory declarative sentence with *the best way to*. In (6.37), the urgency for this advice-seeker, who may have herpes, to use protection in sexual intercourse is stressed by *again* (which refers to the preceding advice *Lucy* gave to have a professional health provider confirm the illness), and *you need to*.[7] Finally, in (6.38), the advisory declarative sentences are preceded with *it's important to* and *it is essential to*. In all of these cases, *Lucy* highlights her advice and thus comes to the fore as an expert, since the reader is reminded of her expertise, which is that of all the health providers working for the Health Services of AEI. The discussion of what contributes to expert talk in 'Lucy Answers' will continue in Chapter 8.

The combinations in which boosting occurs are criticizing-boosting (n = 8), and empathizing-boosting (n = 7), and they are rather rare. The category 'sexuality' uses boosting the least (n = 13), while all other categories use boosting a comparable number of times (n = 22–27). It is striking that the category 'sexuality' once more makes only rare use of the relational work types analyzed here. It therefore seems that in this topic category a more neutral tone is aimed for.

6.3.6 Criticizing

Criticism of a person's beliefs, attitudes and actions constitutes a face-threatening act (Brown & Levinson 1987:66). For this reason, it will often be accompanied with mitigation in many contexts (on avoiding disagreement see Brown & Levinson 1987:113–117). In other speech situations, however, disagreements may be acceptable and expected and do not need to be especially mitigated (cf. Schiffrin 1984; Pomerantz 1984; Kotthoff 1993; Hayashi 1996). In my discussion of a family argument over tuition fees in the United States (Locher 2004), I was able to show that the interactants involved had particular conversational styles, different preferences of ways to express disagreement, and also perceived the force of disagreements differently. I further emphasized that disagreement is a reaction to a prior point and constitutes the possible departure point for a next move by the addressee. A disagreement thus presents the first part of an adjacency pair and the next move will be expected to be a reaction to this disagreement. This observation was of course made for face-to-face interaction in which the recipient of criticism has the chance to react. In 'Lucy Answers', however, we are dealing with a written genre of a question-answer sequence. The advisor team can react to a point made in the question text, but the advice-seeker cannot respond to criticism made by the team in such a way that it would have an impact on the creation of the response text. Since a critique that one cannot respond to is even more face-threatening, the 51 instances of criticism in 'Lucy Answers' are clearly important (Table 6.10). Criticism is also attested in Mininni's (1991) discussion of British and Italian advice columns, as a technique used by the advisors to make their position towards the letter writer clear.

Table 6.10 shows that criticism occurs most often in assessments (n = 23) and in advice (n = 18). The reason criticism occurs in the assessments is clearly because the advice-seeker's situation is evaluated there. (6.39) is such an instance. *Lucy* summarizes information given by the advice-seeker, who wonders why she does not have a boyfriend despite her good looks, and then assesses this point of view negatively:

(6.39) **assessment** <criticizing> You have told Lucy how beautiful, how tall, and how smart you are. But relationships develop based on much more than these objective traits. </criticizing> (LA 1142, relationships, "Beautiful on the outside, but no boyfriend")

Table 6.10 Criticism in the discursive moves in 'Lucy Answers' by topic category, ranked by overall frequency (including combinations; subcorpus)

	Group 1				Group 2					
topic category → discursive move ↓	drugs	fitn./nutrition	gen. health	sexual health	emot. health	relationships	sexuality	total	%	in n dm*
assessment	5	2		1	4	7	4	23	45	400
advice				1	2	11	4	18	35	976
explanation		1			3	2		6	12	278
general information	1	1					1	3	6	502
referral	1							1	2	310
total	7	4		2	9	20	9	51	100	

Links to the content of the questioner's letter also occur in the advice moves, in which a point is repeated and prefaced with *rather than* or *instead of*, as can be seen in (6.40):

(6.40)   **advice type=imp-a** <criticizing> However, instead of being stuck with feeling stuck, </criticizing> take action! (LA, 1684 emotional health, "I want a better job!")

In (6.41) an advisee's position is evaluated and turned into advice. In the question letter to this example, the advice-seeker complains about a flatmate who never joins in any activity, but always wants to be informed about what is going on in the other four flatmates' lives. This girl's behavior resulted in the advice-seeker wanting to find out from *Lucy* how they could *tell her to mind her own business and shut her mouth* and how they could *tell her that* [they] *don't want her to live with* [them] *next year*. In the response to these questions, *Lucy* takes up the advice-seeker's position and comments on it in a critical way:

(6.41)   **advice type=imp-i** <criticizing> Imagine how lonely and frustrating it might feel to always be excluded. </criticizing> **assessment** <criticizing> If your suitemate wrote to Lucy, her letter might look something like this: – Dear Lucy, – Help! My suitemates have been giving me the cold shoulder all year. They are all friends and I am always the odd one out. They go out together all the time and I am never invited (not once!). When I ask them about their plans or how their weekends went, they shut me out again. Every time I try to start a conversation, I get brushed off. I'm not sure if I can take this next year. Please help! – Lonely in a crowd </criticizing> (LA 1873, relationships, "How to tell a nosy roommate to step off")

Lucy thus invites the advice-seeker to change her attitude. This line of argument is continued in this response when *Lucy* includes an entire letter that could have been written by the offending flatmate. This is done to show the advice-seeker that the problem may also be partly due to her own behavior. This criticism is, however, not the only aspect in this response, as *Lucy* also shows awareness of how difficult it can be to live together as flatmates and gives practical advice for how to deal with the problem.

Criticism appears in 29 cases on its own, in eight instances together with boosting, in seven cases together with hedging, six times in combination with humor as a mitigation device, and once with empathizing. Depending on the combinations, the force of the criticism will be either mitigated or boosted. Examples of criticism occurring with hedging were already given in the discussion of "Younger man hot for senior citizens" in Figure 6.1 above. An example of criticism hedged with humor is given in (6.42). The question to this extract is: *Lucy, How do I dump my boyfriend? I have been going out with a guy for over a month and it's just not working, but the problem is I don't know how to dump him. Please help, Emergency in Edinburgh.* Lucy first praises the advice-seeker for not wanting to *linger* in an undesired relationship and then proceeds to comment on the advisee's choice of wording:

(6.42) **assessment** <**criticizing**> Lucy is interested in your choice of words. Do you want to: – a. "dump" your boyfriend like yesterday's rubbish – with no explanation? </**criticizing**><**humor-criticizing**> – b. trash him in soap opera style with a phony blackmail plot involving Madonna and the Scottish Prime Minister? </**humor-criticizing**> – c. end the relationship cordially with minimal reasoning? (LA 1408, relationships, "Breaking up can be hard to do")

There is no doubt that option (c) is preferred by *Lucy* since options (a) and (b) are clearly critical in that they show what connotations come with the phrase *dump my boyfriend* which was chosen by the advice-seeker. I argue that option (b), while still critical, adds a humorous note since the combination of the advice-seeker with Madonna and the Scottish Prime Minister is an unlikely match.

Table 6.10 also shows that criticism occurs mainly in the category 'relationships' (n = 20). The two other categories from Group 2 have nine occurrences, and there are seven cases in the category 'drugs'. The other topic categories in Group 1 feature strikingly little criticism (n = 0–4). 'General health' even shows none at all. This can be explained once more with the observation that the categories 'fitness and nutrition', 'general health' and 'sexual health' deal with problems of a more factual or biological kind that may trigger empathy or bonding, as we have seen earlier, but that do not disclose positions which could be then taken up for criticism by the advisor team to the same degree as other topics. In the case of the category 'drugs', however, the seven cases of criticism are all triggered when the advice-seekers place their health in danger.

6.3.7 The use of humor

In my analysis I have distinguished between humor used as a means of hedging (including mitigation of criticism) and humor used as means to establish a special rapport (bonding) with the reader and/or the wider readership (among others, see Hay (2000) and Holmes (2000) on the different functions of humor). Humor used for mitigation (n = 81) has already been discussed in the section on hedging, and humor-bonding (n = 68) has been presented in the section on bonding. It should be stressed that while the frequency of occurrences of many of the relational work moves discussed in this chapter may not look impressive, their contribution to the overall tone of the site should not be underestimated. Humor may well be one of the qualities that make 'Lucy Answers' attractive to the readership in addition to the information that is provided by the advisor team. With 149 occurrences, a certain awareness of the entertainment value in the responses can certainly be detected in the use of this discursive practice. (This may even be the case when there is no explicit humor, since, according to Hendley (1977: 345), advice columns may be consulted by many readers not only as resources for information, but also to satisfy their curiosity.)

Humor-bonding and humor-hedging fulfill two different functions. Humor-bonding aims at establishing a positive rapport with the readership, while humor-hedging is specifically used to mitigate face-threatening acts. This is also reflected in the place where humor occurs within the responses (Tables 6.11 and 6.12): humor-bonding is predominantly used in the assessment sections (28 of 68), while humor-hedging occurs most frequently in the advisory moves (51 of 81). As pointed out earlier, the category 'relationships' features the most humor-hedging (n = 24), while the other categories have a similar but lower number of occurrences (not above thirteen instances; Table 6.12). In the case of humor-bonding, however, there is no such clear-cut dominance (Table 6.11). The categories 'general health' (n = 15) and 'relationships' (n = 13) use this kind of relational work most often; the categories 'emotional health' (n = 10), 'fitness and nutrition' (n = 10) and 'sexuality' (n = 9) are in the middle range, while the categories 'drugs' (n = 6) and 'sexual health' (n = 5) have fewer instances. Once again, it is in the category 'relationships' that humor-bonding is used most frequently, which shows that humor is especially important in this topic category.

Table 6.11 Humor-bonding in the discursive moves in 'Lucy Answers' by topic category, ranked by overall frequency (subcorpus)

topic category → discursive move ↓	Group 1				Group 2			total	%	in n dm*
	drugs	fitn./nutrition	gen. health	sexual health	emot. health	relationships	sexuality			
assessment	1	1	6	2	7	7	4	28	41	400
general information	3	2	2	1	1		2	11	16	502
advice		4			1	3	1	9	13	976
farewell	1		3	2		1	1	8	12	47
metacomment	1	2	1		1	1		6	9	156
explanation (adv)		1				1		2	3	278
open category			2					2	3	12
own experience			1					1	1	11
referral (imp-a)							1	1	1	310
total	6	10	15	5	10	13	9	68	99	

* dm = discursive move.

Table 6.12 Humor-hedging in the discursive moves in 'Lucy Answers' by topic category, ranked by overall frequency (subcorpus)

topic category → discursive move ↓	Group 1				Group 2			total	%	in n dm*
	drugs	fitn./nutrition	gen. health	sexual health	emot. health	relationships	sexuality			
advice	7	7	6	4	5	18	4	51	63	976
general information	3	2	2	1			3	11	14	502
assessment	1	1		1	1	4	2	10	12	400
explanation (adv)		1	1	1		2		5	6	278
metacomment	1			1			1	3	4	156
referral	1							1	1	310
total	13	11	9	8	6	24	10	81	100	

* dm = discursive move.

6.4 Summary and evaluation

The first question I asked in the introduction to this chapter was what types of relational work are employed in 'Lucy Answers' and the second question aimed at establishing in which discursive moves these types of relational work appeared. In my close readings, the seven relational work types of bonding, empathizing, prais-

Table 6.13 The types of relational work and their preferred appearance in the discursive moves in 'Lucy Answers' for all topic categories together (subcorpus)

location preference → relational work type ↓	1st preference	2nd preference
involvement strategies:		
empathizing	assessment	advice
praising	assessment	farewell
bonding	assessment	farewell
face-saving strategies:		
hedging	advice	assessment
face-threatening strategies:		
boosting	advice	assessment
criticizing	assessment	advice

ing, hedging, boosting, criticizing and using humor emerged. In what follows, I once more consider several points that were raised in my individual analyses of the categories of relational work found in the responses of 'Lucy Answers'. I showed that there are specific discursive moves in which the relational work categories mainly occur. To pursue this finding I checked these preferences for every individual topic category and relational work move, which confirmed the results. Table 6.13 presents the relational work strategies and the two discursive moves with which they are most likely to occur in combination. This ranking is based on frequency.

We can see that the involvement strategies of empathizing, praising and bonding tend to appear in assessments. Assessments are the ideal location to use involvement strategies for supportive relational work in 'Lucy Answers' since it is in this discursive move where the advice-seeker's situation is commented on. The second most frequent location is either advice or farewell. For empathizing and praising, this second choice is not very frequent, while bonding occurs almost equally in the farewell and in the advice sections. All instances of farewell include a type of involvement strategy. Thus, it is also clearly linked to supportive relational work, as the category name of the discursive move already indicates.

The face-saving strategy of hedging appears mainly in the advice moves. This can be explained by the fact that giving advice constitutes the main face-threatening act in 'Lucy Answers'. In Chapter 5, the face-saving strategy of mitigation was also shown to play a role in the syntactic realization of advice. I showed that the preference for advisory declarative sentences and advisory interrogatives over imperatives may be explained by the fact that the two first options are more mitigated, and this then leaves more room for optionality. The advisee can, in other words, choose to ignore the more indirect variants of advisory moves as irrelevant for his or her particular situation. Overall, a strong tendency to mitigate advice can therefore be detected in 'Lucy Answers', which answers the third question raised in the introduction (*If mitigation is used, does it occur at the same time as the actual advice or together with other elements of the answer?*). The second most frequent location for hedges is in assessments where they function as indicators that the advisor team's interpretations of an advice-seeker's problem may be only one of several possible interpretations. Once more this careful phrasing ensures that the advice-seeker can decline the interpretation and the ensuing advice. At the same time, the hedges also protect 'Lucy Answers' because the advisor team demonstrates that they are aware of the fact that several interpretations are possible.

As defined by Holmes (1995:76), boosting intensifies the force of an utterance. Since the boosters found in 'Lucy Answers' occur predominantly in advisory (and referral) moves, it could be argued that they increase the face-threatening aspect of advice-giving. This is because the boosters bring the advisor figure *Lucy* to the fore as an expert and the reader is reminded that 'Lucy Answers' belongs to an institution that offers professional health information. In other words, if *Lucy*, as a representative of this institution which has the well-being of the advisee in mind, highlights a piece of advice, then this decision can be assumed to be based on the expert knowledge of the advisor team. The power difference between the advice-seeker and the advice-givers is thus made visible in the text. It should be pointed out, however, that the level of face-threatening exercised by means of these boosters is modest. The advice-seekers have, after all, voluntarily turned to experts and have engaged in this discursive practice out of their own free will. The primary function of the boosters thus remains to stress the factual content of advice.

Criticizing, finally, is a face-threatening strategy because the addressee is shown that his or her attitudes or actions are judged negatively by 'Lucy Answers'. It is also important that this criticism is made public despite the fact that the advice-seeker remains entirely anonymous. Although the overall number of criticisms is not high as such (n = 51), these instances are clearly important. The main location for criticism is in the assessments. Once more the explanation for this is the content of this discursive move. The advice-seeker's situation is commented on, and this opens up the possibility for criticism. The second discursive move which frequently entails criticism is advice itself. An advisee's position is questioned and turned around into advice; or the advisee is reminded that a different path than the one chosen (and criticized) will lead to a better solution of the problem at hand.

The next question to be studied is which relational work strategies are used in which topic categories. Consider Table 6.14, which is a rearranged form of the overview Table 6.4: for ease of comparison, it shows the groups of relational work strategies and the percentages of the overall usage of the type of relational work within the entire subcorpus (100% = 1,351 relational work moves).

Table 6.14 Relational work moves in 'Lucy Answers' by type and category in percent (including combinations; 100% = 1,351 relational work moves; subcorpus)

topic category → rel. work type ↓	Group 1				Group 2			total %	total % in groups
	drugs	fitn./nutrition	general health	sexual health	emot. health	relationships	sexuality		
involvement strategies:									
empathizing	1	1	1	1	5	4	1	15	
praising	1	1	1	1	1	1	1	5	
bonding	1	2	2	1	2	2	1	12	
humor-bonding		1	1		1	1	1	5	37
face-saving strategies:									
hedging	6	5	5	5	7	10	5	42	
humor-hedging	1	1	1	1		2	1	6	48
face-threatening strategies:									
boosting	2	2	2	2	2	2	1	12	
criticizing	1				1	1	1	4	16
total %	12	13	12	11	19	22	11	100	101

There are two tendencies to be reported here: (1) overall, face-saving strategies (hedging) are most frequent (48%), but involvement strategies (37%) and face-threatening strategies (16%) also contribute considerably to relational work in 'Lucy Answers'. This means that 'Lucy Answers' has taken into consideration the face-threatening aspect of advice-giving, but that there is also an attempt to create a rapport with the advice-seeker and the readership. The use of humor in both involvement and face-saving strategies points to the entertainment factor that is present in 'Lucy Answers'. It was suggested that this contributes to the attractiveness of the site. The presence of boosting, which occurs mainly in the advisory sections, emphasizes the professional and institutional expertise and authority of 'Lucy Answers', and this is also true of the instances of criticism and praise. (2) Generally, the distinction into topic categories of Group 1 and Group 2 which was based on the content structure analysis in Chapter 5 can no longer be observed to the same degree in the analysis of types of relational work. For example, bonding is particularly strong in the categories 'fitness and nutrition' and 'general health' as well as in the categories 'emotional health' and 'relationships'; the use of empathy is clearly preferred in the latter two, but not in the category 'sexuality'. The categories 'relationships' and 'emotional health', however, show similarities and may still be argued to form a unit. These two topic categories differ from the others since they have a distinctly larger share of empathizing and hedging (the latter is especially prevalent in the category 'relationships'). The larger number of empathetic comments made there can be explained by the content of the problems, which very often have emotional rather than biological, physical or reproductive concerns at their core. They thus invite an empathetic reaction. In the case of the category 'sexuality' a similar pattern could have been expected – since the problems discussed there focus on the relationships of people rather than on health issues, but, in comparison with the other two categories of Group 2, the category 'sexuality' features less empathy and is very similar to the other topic categories of Group 1. In my discussion of empathy, I argued that it is a potentially risky involvement strategy that needs to be carefully employed. I hypothesized that it may rarely be used in the category 'sexuality' precisely to avoid embarrassing the advisee.

In the individual sections on relational work my findings were compared to the results and observations made by other researchers, who worked on other advisory contexts. As a final point, it should be stressed that, while the appropriate kind and level of relational work is important, its use does not guarantee the success of the advice given because "an individual's receptiveness to being advised" and judgments about "the content of the advice (usefulness, feasibility and absence of limitations)" are also crucial factors, as MacGeorge et al. (2004:65) point out.[8] In the next chapters I will work with the results from my examination of the content structure of the responses in 'Lucy Answers' (Section 5.2), the linguistic realization of advice (Section 5.3) and the relational work elements identified in this chapter in order to answer more questions about this discursive practice.

CHAPTER 7

The personal and public dimension of advice-giving in the response letters

7.1 Introduction

According to Thibault (2002:91), there are several parties involved in the process of creating an advice column: publishers, editors, (teams of) advisors, the direct addressee and the wider readership. All of these interactants combined create a "web of voices", as Mininni (1991:75) puts it. The nature of the targeted readership is especially crucial and influences the style of the advice column. For example, a column addressing an adult readership is bound to differ from one that primarily addresses children or teenagers. In the case of 'Lucy Answers' the main readership are the AEI students or – due to its public Internet appearance – young adults with similar problems and concerns.

The framework in which the advice column appears is also central. For many commercially run newspapers or magazines, problem pages often increase the publication's attractiveness because of their entertainment factor, and/or because they offer guidance, which is something the readership looks for. Currie (2001:261) found that problem pages in the teen magazines investigated were the favorite reading of young girls, because the adolescents were looking for practical help. The content of the advice in teen magazines shapes a particular ideology of how teenagers ought to behave and be (Currie 2001). There is an (at times hidden) underlying connection between the content of the problem pages – for example in the discussion of concerns about beauty – and products that are advertised or otherwise propagated and discussed in the magazines (cf. Talbot 1992, 1995; Gough & Talbot 1996). The ultimate goal of the magazines is clearly to make a financial profit. 'Lucy Answers', on the other hand, cannot be as directly linked to a profit-making schema. This Internet advice column belongs to a health service program run by a university that offers free access to its site and does not try to sell any products as such. There are also no advertisements on the 'Lucy Answers' site. It is, however, clear that they are very much interested in 'selling' their advice in the sense that they have the declared aim to provide a service to the students that will empower them to make informed decisions about emotional and health concerns. The choice to use a dialogic question-answer sequence in the well-known format of an advice column relies on the popularity of this genre to complete the health program's other services.

In general, it is recognized that the particular format of a problem letter by an individual addressed to a so-called agony aunt offers the reader the added incentive of identifying with the questioner and thereby taking on the role of advisee (Franke 1997:226). The topic is thus individualized by presenting it in the form of a letter from a real human being who is in need of advice. This is the *personal* or *private dimension* in advice columns (cf. DeCapua & Huber 1995). The response letter, while overtly addressing this one particular individual, is in fact aimed at the larger readership to instruct, advise, counsel, etc., and only marginally at the actual, initial advice-seeker. This is the *public dimension* of advice-giving in public contexts, which has been stressed as a subject worthy of study by researchers such as DeCapua and Huber (1995), DeCapua and Dunham (1993), Fleischhacker (1987), and Franke (1997). From the literature review, the reader may recall that Hutchby (1995) has looked at the tension between the public and personal dimension in advice-giving for radio data, which involved a host, an expert and a caller with a problem. He studied how advice was designed to be relevant for a range of participants, "not just the individual advice-seeker (the caller), but the many potential constituencies represented by the overhearing audience" (Hutchby 1995:222), and he identified three ways the interactants modulated their answers:

–   The *expert* displayed "a tendency to answer more than the question and to package advice as a general prescription" (1995:236).
–   The *host*, who, "although not himself a ratified advice-giver, nonetheless can become involved in the provision of advice" by asking auxiliary questions (1995:236).
–   Both host and expert try to return to the caller's particular problem at the end of a call.

'Lucy Answers' will, of course, not give the opportunity to witness this kind of three-party interaction, but will allow us to study how the tension between the personal and public dimensions, i.e., between adhering to the appearance of the format of a personal letter exchange on screen, while clearly aiming at the public readership, manifests itself in the problem and response letters published in 'Lucy Answers'. My discussion will be based on the 280 records in the subcorpus. After identifying the strategies 'Lucy Answers' uses (Section 7.2), I will move to a discussion of the entire corpus of response letters in order to understand the type of changes that have been made to the records in the archive of 'Lucy Answers' over time. This question is of interest for this chapter because any effort made to update the archive by the 'Lucy Answers' team can be argued to be motivated by the aim of improving the advice given for a wider readership. Thus, changes to the archive are particularly relevant to the public dimension of this discursive practice (Section 7.3).

7.2 The tension between the personal and public dimension in the response letters of the subcorpus

In my qualitative close reading of the 280 records of the subcorpus I identified six strategies that are involved in managing the personal and public dimension of advice-giving in 'Lucy Answers'. Three of these are argued to cover *both* the personal and the public dimension simultaneously, while the remaining three strategies are seen as exclusively public. Obviously, no strategy could be identified that is exclusively personal since the question-answer exchanges are all part of the public domain. The strategies are represented in Table 7.1. They are: choice of problem letter to be answered, wording of title, broadening the scope of the response letter, evaluating the questioner's attitudes and actions, bonding with and showing empathy for the advice-seeker, and addressing the wider readership directly. In what follows I shall discuss the strategies one by one.

7.2.1 Choice of problem letter to be answered

The general health services program at AEI offers workshops on topics related to health issues. It also refers students to individual and personal counseling opportunities on and off campus. 'Lucy Answers' is part of this program and presents a public and easily accessible addition to these services. The producers of 'Lucy Answers' have a clear mission statement which was quoted in detail in Chapter 2. Their aim is to provide quality health care information in an easy-to-understand and non-judgmental way. The aim of 'Lucy Answers' is not primarily to help an

Table 7.1 Strategies dealing with the public and personal dimension of advice in 'Lucy Answers'

Strategy	Personal/Public
Choice of problem letter to be answered	public
Wording of title	public
Broadening the scope of the response letter:	
– referring questioners to other sources of information, (further) professional help, or other 'Lucy Answers' records	personal/public
– anticipating follow-up questions	personal/public
– providing more information than is requested	personal/public
Evaluating the advice-seeker's attitudes and actions	personal/public
Bonding with and showing empathy for the advice-seeker	personal/public
Addressing the wider readership directly	public

individual advice-seeker – otherwise the letter exchange would not be public. Instead, its aim is to provide information that is relevant to as many readers of the
target group as possible. The choice of which of the over 2,000 letters that 'Lucy
Answers' receives every week to answer is therefore made on the basis of the perceived needs of the targeted readership, which is the AEI students community. It
is also clear, however, that the five letters chosen to receive answers each week not
only reflect the concerns of this community, but also the 'Lucy Answers' mission
in that the topics treated have to be within the scope of the seven topic categories.

Adherence to the 'Lucy Answers' mission is also the reason there are weeks in
which previously posted records are reposted (marked as 'classic Lucy' or 'retro
Lucy'). In this way the producers ensure that information on, for example, important health risks does not disappear into the archives, but is refreshed in the readers' minds.[1] The choice of the question to be answered is thus strongly influenced
by the public dimension.

7.2.2 Wording of title

A similar argument can be made that the titles given to the question-answer sequences also primarily address the public dimension. Recall that in 'Lucy Answers'
the titles of the records are presented in a hyperlinked form on the main site. There
is even the option to subscribe to a weekly email service that delivers only the hyperlinked headings into one's mailbox, so that readers do not have to go to the
actual 'Lucy Answers' site for updates and new posts. Only once you click on these
links will the question and response letters appear on the screen. It follows, then,
that the titles have to be attractive because they act as *teasers*, i.e., as an invitation to
the reader to follow-up the links (cf. Janoschka (2004) on web advertising). While
the questioners have the opportunity to enter a subject line when submitting their
question, it is likely that the 'Lucy Answers' team is monitoring these titles carefully because of their crucial function in attracting readers. (Examples of titles will
be given below.) The personal dimension – the relevance for the actual individual
who asked the question – can be almost neglected here.

I have reported on Mininni's (1991) and Franke's (1997) comments on differences in cultural traditions earlier. Mininni (1991) found differences between
Italian and British women's magazine headings in that the Italian titles reflected
the answer rather than the question, while the titles for the British exchanges were
drawn from the questioners' letters. Franke (1997: 377) found four types of headings for his more general class of advisory texts: (1) a brief account of the problem
for which the co-text promises a solution; (2) the announcement of a solution of a
problem, without mention of actions; (3) the summary of the solution in the form
of a headline; and (4) triggering the interest of the reader by cryptic formulations
or the use of typographical means.

The wording of the titles in 'Lucy Answers' also needs to be investigated more closely. I found three different types of titles in the subcorpus (N = 280): impersonal statements, statements that describe a problem of a person or persons, and questions. The titles which are impersonal statements can best be described as neutral subject headings from which the reader can immediately infer the topic of the record. Examples (7.1) to (7.6) illustrate this usage.

(7.1)   Marijuana and driving (LA 1651, drugs)

(7.2)   Aspirin therapy (LA 463, drugs)

(7.3)   Alcohol use and memory loss (LA 887, drugs)

(7.4)   Spontaneous orgasms (LA 632, sexuality)

(7.5)   Sex therapy and insurance coverage (LA 1453, sexuality)

(7.6)   Videos and other resources about sexuality for kids to watch at home (LA 1807, sexuality)

The next title category contains an explicit mention of a problem in the form of a statement. For illustration, I have chosen three examples from the category 'relationships':

(7.7)   My mom found my contraceptives! (LA 1487, relationships)

(7.8)   Girlfriend gets scared every time I say, "I love you" (LA 1738, relationships)

(7.9)   My partner feels more strongly about me than I do about him (LA 2589, relationships)

While the wording of the titles in (7.7) to (7.9) still allows the reader to come to an immediate decision of whether or not the topic is of interest to him or her, the titles also identify a problem that is clearly personal. In this way they invite the reader to identify with the advice-seeker. This is also the case when the titles are formulated in the form of (elliptical) questions, since the reader is invited to imagine that he or she may have asked the same question:

(7.10)   Build muscle mass? (LA 37, fitness and nutrition)

(7.11)   Women, calcium, and osteoporosis? (LA 92, fitness and nutrition)

(7.12)   Male contraceptives? (LA 544, sexual health)

(7.13)   What is Colposcopy? (LA 987)

Table 7.2 shows the percentages of the individual types of titles in each topic category. The categories 'drugs', 'emotional health', 'general health' and 'sexuality' use more impersonal statements than questions, while the categories 'fitness and nutrition', 'sexual health' and 'relationships' use more questions than impersonal statements. The category 'relationships' is the only one to use problem statements in almost half of all titles (45%). The categories 'emotional health' and

Table 7.2 Number of syntactic realizations of titles by topic category in percent (subcorpus; N = 280; n = 40 per topic category)

title types → topic categories ↓	impersonal statement	problem statement	question
Group 1:			
drugs	58	13	30
fitness/nutrition	45		55
general health	40	25	35
sexual health	43	3	55
Group 2:			
emotional health	40	25	35
relationships	25	45	30
sexuality	55	13	33
total (N = 280)	122	49	109
%	44	18	39

'general health' also use them, while the categories 'fitness and nutrition', 'sexuality', 'sexual health' and 'drugs' have hardly any problem statement titles at all. These preferences could not be explained by the topic of the categories and the groups previously established.

If we look at the overall picture, Table 7.2 shows us that, from the 280 titles in the subcorpus, 122 (44%) are formulated as impersonal statements, 109 (39%) as questions, and 49 (18%) as statements pointing to a problem. If we combine the two statement categories, they represent 62 percent of the titles. However, if we combine the questions with the problem statements, we see that 57 percent of the titles offer the reader a chance to identify with the questioner. For 'relationships' this percentage even goes up to 75, which means that the reader is clearly encouraged to take on the role of advice-seeker, because the problem is the focus rather than the promise of information.

The incentive to click on the hyperlink – in addition to the promise of receiving information inherent in the frame of 'Lucy Answers' – could also be achieved through the use of humor in the titles. This is the case in 28 instances. Examples are given in (7.14) to (7.16):

(7.14)   Bashful bladder (LA 873, emotional health)

(7.15)   The health of a couch potato (LA 2590, general health)

(7.16)   Longing for love poems (LA 1443, relationships)

It is striking that the use of humor coincides with impersonal statements in the majority of cases (n = 16). (This is the case in the examples just quoted.) This means that this type of title can be made more attractive by the use of humor. To conclude, we can say that more than 60 percent of the titles in 'Lucy Answers' are phrased in such a way that they either attract interest because they invite the reader to identify with the advice-seeker's problem or because they are humorous. The remaining titles focus on the topic in a neutral way and are thus fulfilling their function in a straightforward, but also more detached, manner.

7.2.3 Broadening the scope of the response letter

Based on his radio data, Hutchby (1995: 236) was able to state that the expert often answered more questions than just the one posed by the caller. This is also the case in 'Lucy Answers' and I called this strategy 'Broadening the scope of the answer'. It is classified as part of both the personal and the public dimension, because the advisor team broadens the scope of the answer for the benefit of the larger public, but this information may also be relevant for the individual who asked the question. Broadening the scope is achieved in three different ways: (1) by referring questioners to other sources of information such as websites or books, (further) professional help, or 'Lucy Answers' records, (2) by anticipating follow-up questions, and (3) by providing more information than is requested in the problem letter. The first strategy is represented in (7.17), in which a questioner and the readership are directed to further information to be found in a book:

(7.17) For more information on the subject of body building and nutrition, Lucy recommends the book *Built on Balance*. It was written by Carol Emich, a female champion body builder who only competes in steroid-free competitions. (LA 37, fitness and nutrition, "Build muscle mass?")

Referring readers to other resources of help and information occurs frequently in 'Lucy Answers'. As we have seen earlier, I have assigned a specific category (referral) to this kind of practice in the analysis of advice in Chapter 5.

In (7.18), the second strategy can be observed: anticipating follow-up questions. "Worried and Wondering" asks about how to properly sterilize injection needles. This issue is addressed in the first paragraph of *Lucy's* answer. The second paragraph, however, broadens the scope of the answer because *Lucy* poses follow-up questions connected to cocaine misuse (italicized), which were not raised in the questioner's letter. The paragraph ends with referral information.

(7.18)   "Shared needles for cocaine?" (LA 0013, drugs, italics added)*

Lucy –

Recently my boyfriend began injecting cocaine. I've noticed that he and his friends share their needles, but "clean" them first with bleach and water. Is this a valid way to avoid contamination?
Signed – Worried and Wondering

Dear Worried and Wondering,

Oh, boy! There's quite a few levels to this question. First of all, cleaning shared needles can be an effective way to prevent transmission of HIV (Lucy assumes that this is what you mean by contamination). But, by putting cleaning in quotation marks, you put into question its definition. To prevent HIV transmission, your boyfriend and his friends must clean the complete works, including syringe and cotton, not solely the needle. Bleach should be drawn into the syringe, and then emptied and flushed with water, at least three times. A recent news report questioned the effectiveness of this technique. The NYC AIDS hotline still recommends it, although there is no scientific research to support either conclusion.

Lucy would like to ask you to think about some things… How does your boyfriend's drug use affect you – emotionally? physically? Do you use a condom every time you have sex? Is he aware of the potential dangers of shooting coke – Are you? It's different than snorting it, or free basing. Lucy will stop here because you didn't ask her about these things. But, if you need a place to talk, feel free to call Counseling and Psychological Services (CPS) at xx-xxxx, and make an appointment with a counselor.

Lucy

* The examples in this chapter are not presented in their tagged form (cf. Chapters 5 and 6) to save space and because the additional information gained from the tree structure is not relevant to my argument here.

The sentence *Lucy will stop here because you didn't ask her about these things* demonstrates that, in this record, the advisors show that they are well aware they are broadening the scope of the answer. This statement in combination with the introductory sentence in the paragraph, which displays mitigation (*would like*; the ellipsis acknowledging the face-threatening character of what is to come), contains the implicature that *Lucy* is aware of the fact that broadening the scope of the response might not be considered appropriate by the advisee. The reader is nevertheless invited to follow up the issues raised.

The final strategy is the provision of more information than is requested in the question. In "The health of a couch potato", *Lucy* responds to a person who asked *What are the health implications of a sedentary life?* Not only does *Lucy* give an appropriate answer to the question by listing the physical and medical drawbacks that ensue when there is *too much bonding time with the couch and TV remote control*, but she also takes the opportunity to point out ways in which to get active. In fact, three of the five units in this answer are filled with concrete suggestions to motivate the readers to lead an active life. The final unit of the letter illustrates this in (7.19):

(7.19)   An excellent way to stay healthy is to stay active – with or without a friend or exercise buddy – whether you're swimming, rock-climbing, working up a sweat at the gym, dancing, walking around the neighborhood, taking the stairs rather than the elevator, and/or getting off at an earlier subway or bus stop. You can get moving in so many ways that you are certain to find one or more that you enjoy and can stick with. Anything that makes you put down the remote and get off of the couch is a step toward a healthy, more fulfilling, and longer life. (LA 2590, general health, "The health of a couch potato")

A more subtle form of broadening the content of an answer is given in (7.20). A questioner who identifies herself as an East Asian woman asks how to respond to her mother's finding of her contraceptives:

(7.20)   "My mom found my contraceptives!" (LA 1487, relationships, italics added)

> Dear Lucy,
>
> A few months ago, my boyfriend and I went to the hospital to get the "morning after pill." I had two extra pills in case I vomited the ones I took. Stupidly, I kept them and recently, my mom found them. She has not confronted me about them yet but I'm freaked out!! Being East Asian, my parents are pretty conservative, so I can't possibly tell them "Oh mom! I had sex behind your back and the condom broke!" They'd flip out! What should I tell them?
>
> ---
>
> Dear Reader,
>
> So far, your parents haven't asked you about finding your emergency contraception pills, and, in fact, they may not. *Asian families tend not to talk about sex, contraception, and other related matters considered taboo* (*many non-Asian families are uncomfortable about these kinds of discussions as well*). So, if your parents don't bring it up, you don't have to either. In case they *do* want to talk with you about it, you have some choices about what you say and how you respond. Practice by making a list of what you think they might ask you, or how they may bring up the topic, and the various ways of responding to their questions or hints. Then decide which

> of these answers are appropriate and comfortable considering your family
> and cultural values. This way, if your parents do bring up the subject,
> you're prepared. Remember to listen carefully to what they are asking. Also
> keep in mind that the key is to respond, not to react.
>
> You seem to be pretty responsible. And, you deserve some privacy. Good
> luck.
>
> Lucy

In (7.20) the sentence *Asian families tend not to talk about sex, contraception, and other related matters considered taboo* (*many non-Asian families are uncomfortable about these kinds of discussions as well*), which is italicized in the answer, is of interest. The content of this sentence is only marginally relevant to the individual who was looking for advice. After all, she is well aware of the fact that she is from an Asian family and that talking about sexuality is difficult for her. In fact this is why she turned to 'Lucy Answers' for help in the first place. We can conclude that this sentence is therefore included for the benefit of the wider readership which may lack this kind of background information. The three broadening strategies together ensure that the targeted readership's informational needs are addressed as well as possible.

7.2.4 Evaluating the advice-seeker's attitudes and actions

Evaluations allow the team of advisors to address the personal individual advice-seeker more explicitly by stating the kind of behavior the advisors consider commendable or objectionable. Both praise and criticism have been addressed in earlier discussions (cf. Chapter 6). At this stage, I want to illustrate with two examples how, by necessity, these evaluations address the letter writer as well as the larger audience. Both the public and private dimensions are therefore involved. In (7.21) *Lucy* praises the questioner's willingness to seek information. By doing this, she encourages other readers to act in a similar way:

(7.21) Dear Gathering info, Good alias… and smart strategy. (LA 1205, drugs, "Hungry for heroin information", periods in original)

Lucy can also choose to be critical, thus showing the readership what kind of behavior is deemed objectionable or debatable. In (7.22) an advice-seeker worries about whether her boyfriend is gay or not. In the first paragraph of the answer, the tone is clearly critical in that the advice-seeker is confronted with a number of questions that force her to reconsider her own role in relation to the problem at hand:

(7.22) "Gay, a tease, or just unavailable" (LA 1403, relationships, italics added)

> Dear Lucy,
>
> I'm worried about my boyfriend. A lot of people have told me that he is probably gay, because he looks good and most guys who look real good are. I didn't believe any of it at all because he doesn't act or talk gay. The ones telling me this are also guys. Could it be that they are jealous? Because I'm getting ready to believe it. I say that because every time we are alone, he knows how to get me really turned on, he gets me turned on, and then refuses to "DO" anything.
>
> What's going on? Is he or is he not?
>
> ---
>
> Dear Reader,
>
> *Lucy does not know whether or not your boyfriend is gay, but wonders why you are with someone who teases you – whatever his sexuality. Why are you with someone who suggests sex but won't follow through?* A frank discussion with your boyfriend will be your best shot at answers to your questions – maybe something like this:
>
> [..]

The italicized comments in (7.22) clearly invite the general readership to ask similar questions in case they find themselves in a comparable dilemma, and to accept the inherent criticism. However, since the criticism is addressed to the letter writer, the personal dimension emerges in a much stronger form than in the other strategies discussed until now. For this reason, a member of the general readership may easily choose to ignore the criticism involved. The format of a 'personal' response to a 'personal' problem letter thus emerges as representing a form of mitigation for the benefit of the wider readership.

7.2.5 Bonding with and showing empathy for the advice-seeker

Both bonding with the advice-seekers as well as showing support for them and an awareness of their situation (empathy) emphasize the personal dimension of the response letters. This is because bonding and empathizing express a personal connection with the advice-seeker (cf. Chapter 6). These aspects of relational work are hence less 'instructional' than praising and criticizing in 'Lucy Answers'. Examples (7.23) and (7.24) illustrate the ways support is offered to the advice-seeker:

(7.23) Dear Want to break out of the shell!, You are not alone in feeling shy – although it probably feels that way. (LA 238, emotional health, "Shyness?")

(7.24)   Dear Heroin Hater, Living with an addict in the family is difficult and stressful, regardless of whether or not you live under the same roof with that
person. (LA 1306, drugs, "Dealing with a brother addicted to heroin")

In (7.23) the advice-seeker is reassured that he or she is not alone with the feeling
of shyness, while in (7.24) the situation of the advice-seeker is acknowledged to be
a difficult one. It was argued earlier that the choice to publish a real question posed
by a real individual functions as an invitation to the readership to identify with the
advice-seeker. This invitation is reinforced when the advisor *Lucy* shows support
and empathy towards the advice-seeker. A potential reader with a similar concern
will then feel reassured not only by the fact that there are other people with the
same problem, but also by the fact that this problem is recognized as serious and
deserving an answer in public. However, the individual who wrote the problem
letter is likely to benefit even more from such support.

In the case of bonding, I argue that it is again the original advice-seeker who
benefits most strongly from this relational work. At the same time, however, the
wider readership is of course invited to participate in this created connection, if
they can identify with the advice-seeker. This is the case in (7.25), in which *Lucy*
offers the following assessment to an advice-seeker who performs in three bands
as a singer and has problems with his or her voice:

(7.25)   You may not be a rock star... yet, but it looks like you have the performance
schedule of one. (LA 2420, general health, "Secrets of singers who shout their
brains out?")

The element of bonding lies in the ... *yet*, which acknowledges that the advice-
seeker may have the potential for a rock star. Since this aspiration is shared by
many young adults, this comment will also work to create a bond with members
of the wider readership.

In general, the assessment sections deal with the particular situation of the
advice-seeker and offer interpretations of this situation. The assessment is therefore the discursive move that can most easily be connected to the personal dimension. In Chapter 5 it was argued that these sections create relevance for the
advice-seeker because he or she can agree or disagree with the interpretation and
consequently take or leave the ensuing advice. The same argument can be made
for the wider readership. If readers identify with the situation of the advice-seeker
as discussed in the assessment sections, they will interpret the advice that is designed for this particular situation as important for themselves. As explained in
this and the last section, supportive relational work, such as praising, empathizing, and bonding, that often occurs in this discursive move (cf. Chapter 6), offers
a particular invitation to identify with the advice-seeker, and thus covers both the
personal as well as the public dimension of advice-giving in 'Lucy Answers'.

7.2.6 Addressing the wider readership directly

In several instances keeping up an illusion of a 'personal' answer is disrupted when *Lucy* explicitly addresses readers other than the original advice-seeker. This kind of usage opens up a direct link to the wider readership. In (7.26) *Lucy* directs not only the questioner but also *everyone else* to question-answer sequences in the archive. In (7.27) the possibility that there may be more people than just the advice-seeker who do not know of the ACOA (Adult Children of Alcoholics) organization is acknowledged by writing *for those of you unfamiliar with ACOA*, and in (7.28) – one of the rare records dealing with suicide[2] – *Lucy* maintains that the questioner's expression of feelings will serve as an example *for others out there*. In this way *Lucy* explicitly points to the fact that these records are read by a wider readership and are therefore public rather than personal.

(7.26) You *and everyone else at AEI!* Please see the answers to "Uncomfortable with college stresses," "Problems sleeping," "Managing stress?" "Insomnia", and "Stress management." (LA 155, emotional health, "Stressed out!", italics added)

(7.27) *For those of you* unfamiliar with ACOA, children who grew up in alcoholic households often adapted to their situation by learning patterns of inter-action and methods of coping that helped them survive in childhood, but that didn't, and don't, support their own healthy environment. (LA 5, drugs, "Adult children of alcoholics group at AEI", italics added)

(7.28) No doubt, your expression of your concerns here will make it easier *for others out there* to say, "I need help, too." (1574, emotional health, "Thinks about killing others and self", italics added)

Table 7.3 shows that there are only 34 instances of such an explicit mention of the wider readership of 'Lucy Answers'. The majority of these occur within the advice and referral sections. The small number of such direct addresses of the wider readership means that 'Lucy Answers' adheres closely to the format of a personal

Table 7.3 Explicit mention of the wider readership in discursive moves in the subcorpus of 'Lucy Answers'

Discursive move	n	%
advice and referral	16	47
assessment and disclaimer	8	24
general information	5	15
metacomment	2	6
open category	2	6
explanation-advice	1	3
total	34	101

letter exchange by maintaining its forms of address in the majority of cases. In Section 7.4, I will present a summary and evaluation of the results of my discussion of the tension between the personal and public dimension in the response letters of the subcorpus of 'Lucy Answers'.

7.3   'Lucy Answers' over time: A comparison of new and old response letters in the archive

After this discussion of the six strategies identified in the close readings of the response letters in the subcorpus, we now turn to the records in the entire archive of 'Lucy Answers'. In the description of the material, it was stressed that the archive is an integral part of the site as the advice-seekers are clearly encouraged to browse the archive first and only then ask questions. For such an archive to work as a reliable source of information, it needs to be constantly updated. The focus in this section is on these updated records, which are, once again, taken to reflect the consensus of a team of health counselors rather than to be the result of an individual's initiative. Data collection from the 'Lucy Answers' website took place at two different times: August 2002 and March 2004. During the nineteen intervening months, the 'Lucy Answers' archive changed because the responses are regularly updated by the team. Since the entire archive was at my disposal at both times of collection, it was possible to compare the older archive with the newer one. With the help of a computer program (WinMerge), I identified 327 records as having been updated. They were then analyzed manually, and this resulted in the identification of different types of alterations. My first interest in these comparisons is to study what kind of changes were made. Second, the comparison should reveal whether these changes are systematic ones. Either they contribute to the voice of the advisor *Lucy,* as will be discussed in Chapter 8, and/or they are due to the site's orientation to the wider Internet readership. This would pay tribute to the public dimension of this discursive practice in general and to the increasing popularity of 'Lucy Answers' outside the AEI community in particular. The latter idea was originally triggered by the following example:

(7.29)   Sounds like you had an AWESOME summer… *Welcome Back to AEI!* (2002, LA 1, sexual health, "Two virgins – Use condoms?", italics added)

Sounds like you had an *awesome* summer! (2004, LA 1, sexual health, "Two virgins – Use condoms?", italics added)

In (7.29), the 2002 version contains an explicit mention of AEI, the home university of the health program; in the 2004 version, this mention has been removed. It is argued that this removal opens up the potential for readers to identify with the addressee to a wider number of people and may be motivated by the increasing popularity of the site over time. The history of the site may thus have an impact on the design of the response letters.

Broadly speaking, the changes that were identified can be classified into changes in content and changes in style. Ultimately, it can be argued that both types of changes are due to the public dimension and, more specifically, to the public agenda that 'Lucy Answers' adheres to. Since it is their mission to provide quality advice and since the archive is designed as an integral part of the site to which readers are referred, it is in the interest of the advisor team to work constantly on the quality of the texts – whether this work is on content or style. The content changes concern (1) referral information, (2) the informational content more generally, and (3) the addition of a link to the specific reader response contributions. The three categories will briefly be illustrated.

In 138 records I found changes that update referral information on names of services, phone numbers, addresses and hyperlinks. The majority of these changes rename services at AEI. For example *Women's Health* becomes *Primary Care Services,* or *Health and Related Services* is changed to *Health Services* as in example (7.30):

(7.30)   If you are an AEI student, the Women's Health clinic of <u>Health and Related Services</u> (xx-xxxx) can also answer your questions directly. (2002, LA 1139, sexual health, "Are two condoms better than one?")

If you are an AEI student, the Primary Care Medical Services division of <u>Health Services</u> (xx-xxxx) can also answer your questions directly. (2004, LA 1139, sexual health, "Are two condoms better than one?")

These changes can be categorized as 'referral informational' since they assure that readers will still be able find the places or sources of information mentioned.

The next category involving content entails actual changes in informational content. This is the case in 77 records. These changes ensure that the information contained in the answers is still current. For example, if new medical insights were gained between the date of the original publication and the time of revision, this information is included in the update. Example (7.31) on low cholesterol is a case in point. Between the original posting in 1995 and the update in 2003 studies were made which led to new scientific results. This is reflected in the first paragraph of the answer and in the listing of 'Related Q&As' (see italicized passages).

(7.31) "Low Cholesterol?" (LA 514, fitness and nutrition, italics added)

> Dear Lucy,
> What are the implications of low cholesterol? Mine has been running between 100–110 for several months. Do I have anything to worry about?
> – Skinny

2002-Database	2004-Database
Dear Skinny,	Dear Skinny,
You have nothing to worry about. If you don't eat enough cholesterol in your diet, your body manufactures whatever additional cholesterol it needs to function. The dangers are of high cholesterol levels, as your body does not have mechanisms for getting rid of the excess. Stay healthy!	*In 1999, a flurry of news began as a result of a paper that was presented to the American Heart Association linking low cholesterol with increased risk for stroke. More recent published research supports many experts' skepticism regarding the claim and that original study.*
Lucy	If people don't take in enough cholesterol from their eating plan, their bodies manufacture whatever additional cholesterol they need to function. The dangers exist when individuals have high cholesterol levels, as their bodies do not have mechanisms for getting rid of the excess.
[date 1], 1995	*For more information about cholesterol, take a look at the Related Q&As listed below.*
	Lucy
	Related Q&As
	Concerned with low HDL
	Concerned with high cholesterol
	Cholesterol?
	Good and bad cholesterol
	Updated [date 2], 2003 / [date 1], 1995

Other changes in content can also be due to the growing number of records in the 'Lucy Answers' archive that deal with similar questions. In (7.32), entitled "More about melatonin", taken from the category 'fitness and nutrition', the content of the answer is drastically shortened since the same information can be found in other responses concerned with melatonin, which are listed at the end of the new version. The first four paragraphs in the old version have not been included in the new version. The fifth paragraph still exists (❶ corresponds to ①), while the referral information at the end of the answer is reorganized (❷, ②). There is, however, a new paragraph added to the new version which in fact provides a more direct answer to the question about melatonin as a dietary supplement than does the older version of the answer (see italics). Updates in content can therefore result in the deletion of previous text, additions or even a complete reorganization of the text. All of these changes are motivated by an attempt to inform the wider readership in the best possible way and to take into account the growing number of records in the archive. The history of the site, made constantly available by means of the Internet archive, thus has a direct impact on the way in which the response letters are updated, and, by analogy, also on the creation of new letters.

(7.32)   "More about melatonin" (LA 1383, fitness and nutrition)

> Dear Lucy,
> Do you recommend any natural remedies (Melatonin, etc.) as dietary supplements for healthy living?
>
> ---
>
> **2002-Database**
> Dear Reader,
> If your night time activities include rolling around restlessly in bed and staring at an alarm clock, melatonin could be an answer sent from heaven. Melatonin is a hormone produced naturally by the pineal gland at the base of the brain. The hormone is usually released in large amounts at night or when there is little light available. Melatonin elicits drowsiness and deep sleep. This action explains why individuals get sleepy in a dark classroom or a pitch-black movie theater.
>
>   The hormone is commonly used to correct sleep-associated problems, such as jet lag and insomnia. Animal studies have shown that melatonin use may indirectly increase the life span. Extra sleep could accomplish this feat by increasing time for the body to repair its tissues and by reducing the amount of stress placed on the body due to physical and mental activity.
>
>   Clinical trials have not shown any serious adverse effects caused by the consumption of melatonin. However, the product is still experimental. It has not been used on the consumer market for
>
> **2004-Database**
> Dear Reader,
> *For healthy living, it's important to take care of your physical, emotional, and sexual self, which includes healthy eating, regular exercise or physical movement, getting enough rest, and managing stress. Taking supplements regularly as a component of this regimen is something to talk about with your health care provider. It's also important to investigate any herbal products or hormonal supplements thoroughly with your health care provider before you begin taking them. Herbal and hormonal supplements can have side effects, are not be used by women who are pregnant or by those who have certain conditions, and can interact with prescription drugs an individual might be taking at the same time.*

an extended length of time. Drowsiness is the most evident side effect (do not take it during the daytime, and don't drive a car or sail a ship when under the influence of the drug). Also, a small percentage of users have reported vivid nightmares and dreams, decreased sex drive, mild depression, and morning sluggishness.

The most important bit of advice to remember when choosing an over-the-counter (OTC) drug or an herbal supplement is to consult with a doctor before starting the regimen. S/he can explain the possible benefits or risks of treatment on a personal basis. If using melatonin, a doctor should be advised if an individual is pregnant or has a history of depression, diabetes, autoimmune problems, or allergies.

❶ Herbal remedies are as old as time itself; however, Lucy reminds you that herbal "medicines" are not regulated by the U.S. Food and Drug Administration (FDA). There is no guarantee of the ingredients' quality or quantity. So, choose wisely and carefully.

❷ Read Melatonin and Melatonin – Jet Lag? in Lucy's General Health archives. Also check out the following organization for more info on melatonin:
Society for Light Treatment and Biological Rhythms (SLTBR)
10200 West 44th Ave.,
Suite 304, Wheat Ridge, CO 80033-2840
E-mail SLTBR

Lucy

① Many herbal remedies are as old as time itself; however, herbal "medicines" are not regulated by the U.S. Food and Drug Administration (FDA). There is no guarantee of the ingredients' quality, quantity, or safety. So, choose wisely and carefully.

② For more information on the specific hormonal supplement you mentioned, melatonin, read the Related Q&As listed below.

Lucy

Related Q&As
Melatonin
Melatonin – Jet lag?
Gingko – What d'ya thinko?
Kombuchia – Diet supplement?
Echinacea
Ephedrine
St. John's Wort

Updated [date 2], 2004 / [date 1], 1998

> [Material adapted from:
> _Medical Sciences Bulletin_ (August 1995)
> "Melatonin: Hormone of the Night"
> available at the Pharmaceutical
> Information Network (PharmInfoNet)]
> [date 1], 1998

The final category of informational updates is the addition of a hyperlink to reader response contributions to the particular record in question. In 74 records this was the _only_ change found in the updated version. They are regarded as content additions since they link to new points of view which were previously not directly accessible. Contributions by the public readership are thus given more prominence than before, and this can be interpreted as an attempt to adjust to the popularity of 'Lucy Answers'. These links also emphasize that the records belong to the public domain: the 'personal' letter is published and thus belongs to the site and its archive, and is open to comments from other parties. This brings to the fore that the format of a 'personal letter' is used as a vehicle to pass on information – a convention which both the makers and readers of 'Lucy Answers' adopt.

In 97 records I identified changes in style. This means that the factual content of the answer is hardly affected by these changes, but the way the answer is visually or stylistically presented is altered. Such changes include the addition or deletion of relational work strategies. The first stylistic changes found are in reformulations of titles. There are only three cases in which this occurs, and they are listed in Table 7.4. The first change clarifies the abbreviation TA by giving the words it stands for. Readers from a non-American and/or non-academic background are particularly likely to benefit from this change. The second alteration concerns the record on melatonin (see (7.32) above). As I have shown in my discussion of this record, the content has changed quite drastically and the new title better reflects this new content. The last title change could at first sight be explained by the mission of 'Lucy Answers' that aims at facilitating decision-making rather than at offering recommendations. The actual content of this record, however, in both cases consists of providing referral information, i.e., it tells the advice-seeker and general readership where to _get_ recommendations rather than providing information it-

Table 7.4 Changes in titles

Record	2002 Title	2004 Title
193	Girlfriend or TA	Girlfriend or teaching assistant
1383	More about Melatonin	Are there dietary supplements that promote healthy living?
1552	Meningitis vaccine recommendations	Meningitis vaccine decision-making

self. It can therefore also be claimed that the new title better fits the content of the record.

Stylistic changes can also be of a more technical nature or, more importantly, they may change the tone of an answer. More technical alterations include turning bold face into italics for stress, turning % into *percent*, or changing the visual presentation of lists (capitalized versus non-capitalized items). There are also recurring vocabulary changes, e.g., *look like* becomes *look similar to*. The updated record versions also consistently move references to other problem and response letters from the main text into the 'Related Q&As' section at the end of the answer, as can be seen in (7.32) above (② and ❷). This facilitates quick access to further information and thus serves the wider readership.

Another set of stylistic changes is in the use of pronouns and/or reference to *Lucy*. The latter set will be discussed in Chapter 8. In the use of pronouns to refer to the questioner and/or wider readership, we have seen in Section 7.2.6 that the reader is usually addressed with the second person pronoun *you* and only in rare cases is the wider readership *directly* addressed with phrases such as *for those of you* or *everyone else*. In the updates, there were several records in which a tendency to formulate in a more impersonal style could be observed, as can be seen in example (7.33) on low cholesterol. The two versions of the letter were already introduced earlier in (7.31) and here only a part of each letter is included:

(7.33)   You have nothing to worry about. If *you* don't eat enough cholesterol in your diet, *your* body manufactures whatever additional cholesterol it needs to function. The dangers are of high cholesterol levels, as *your* body does not have mechanisms for getting rid of the excess. Stay healthy! (2002, LA 514, fitness and nutrition, "Low cholesterol?", italics added)

If *people* don't take in enough cholesterol from their eating plan, *their* bodies manufacture whatever additional cholesterol they need to function. The dangers exist when *individuals* have high cholesterol levels, as *their* bodies do not have mechanisms for getting rid of the excess. (2004, LA 514, fitness and nutrition, "Low cholesterol?", italics added)

Apart from the other stylistic changes, we can see that the direct address to the reader (*you, your*) is dropped in favor of a more impersonal address form (*people, their, individuals*). The same change can be observed in an extract, (7.34), from an answer to the question of what a swing club is.[3] This record is one in which the wording is changed drastically, and in which references to *Lucy* as an individual have been deleted as well (cf. Chapter 8 for a discussion). The example reproduces the last paragraph in the response letter:

(7.34)   A former swinger told Lucy that many people in the swing club scene believe their "community" doesn't have any diseases and they believe they won't contract anything. This type of ignorance and resistance to the truth can make sex at swing clubs risky. However, *you* can go to a swing club and have sex with the partner who accompanied *you*. In this way *you* can still be monogamous and safe. If *both of you* know you are free of any infections and are protected from pregnancy, if applicable, then safer sex will not be an issue. If *you* change partners, Lucy recommends always practicing safer sex – whether oral, vaginal, or anal. By practicing safer sex techniques, *you* will certainly reduce the risk of any sexually transmitted diseases. (2002, LA 831, sexuality, "More on commercial party houses", italics added)

If monogamy and risk reduction are important *to couples, they* can go to a swing club and have sex with their accompanying partner. In this way, *a person* can still be monogamous and safe. If *both people* know they are infection-free and protected from pregnancy, if applicable, then *they* may not need to have safer sex. If partner(s) are changed or added, and they have oral, vaginal, or anal sex, precautions, such as condoms and other safer sex strategies, can help keep all involved healthier. (2004, LA 831, sexuality, "More on commercial party houses", italics added)

Again we can see that the direct address form *you* for the advice-seeker and public readership is exchanged for a more neutral wording (*couples, a person, people, they*). The choice of these terms can be said to create a distancing effect. While *Lucy* still reports the facts about swing clubs, she avoids giving the impression that the readership is invited to identify with visitors to such clubs. This effect is strengthened in the content of the rest of the answer, in which *Lucy* cautions more elaborately about the health hazards in swing clubs.[4] However, there are quite a number of counter-examples in the updated records, which make it impossible to argue that the 'Lucy Answers' team now consistently makes its advisory text more impersonal by avoiding the second person pronoun. It is therefore not possible to speak of a general tendency and the result reported on in Section 7.2.6, i.e., that the advisor team adheres to the format of a personalized letter exchange with respect to the forms of address in the majority of cases, is not contradicted by an examination of changes to the archive.

In several records, only the paragraph sequence is revised, which results in a different style of the response. Example (7.35), "Dating First Cousin", is one of those records in which the old paragraph sequence is reorganized, but there are also other changes with respect to wording as well as content within paragraphs (cf. especially paragraphs ❸/③ and ❹/④). There are also two more substantial additions to the new version, which are marked with curly brackets and are italicized. These changes results in a much clearer, more precise and specific answer, while more support is offered to the questioner in the additions.

(7.35)   "Dating first cousin" (LA 706, relationships, italics added)

Dear Lucy,

What are the pros and cons (legally and morally) of dating your 1st cousin? To make a long story short, my cousin and I became close friends then fell in love with each other. We have that "don't care" attitude on what others say or think about our relationship, but are curious anyway.

Signed, Jus' need advice from a 3rd party…

2002-Database

Dear Jus' need advice from a 3rd party,

❶ There is no law that prohibits dating between first cousins. In fact, there is no law that prohibits a rendezvous with absolutely anyone you choose, given they're of the legal age of consent in your state. However, should you consider marriage with a first cousin, laws vary by state. In most states, the marriage of first cousins is prohibited. You can find out more about family law in your own state by contacting a legal services office, a law school that offers legal services to students and the public, or you can look it up yourself under "marriage" or "domestic relationships" in the legal statutes for your state (found in a state government office).

❷ In regards to your question of the moral consequences of dating your first cousin, YOU must first decide what your values are, where your and your cousin's interests lie, what you are thinking about in terms of your future, etc. This is a very personal decision, although, as you already know, people will always have their own opinions and make

2004-Database

Dear Jus' need advice from a 3rd party…,

③ Negative reactions to cousins who pair off come largely from the belief that offspring from such relationships may have physical and/or mental abnormalities. ④ Children with genetic disorders such as spina bifida or cystic fibrosis are more likely to be born of blood relatives because previously unexpressed recessive genes are more likely to appear. Recessive disease-causing genes that don't affect parents who only carry a single copy can cause disorders in children who inherit a copy from each parent. Studies of first cousin offspring show that there is a 6 to 8 percent chance that the child will have a birth defect, in contrast to the 3 to 4 percent rate of birth defects in children born of couples who don't share a common grandparent. If cousin couples happen to be carrying known genetic diseases, the risks faced by their offspring can jump. Experts say 1 out of 4 such children will have some sort of disorder.

① Legally, you can date your first cousin, but if you are considering marriage, laws vary by state and country. Twenty-four states legally forbid first cousins from marrying, and another seven require genetic their own comments. ❸ Most often people are apprehensive about first cousins, or family relatives who fall "in love" because there are very often negative biological consequences in the offspring of blood relations. The ramifications of offspring from second cousins or more distant relatives are minimally greater than for offspring of non-relatives, but for those more closely related than second cousins, there are tremendous disadvantages to their consanguineous consummation. ❹ Physically or mentally impaired children are frequently born of blood relatives because previously hidden recessive genes are more likely to appear. The closer the parents are in blood relation, the higher the chances are that they share similar genes. "Hidden genes" may contain beneficial traits, but they are more likely to contain detrimental traits because recessive gene mutations are most often a result of their inefficiency. Studies of first cousin offspring show that there is a 6 to 8 percent chance that the child will have a birth defect, in contrast to the 3 to 4 percent rate of birth defects from children born of non-relatives. In other words, the descendants of first cousins are almost two times more likely to suffer an abnormality or death than children of the average couple. ❺ For more information and counseling before legal union can take place. You can find out more about family law in your own state by contacting a legal services office, a law school that offers legal services to students and the public, or searching your state's homepage on the Internet. You can also look it up under "marriage" or "domestic relationships" in the legal statutes for your state (paper copies are found in a state government office).

② Regarding your question of the moral consequences of dating your first cousin, it's up to the two of you to know what your values are, what you're thinking about for the future, and what's best for you as individuals, a couple, and a family. As with all moral decisions, this is a personal, but complicated, matter, given societal norms and the many who see cousin marriages as taboo.

{1} *If you are considering having children together, it makes sense to get genetic counseling. A genetic counselor is a nurse or doctor with special training or expertise who will perform tests and learn about you and your partner's family history. With a clearer picture of the risks your offspring might face, a counselor can help you reach a decision that makes sense for you, your partner, and if you choose to go down that path, your children as well. You can learn more about genetic counseling by visiting the March of Dimes Birth Defects Foundation.* ⑤ For more general information and studies on the effects of blood related unions, visit the March of Dimes Birth Defects Foundation web site.

studies on the effects of blood related unions, contact the March of Dimes Birth Defect Foundation at x-xxx-xxxx.

Lucy

[date 1], 1995

{2} *All that said, it sounds as though you and your partner have found something special in each other. You say you have a "don't care" attitude, but you are smart to ask about the risks – legal, moral, and medical. No one knows where your dating relationship will lead – but it's good to be aware as you explore your closeness and make choices.*

Lucy

Updated [date 2], 2003 / [date 1], 1995

In the newer version, the first paragraph focuses directly on the biological likelihood that offspring from a relationship of first cousins may have *physical or mental abnormalities*. This first paragraph corresponds to paragraphs ❸ and ❹ in the old version and is shortened and updated. It is interesting to see that the evaluation in paragraph ❸ is left out (*there are tremendous disadvantages*). In the newer version, this conclusion is left to the reader to make. Then the new version of the response moves to legal issues followed by the moral question of dating one's first cousin. The penultimate paragraph is partly new {1} and offers actual advice about what to do in case the questioner really wants to have children. This is presented in a factual manner. This information is an important addition since the reader was largely left on his or her own with the information provided in the first version. Only in the last paragraph, which is again an addition to the earlier version {2}, do we see some acknowledgement of the questioner's difficult situation (*All that said*) and a recognition of the special case of the couple in question (*it sounds as though you and your partner have found something special in each other*). *Lucy* even praises the questioner in a straightforward manner for seeking information. This comment is in line with the official 'Lucy Answers' mission: *No one knows where your dating relationship will lead – but it's good to be aware as you explore your closeness and make choices*. The revised record is thus more informative than the initial record, and presents an additional suggestion of where to turn to for help. The relational work in the updated version is also changed since *Lucy* now offers empathy to the advice-seeker and clearly leaves the final decision about this relationship to the advice-seeker him- or herself.

Admittedly, all of these stylistic changes are very subtle and their effect on the reader is open to interpretation. In addition, every response has to be looked at individually and in its entirety to see how its elements interact. In this section I have only given a few examples to illustrate the categories of changes. In general, however, we can say that the content changes aim at increasing the quality of the factual information for the benefit of the wider readership. There is no such clear result from the examination of the stylistic changes. While there is, for example, more empathy offered in (7.35), bonding comments have been removed in (7.31) on low cholesterol, in which the framing remarks *You have nothing to worry about* and *Stay healthy!* do not appear any longer in the revised version. Such contradictions make it impossible to identify a clear direction for the stylistic changes in the response letters.

7.4 Summary

The archive of question-answer sequences is an integral part of 'Lucy Answers' and this is the place where the public dimension of this text genre comes to the fore. In order for the archive to function properly as an up-to-date source of information, the records need to be constantly revised. These revisions have been of interest in this chapter since it can be assumed that they are motivated by the wish to improve the quality of the response letters for the benefit of the wider readership, while the format of a 'personal letter' response is still adhered to. The fact that data collection for this project took place at two different times allowed me to compare the first collection with the second. This resulted in an examination of 327 records which had undergone changes during the time period between collections. They were analyzed and different kinds of alterations were identified.

The first set was categorized as content changes and includes substantial updates on the informational subject matter of the answers, keeping referral information current and adding reader response contributions. The first two categories of change are central to the practice of 'Lucy Answers'. Without these changes the archive could no longer function as a source of accurate and helpful information and they can be argued to serve the needs of the wider and growing readership. It was also claimed that the inclusion of a link to the reader responses emphasizes the public character of the records, highlighting the public dimension of 'Lucy Answers'. This can also be argued to be due to the increasing popularity of the site. The AEI readership, however, still seems to be the prime target readership as can be most clearly seen in the many pieces of referral information that are updated and geared only towards AEI students.

The second set of changes is of a stylistic nature. Some alterations are of a more technical kind, and affect the visual presentation of the answer, such as turning bold face into italics for stress, % into *percent*, the visual presentation of lists, or the removal of the mention of the 'Related Q&As' from the main text and placing it at the end of the answer. Other stylistic changes are connected to finding or improving the voice of 'Lucy Answers'. At times, the paragraph composition of an answer is rearranged in order to round the text off better, to stress or merge ideas. References to *Lucy* as an acting character seem to decrease over time (see Chapter 8), while there is no clear pattern to decisions to use either the second person singular pronoun to directly address the questioner/reader, or to use the more impersonal, detached forms of reference. At the end, it was argued that every problem and response letter sequence has to be looked at as a composition in its own right and that changes in the tone of an answer, and in the relational work invested, can only be interpreted if the text is looked at in its entirety. It was, however, not possible to identify general tendencies for the direction of the stylistic changes.

The study of the updated records in the archive has highlighted the influence of the medium of the Internet on the discursive practice of 'Lucy Answers'. Unlike the readers of an advice column in a newspaper or magazine, the readers of 'Lucy Answers' have the entire archive of question-answer sequences at their disposal by mouse click. The makers of 'Lucy Answers' are aware of their site's 'history' as presented in the question-answer sequences in the archive. It was shown that when updating a record not only is external factual information taken into account, such as new medical insights gained in a particular field, but the record is recomposed with the other letters in the archive in mind. The history of the site thus has a direct bearing on the composition of all the response letters – both new ones and updated ones.

My discussion of the tension between the public and personal dimension in the records of the subcorpus of 'Lucy Answers' centered on six different strategies: the choice of question to be answered, the wording of titles, the broadening of the scope of the answer, the evaluations of the questioner's attitudes and actions, bonding with and showing empathy for the advice-seeker and, finally in a few cases addressing the wider readership directly. The strategies employed by the expert and host in a call-in radio show to account for the public audience identified by Hutchby (1995) can to a certain degree also be observed in 'Lucy Answers'. Answering more than the question (expert), as well as the auxiliary questions (host) are similar to two of the subcategories of 'broadening the scope of the answer', i.e., 'providing more information than is requested' and 'anticipating follow-up questions'. There is no direct strategy in 'Lucy Answers' that would equal the final strategy identified by Hutchby, namely that the host and expert try to return to the caller's particular problem at the end of a call. It is possible to argue, however, that this link to the individual, original advice-seeker is never entirely severed in 'Lucy Answers', since there are enough strategies to ensure that relevance is created for the advice-seeker as well as the wider readership (e.g., in the assessment sections, the conditional clauses in the advisory moves, the relational work such as bonding, praising, criticizing or empathizing; cf. Chapters 5 and 6).

Not all of the strategies discussed in this chapter have to occur in every question-answer sequence. Their presence, however, assures that the general readership's needs are covered true to the mission of 'Lucy Answers' in the best and broadest manner possible, while the appearance of a private and personal exchange is sustained. As a final point it is worth mentioning once more that the advice column format of a 'personal' problem letter followed by a seemingly individualized response letter functions nicely as a conveyor of advice and information that the general readership can either take or leave. The format itself therefore represents a form of mitigation: the wider readership is meant to be reached and invited to identify, but this is done in an indirect manner by means of a 'personalized' letter exchange.

CHAPTER 8

Lucy's voice

Constructing the identity of an expert advice-giver*

> He might listen if you speak from the heart and not from a medical encyclopedia.
> (*Lucy*, LA 1311, drugs)

8.1 Introduction

Lucy's "voice", or rather, the linguistic strategies that contribute to the construction of the advisor-identity *Lucy*, are at the heart of this chapter. It will be shown how the central concern in the discourse of 'Lucy Answers', which is the negotiation of its professional expert advice in a way that is optimally acceptable and relevant to its target audience, results in the formation of a particular advice-giving identity for *Lucy*. 'Lucy Answers' is a professional Internet site designed to provide a larger audience with quality health information (cf. the mission statement quoted in Chapter 2), yet, as we have seen, information transfer is not the only function of *Lucy*'s answers since she clearly provides 'advice'. She is therefore much more than a source of electronically stored information, as she engages in an interactive exchange, and can thus be argued to represent a professional expert who tries to have a positive effect on the attitudes and actions of the readers. Thus, not only is the transfer of information important, but also the creation of an atmosphere in which the addressee feels he or she has been taken seriously. For this reason, it must be in the interest of the 'Lucy Answers' team to create a voice for *Lucy* that the readers of the site can relate to. This could, for example, be achieved by constructing her persona as somebody who is neither too sociable nor too distant. A professional site has an interest in creating an appropriate advisor for its target readership because the way in which he or she gives advice may be the reason readers return to the site (in addition to the actual information that can be found there).

   Lucy is, of course, an artificial construct which has a voice that is the result of the linguistic choices made by a team of advisors. This fact is of special interest because it allows us to take the linguistic strategies that contribute to the emergence of *Lucy*'s identity to be the consensus of more than just one individual person. It is important to point out that the advisor team could also have decided to sign their response letters with "your AEI health program team". Instead, they have chosen a female name as a pseudonym. The fact that *Lucy* is not a real person is not concealed from the readership, but this information is also not visible on the main page. The reader can click on the link 'about Lucy Answers' (cf. Figure 2.1) and is then directed to an explanation about the team of advisors who compose the responses and sign as *Lucy*. There is also no picture of a fictional advisor on the 'Lucy Answers' site, as is the case for many advice columns on the web or in magazines. Mininni (1991:78) reports that in the two British magazines of his study such pictures were accompanied by a caption that listed the credentials of the advisor, which meant that the advisor was clearly identified as an expert. In the case of 'Lucy Answers' there is no such picture, nor a caption or headline praising *Lucy*'s qualities. However, in the top right-hand corner of the main frame there is an icon that links to 'AEI Health Services', which tells the reader that this is the source of the expertise and credibility (cf. Figure 2.1). The design of the website therefore implicitly invites the readers to accept *Lucy* as an expert advisor.

I will now look more closely at the concept of identity and in particular at what might constitute an identity of an advisor. As pointed out earlier, identity is a difficult concept to define because it is "neither categorical nor fixed" (Schiffrin 1996:199) and "people adhere to multiple and shifting identities" which "are displayed in and negotiated through interaction" (Adelswärd & Nilholm 2000:545). Davies and Harré (1990) put it as follows:

> An individual emerges through the process of social interaction, not as a relatively fixed end product but as one who is constituted and reconstituted through the various discursive practices in which they participate.   (Davies & Harré 1990:46)

It is thus important to look carefully at the specific discursive practice under investigation. De Fina (2003), in her study on identity in narratives of immigrant discourse, points out that

> [i]dentities emerge through the narrators' manipulation of linguistic choices that construct specific relationships with aspects of the story worlds depicted, of the interactional world in which the stories are told, and of the social context that frames the more local context.   (De Fina 2003:220)

Any analysis of linguistic strategies will thus have to be seen and discussed in connection with the discursive practice as a whole, and in particular with the ideologies determining this practice.

An advice-seeker, when soliciting advice, grants the advice-giver a position of authority or expertise. However, there are more facets to an advisor-identity than just the possession and sharing of knowledge. DeCapua and Dunham (1993:519) point out that meaningful advice also depends on credibility, trustworthiness and

reliability. Thus advice is most likely to be elicited and accepted from an authority figure whose opinion is valued and trusted. Such a person has the ability to
influence the conduct or attitudes of others. An insensitive person who chastises
others for being ignorant may issue directions but will generally not be consulted
for genuine advice – nor would his or her advice be read.[1] However, while advising is clearly linked to trust, competence and knowledge, it does not necessarily
involve a hierarchical status difference between the interactants. DeCapua and
Huber (1995) report that the 26 subjects questioned in their study prefer to turn
for advice to family and friends whom they perceive as more knowledgeable, but
not necessarily as more powerful. An important aspect of advice is thus not only
the transfer of information, but also the creation of an atmosphere in which the
interactional partners feel they are being taken seriously.

The notion of identity that is used in this chapter is one that sees identity as a
construct that emerges interactively, i.e., in the case of 'Lucy Answers', when readers repeatedly engage in reading the advisory texts. In this institutional health care
service, advice-giving will ideally be designed in such a way that it serves its institutional goals best. The texts are thus likely to be carefully constructed by the
advisor team so that readers will not only be confronted with the actual factual
content of the advice given (that will be indicative of the advisors' understanding
and evaluation of the problem at hand), but also with the way in which this advice is designed. According to Joseph (2004: 21), people's identity "inheres in their
voice, spoken, written or signed" (emphasis in original). Thus, when examining
the construction of an expert advisor identity, it will be necessary to investigate
both the action of advice-giving itself, as well as the relational and interpersonal
level that accompanies it.

At first sight, it might seem inappropriate to use the notion of 'interactivity'
for identity construction in an Internet advice column. It is, of course, true that
'Lucy Answers' uses a format of written question-answer sequences which is not
interactive in the way that face-to-face communication is. However, it is important
to point out that the emergence of *Lucy*'s identity depends on interaction with
the readership or the analysts. It should be stressed that *Lucy*'s identity does not
emerge in the reading of one single record, but over time, in the reading of the
weekly publications of new exchanges of problem and response letters or in using
the archives, which are an integral part of 'Lucy Answers'. In the same vein, it can
be argued that the team creating the advisor persona *Lucy* is well aware of the
historicity of the site and continually re-creates *Lucy*'s voice in the response letters
by considering the previously published responses, which are, after all, the cause of
the success of the site. In the end, however, there is no guarantee that the identity
which emerges through the exposure to *Lucy* is the same for every reader. There
can be no last word on *Lucy*'s voice, but my aim is to point to linguistic patterns
that I deem to *contribute* to its emergence in the texts.

8.2 Results and discussion

In my analysis seven factors have emerged which contribute to the construction of *Lucy*'s voice in the 280 response letters in the subcorpus of 'Lucy Answers':

1. *Lucy*'s name, self-reference and address terms.
2. *Lucy* presents herself as a competent and knowledgeable source of accurate information.
3. *Lucy* makes readers think and gives options when she presents her advice.
4. *Lucy* chooses an easily accessible, informal and inoffensive range of vocabulary.
5. *Lucy* has an opinion (positive and negative evaluations).
6. *Lucy* shows awareness of difficult situations (empathy).
7. *Lucy* has a sense of humor.

Many of these linguistic strategies will already be familiar to the reader from previous discussions. In this part of the analysis, however, they will be investigated to discover what they contribute to *Lucy*'s advisor identity. The seven strategies contribute to *Lucy*'s particular voice on different levels. Point one is related to identity because an individual's name and the way he or she conceives a position towards others are part of the manner in which image is portrayed. Point two deals with the aspect of an *expert identity* that plays an important role in the discourse of health related issues and one which was argued to be crucial in advice-giving situations. Points three and four are concerned with aspects of how advice is realized linguistically that have an impact on the advisor identity. Points five to seven are interpersonal strategies that are of importance when the qualities of an advisor are considered. In what follows, I will illustrate and discuss the seven strategies.

8.2.1 *Lucy*'s name, self-reference and address terms

Since the names of the advice column and the fictitious advisor have been changed for this study, I cannot discuss in detail the connotations that the original name may evoke in the readership. I have, however, taken care to choose a female first name as a pseudonym which may carry some of the original associations.[2] First of all, it is important to stress that the advisor is portrayed as a woman. The choice of a female name ties in with a long standing tradition in the United States that women occupy the role of advice columnists. A fictional example can be found in Nathanael West's (1933) novel *Miss Lonelyhearts*. Well established, if not to say institutionalized, columns were run over decades by *Dear Abby* or *Ann Landers* for an American readership. The choice of first name is also not uncommon as we can see from such popular advice authorities as *Dr. Ruth* or *Dear Abby*. The female first name as a pseudonym thus places our advice-giver in the tradition of female advisors in the genre of advice columns. It is also telling that there is no title

(*Dr.*) attributed to her name, which would have stressed a hierarchical difference between the readership and the advisor persona. Instead, the first name without title or surname does not emphasize status differences and implies that this advisor is approachable.

De Fina (2003:52) points out that "[t]he investigation of the use of pronouns as a window into the analysis of identity has a long-standing tradition in linguistics." In addition to their referential function, which links the text to its specific context, the choice and manipulation of pronouns can "also convey subtle social meanings that relate to [the speakers'] social identities or to their positions with respect to other interlocutors, both present and absent, and to the experiences and topics that are being discussed" (De Fina 2003:52). It is therefore important to see how *Lucy* refers to herself and how she addresses the questioner and other readers. This issue has already been partially addressed in Chapter 7.

Lucy addresses the questioner either with *Dear Reader* or with the pseudonym chosen by the questioner as a signature. In the body of the answer *Lucy* typically addresses the questioner with *you*. Since the site's aim is to reach a larger readership than just the questioner, the quality of the English pronoun *you* to refer both to the singular as well as to the plural is an advantage. The reader can thus either identify him- or herself directly with the questioner or as part of the plural *you*. In some cases, *Lucy* also addresses the readership directly by saying *those of you* or *everyone else*, as shown in Section 7.2.6. Usually, however, *Lucy* adheres to the format of 'reply to a personal question', a finding which was also confirmed in the analysis of the updated response letters (cf. Section 7.3).

More revealing for the study of the way *Lucy*'s identity is constructed is the finding that *Lucy* refers to herself as *Lucy*, i.e., she uses third person singular constructions. The first person pronoun *I* is avoided and appears only in five instances in the 280 records analyzed. Apart from the signature *Lucy*, her name appears 213 times. Fifty of these uses occur in connection with the archive that is an integral part of 'Lucy Answers'. (8.1) and (8.2) illustrate this usage:

(8.1) For more information, check out Marijuana and health in Lucy's Alcohol, Nicotine, and Other Drugs archive. (LA 1651, drugs, "Marijuana and driving")

(8.2) For more information about the Pill and other forms of contraception, go to the contraception section of Lucy's Sexual Health archive. (LA 1968, sexual health, "Needs birth control pills, but fearful about doc's evaluation to get them")

In 35 cases *Lucy*'s name is mentioned neutrally but not in connection with the Internet service as such, as can be seen in (8.3):

(8.3)   Tell him what you told Lucy: "It's just not working." (LA 1408, relationships, "Breaking up can be hard to do")

The more important cases of mentions of *Lucy* are those that occur in combination with relational work moves (n = 128, 60%), i.e., with hedging (n = 54), boosting (n = 35), empathizing (n = 16), praising (n = 9), bonding (n = 17), both types of humor (n = 9), and criticizing (n = 7).[3] Examples (8.4) to (8.10) represent typical usages:

(8.4)   Lucy assumes that by not "liking" them, you mean not liking them sexually. (LA 1386, sexuality, **hedging**, "Gay men having sex with women?")

(8.5)   One doctor recommends eating at least one "healthy serving" (Lucy assumes this means a LARGE portion) of steamed cabbage once a day for about two weeks. (LA 953, fitness and nutrition, **humor-hedging**, "Natural ulcer remedies?")

(8.6)   Lucy understands your concern about not wanting to make your boyfriend mad. (LA 1401, relationships, **empathizing**, "Should I tell my partner I was raped when I was a virgin?")

(8.7)   Lucy is glad to hear that you take protection seriously and use condoms when appropriate. (LA 957, sexual health, **praising**, "More about bumps and lumps on penis")

(8.8)   Lucy also wishes you the best on your first sexual experience, whenever it may occur. (LA 990, sexual health, **bonding**, "White spots on penis and tight foreskin")

(8.9)   Lucy recommends that you have this checked by a health care provider who can diagnose and determine the appropriate treatment for you, if any. (LA 997, sexual health, **boosting**, "Penis bump – wart?")

(8.10) You have told Lucy how beautiful, how tall, and how smart you are. But relationships develop based on much more than these objective traits. (LA 1442, relationships, **criticizing**, "Beautiful on the outside, but no boyfriend"; (6.39))

In the 213 mentions of *Lucy*, there are eleven cases in which *Lucy* offers a particular personal experience, such as in (8.11):

(8.11) Everyone will not agree with Lucy, but Lucy pumps up her vitamins, taking a stress-B formula. (LA 24, general health, "Can't sleep")

With only eleven occurrences such personal remarks are rare. However, they are also particularly important since *Lucy* does not exist as a real person, but nevertheless is constructed as having a personal history.

Referring to herself in the third person is a striking feature. The few instances of the first person pronoun *I* are clearly noticeable to a readership familiar with

'Lucy Answers', in the sense that they are a slip in tone or register, especially because two of the five cases even occur in combination with a reference to *Lucy* in the third person. It is argued that this strategy simultaneously serves two functions. First, it is a way to point to the team of health educators that stand behind the pseudonym *Lucy*. This reinforces her identity as an authoritative expert. At the same time it is also an honest way of reminding the reader that *Lucy* is not real. Secondly, the frequent mention of her name calls *Lucy* into being, so to speak.[4] This happens only over time, if readers access the site repeatedly.

In Section 7.3 it was mentioned in passing that references to *Lucy* in the updated texts were sometimes changed. In (7.32) on melatonin, we could see that the sentence *Lucy reminds you that* is deleted in the newer version, as indicated in Table 8.1. This has been observed in other records as well. Table 8.1 shows further examples from a response letter entitled "Men's legs and shaving", taken from the category 'general health': references to *Lucy* are removed two out of three times (see italics). The first reference is simply deleted, while the second is replaced with a more impersonal, detached realization (*Lucy doubts that* becomes *it's doubtful that*). In the third case, however, the reference to *Lucy* is left intact (*a painful... a very painful... did Lucy say painful, procedure*). It is hypothesized that this is because of the humorous effect that this last comment evokes, which the authors did not want to lose.

It has just been argued that reference to *Lucy* in the text of the answer has a dual effect: it points to the team of health educators who stand behind the pseudonym *Lucy*, thus reminding the reader that *Lucy* is not real, and it contributes to *Lucy*'s identity by talking her into being through the recurrent mention of her name. Because of the evidence that there might have been changes in this habit, it was important to see whether the team have adjusted their style by making changes of a more systematic nature. In order to see if there is any change in the frequency of references to *Lucy* as 'a person' over time, I looked at the first 150 records of the entire database (totaling 2,286 records), that were not changed after 2002, and at the last 150. Fifty percent of the first 150 records have been updated at various points in time before 2002 (this information is given in every record), which means that I am actually comparing the state before the first data collection (2002) with that of the usage in between the two collection times (cf. Section 7.3 for more information). The result of this comparison can be seen in Table 8.2.

In the first 150 records of the database there are 52 response letters which include at least one reference to *Lucy* combined with a verb in the third person singular. In the records published between April 2003 and March 2004, however, there are only fourteen answers with such a usage. It is therefore likely that the changes observed in the comparison of the 2002 database with the updated records of the 2004 database indicate that the 'Lucy Answers' team use references to *Lucy* as an active agent more sparingly. At the same time, however, we can say that not

Table 8.1 Examples of references to *Lucy* in updated response letters (italics added)

"More about melatonin" (LA 1383, fitness and nutrition)

2002-Database	2004-Database
Herbal remedies are as old as time itself; however, *Lucy reminds you that* herbal "medicines" are not regulated by the U.S. Food and Drug Administration (FDA).	Many herbal remedies are as old as time itself; however, herbal "medicines" are not regulated by the U.S. Food and Drug Administration (FDA).

"Men's legs and shaving" (LA 895, general health)

2002-Database	2004-Database
When it comes to removing body hair, whether it's on top of your head, under your arms, or on or between your legs, *Lucy feels that* there's no incorrect decision because the act is naturally reversible.	When it comes to removing body hair, whether it's on top of your head, under your arms, or on or between your legs, there's no incorrect decision because the act is naturally reversible.
So, since hairless supermodels are in vogue, *Lucy doubts that* you will become a shaved-legged laughing stock at this summer's beach parties and barbecues. And yes, you may even discover that few notice your nakedness, as many guys have very little hair on their legs, arms, chests, etc. from the get go.	So, since hairless supermodels are in vogue, *it's doubtful that* you will become a shaved-legged laughing stock at this summer's beach parties and barbecues. And yes, you may even discover that few notice your nakedness, as many guys have very little hair on their legs, arms, chests, etc. from the get go.
Short of waxing (a painful ... a very painful ... *did Lucy say painful*, procedure where your hair is professionally removed above and below the skin surface as a method for delaying re-growth), be aware that everyday shaving may leave you with a prickly, bumpy surface, rather than the silky, smooth skin you see on TV.	Short of waxing (a painful ... a very painful ... *did Lucy say painful*, procedure where your hair is professionally removed above and below the skin surface as a method for delaying re-growth), be aware that everyday shaving may leave you with a prickly, bumpy surface, rather than the silky, smooth skin you see on TV.

Table 8.2 References to *Lucy* as a person (third person singular verb)

Records	*Lucy* with 3rd person sg. verb	Period of time
first 150	52	before 2002
last 150	14	April 03 – March 04

every reference to *Lucy* in the third person singular has been deleted, and that the usage of the first person pronoun *I* for the advisor voice is still avoided – in fact in one response which includes one of the rare instances in which *I* is used, we have evidence for this consistent avoidance because *I would highly recommend that* has been altered to read *it's highly recommended that*. The general pattern in 'Lucy

Answers' to refer to the advisor *Lucy* as an active agent in the text is thus still there but seems to be decreasing slowly.

8.2.2 *Lucy* presents herself as a competent and knowledgeable source of accurate information

As I have demonstrated in Chapter 5, *Lucy*'s replies consist of several discursive moves. I argue that the general information and the referral moves are especially important for the construction of an *expert* voice, since *Lucy* can present herself as a competent and knowledgeable source of accurate information. *Lucy* displays her encyclopedic knowledge, as she presents facts, describes symptoms, enumerates side effects (in the case of drug related questions), etc. and is able to refer the reader to helpful resources. This can be seen in (8.12) in which *Lucy* answers a question from someone who is worried about a partner's panic attacks and wonders how to be supportive.

(8.12) "Panic attacks" (LA 832, emotional health)

> Dear Lucy,
>
> I need some information about panic attacks. My partner moved with me to NY and, at the time of moving, experienced several attacks of extreme fear.
>
> This has paralyzed her to the extent that she no longer goes to work, her career is on hold, and she requires help traveling, if she travels at all. As well as being incredibly distressing for her, it's not helping our relationship either.
>
> My question relates to my role in helping her recover from this. At present I frequently 'overlook' the problem by going everywhere with her and being as supportive as possible. Am I an 'enabler'? Should I make her 'tough it out,' or will she just get better?

> Dear Reader,
>
> Panic attacks are periods of heightened anxiety often coupled with an extreme fear of being in crowded or closed places. At first, these attacks are sudden and unexpected, but, if they continue, are often triggered by environment, like going through tunnels, traveling across bridges, or being in crowded elevators. Accompanying symptoms include a sense of chest pain, shallow breathing, lightheadedness, dizziness, sweating, a pounding heart, chills or flushes, nausea, and even tingling or numbness in the hands. A sense of impending doom is usually part of the experience.
>
> Panic attacks are common, frequently linked to feelings of loss. Panic attacks vary in intensity and tend to be exacerbated by stressful periods.

> Psychotherapy, with and without medication, is effective for as many as 90 percent of people affected with panic attacks. Cutting back on caffeine may make a difference, too.
>
> While your support may be comforting to your partner, it would be wise for her to get professional counseling, especially since her panic is affecting your relationship. With counseling for yourself as well, you may be better able to help your partner. If you are at AEI, call Counseling and Psychological Services (CPS) at xx-xxxx.
>
> *Lucy*

The first two paragraphs of the response letter give general information about panic attacks in the form of a concise explanation and a list of symptoms. *Lucy* thus displays that she has researched the topic (notice the percentage figure in the second paragraph) and is knowledgeable about the ins and outs of this problem. *Lucy* offers advice only in the third paragraph, in which she suggests that the questioner and the person who suffers from the panic attacks should seek professional counseling. *Lucy* also provides a phone number and thus displays knowledge of where to direct the questioner for further help. Records such as (8.12) contribute to *Lucy*'s identity as an informed advice-giver.

This dedication to provide well-researched information, which is of course part of the agenda of 'Lucy Answers', also manifests itself in *Lucy*'s attempts to answer comprehensively. As discussed in Section 7.2, *Lucy* may broaden the scope of the answer by giving more information than is requested in the question, by asking follow-up questions and answering them herself, and by referring the readers to other sources of information such as book titles, other websites, addresses, or links to previous *Lucy*-records. All three strategies show that *Lucy* takes her task to provide 'factual, in-depth, straight-forward, and nonjudgmental information' seriously (Lucy Answers, mission).

This dedication can also be seen in (8.13) (from the category 'drugs') in which *Lucy* informs several concerned questioners[5] that the rumors they heard about a party drug which leads to girls being raped and sterilized are in fact a hoax (*Much research was done on the matter; no evidence of the existence of such a drug was substantiated by veterinarians, pharmacists, and researchers at the following agencies and institutions*). *Lucy* lists the sources where she sought but did not find any information about this drug. In the following paragraphs she provides information on drugs that may cause behavior related to the fears of the questioners and lists links that lead to further information. *Lucy* then condemns in a distinctly annoyed tone individuals who start myths which frighten large numbers of people. This last passage is reproduced in (8.13):

(8.13) "'Progesterex': Horse and human sterilizer, date rape drug, or urban legend?"
(LA 1597, drugs, italics added, abbreviated)

[four individual questions on the same topic]

Dear Readers,

[research history; the reports on the drugs are a hoax]
[information on drugs that have a similar effect; links to further information]

'Lucy Answers' and AEI were not the only places on the 'Progesterex' case this week. Many *other educators and health care providers* around the country received similar messages, were concerned about what they read, and *took action* to find out whether or not what they were reading and hearing was legitimate. This isn't the first time that seemingly-implausible situations have popped onto the scene, and it no doubt won't be the last; who's rectum will a gerbil find its way into tomorrow? Whose image, sense of security, and peace of mind will be sacrificed next year just for laughs? Yes, the volume of information and the speed at which it can travel 'round the world sometimes makes it more difficult to separate the truth from the crap. *Some sound research from reputable resources is a good tool to have along to reach reality.*

This current situation certainly seems like a hoax; its creator(s) might be reading this, laughing, and basking in his/her/their fifteen minutes of Internet fame. If so, there are some other things you might try when you next find yourself with some time on your hands: teach disadvantaged kids to read; volunteer at a soup kitchen; raise money for earthquake victims; or, just take a nap.

Lucy

In (8.13), *Lucy* chooses to show her annoyance at people who frighten others and cause a lot of work for people who take their job seriously. She does so by asking a set of rhetorical questions referring to earlier hoaxes (also notice the lexical items *just for laughs* and *crap*) and by suggesting that such people should spend their time in a better way. *Lucy*'s criticism emphasizes that *Lucy* is to be taken seriously and that *Lucy* takes her questioners and their problems seriously (cf. my discussion below of *Lucy*'s opinions). It is interesting to us here that *Lucy* offers us a glimpse of how her research is conducted. Furthermore, she describes her work as 'taking action' and herself as being a member of *educators and health care providers*, and defines 'Lucy Answers' as a *reputable resource* that offers *sound research* (see italics in (8.13)). In her study of postings to asynchronous newsgroups on the Internet about risks related to the use of cell phones, Richardson (2003:172) points out that credibility and trust are at the core of whether an individual's contribution is accepted or not. In her data, newsgroups users therefore engaged in 'warranting strategies', i.e., in strategies "designed to give fellow participants reasons to take the information seriously", for example by referring to (presumably reputable) sources (2003: 172). As extract (8.13) shows, the use of such strategies can be observed even by *Lucy*, whose expertise is less likely to be called into question because of her role as an institutional helper. The team behind *Lucy* thus works to create her identity as a trustworthy source of well-researched, quality advice.

8.2.3 The realization of advice: *Lucy* makes readers think and gives options

We have seen in the previous section that *Lucy* provides background information. Let us now look at the sections in her answers in which she gives advice. As discussed in detail in Chapter 5, I found that *Lucy* gives advice by making use of all three principle syntactic types: declaratives, imperatives, and interrogatives. It was argued that the latter represent an invitation to the reader to reconsider problems and to look at them from different angles. *Lucy* may thus place the ball back in the reader's court by asking questions herself. In this way, *Lucy* emerges as involving her readership actively. Interrogatives can also function as suggestions for future action as well as invitations for introspection. *Lucy*'s usage of imperatives is also classified further into imperatives inviting future action and those inviting introspection. When declarative sentences are used to realize advice, they can best be described as suggestions. To briefly illustrate these options once more, I will give one example from each main category:

(8.14)   If there is no significant stress in your life (work, school, relationship, family, etc.), and the amount you are masturbating isn't hurting you, why not just enjoy yourself? (LA 26, sexuality, **interrogative**, "Long-term masturbation effects?")

(8.15)   Eating three regular meals a day can make a difference. (LA 2106, fitness and nutrition, **declarative**, "Weight loss tricks for big and chunky teens?")

(8.16)   – Establish a regular sleep time. Try going to sleep the same time each night, and waking up the same time each day, within an hour, more or less. Make an effort to keep the same sleep times on the weekends in order to set your body's rhythm. – Create a personal sleep environment – dark, quiet, free of distractions, and not too warm. Use an autotimer to shut the radio or TV off after you have fallen asleep. – Give yourself time to wind down before going to bed. (LA 99, emotional health, **imperatives**, "Can't wake up in the winter")

Giving advice, as pointed out earlier, is potentially very face-threatening in Western cultures (cf. Chapter 6). The way you give advice thus says something about whether you are a considerate advisor. The results from my previous discussion showed that advice in the form of declaratives accounts for 52 percent of all instances. Advice realized with imperatives follows with 36 percent, and questions make up 11 percent. *Lucy* thus alternates methods in her realization of advice. This means that she plays with the level of indirectness. Interrogatives and declaratives (63%) are less straightforward than imperatives in their directive force. They leave the opportunity open for the reader to interpret the utterances as options. However, even imperatives often occur in combination with hedges that soften their directive force. For example, the list of imperatives with detailed instruction on how to improve sleep patterns in (8.16) is prefaced by a statement marking the instructions as suggestions (*Here are some suggestions for creating healthful sleeping habits for yourself*; LA 99, emotional health). While there is clearly a preference for mitigated rather than straightforward advice-giving in 'Lucy Answers', it should be stressed that the use of imperatives at 36 percent is part of the discursive practice established on this site and contributes to what is deemed appropriate advice-giving in this context (cf. Note 4, Chapter 6).

An explanation for *Lucy*'s preference for displaying optionality can be found in the stated aim of 'Lucy Answers' to provide information "to assist readers' decision-making" (Lucy Answers 2004), which reflects the ideal of non-directiveness in some counseling contexts as reported by He (1994), Sarangi and Clarke (2002) or Vehviläinen (2003). This implies that the team of health educators aims at *facilitating a decision process* in the readers' minds, rather than at giving straightforward directions. This position is neatly summarized in a response letter in which *Lucy* ends her explorations on risks of being infected with HIV by saying *You now have the information – let each student make good, intelligent, informed decisions for themselves* (LA 93, sexual health). *Lucy* is thus constructed as someone who gives options and not directions and who considers the questioners to be responsible for their own decisions.

8.2.4 *Lucy* chooses an easily accessible, informal and inoffensive range of vocabulary

Originally the target readership of 'Lucy Answers' was the students of AEI. However, as the site is accessible worldwide by means of the Internet, the range of possible advice-seekers has vastly expanded. Nevertheless it is still the site's primary aim to reach young adults and particularly the students of the university which hosts the web-site 'Lucy Answers'. It is therefore of interest to see whether this is reflected in the kind of vocabulary used.

First of all, it is striking that the question-answer pairs found on 'Lucy Answers' largely conform to the conventions of standard written American English. This is in stark contrast to the type of language use found on many other sites with a comparable target audience. As a case in point, consider (8.17), which is a typical question-answer pair found on the 'Studentcenter' (SC),[6] a forum where teenagers can seek advice from peers in the same age group:

(8.17) [question]
I have a million friends. But there is one that NO one can get along with... we say we can never be her friend but always are... seh has called us brats and snobs and preps and almost everything imagainable. She has even gone as far as to get her mom on the phone and her mom even called us that. We dont know what to do becuase one moment she is all nice and then next she is evil kenevil... We would like to be her friend but cnat WHat do we do?'

[answer]
If you have a million friends and shes being a bitch then dont be friends with her. If shes so mean then you shouldnt have to put up with her evilness. Youll be much happier without that problem in your life. Hope this helps, [name] (SC, 2002)

This extract has clearly not been edited and it contains a whole range of non-standard spellings (*shes, dont, youll, shouldnt*) as well as obvious typing errors (e.g., *becuase, cnat* instead of *because* and *can't*). The response also does not elaborate on the problem as *Lucy* would be likely to do.

While an exchange of the type shown in (8.17) may indeed be adequate for some purposes, it is clearly incompatible with *Lucy*'s mission of providing quality health care information. Instead, by adhering to standard spelling rules and conventions and by presenting her well-structured answers in fully grammatical English, *Lucy* underscores the impression that she is competent and trustworthy. Her choice of vocabulary, however, has more complex implications. On the one hand, ample use of specific technical terminology would show readers that *Lucy* has the required level of knowledge to give competent answers. On the other hand, over-use of such terminology might increase the distance between *Lucy* and the reader and thereby reduce the impact of her advice. A more detailed look at the type of vocabulary used is thus necessary.

For this reason, word frequency lists were created for the entire corpus of *Lucy*'s responses (2,286 records). In addition to a general frequency list, individual word-class based lists were also compiled.[7] Frequency lists offer the researcher an opportunity to quantitatively assess some aspects of language use which would necessarily escape attention in the course of a purely qualitative analysis. Such lists can also be used to compare language use across several text collections, in order, for example, to isolate particular stylistic features which are typical of an individual text domain or discourse context. In order to find out which aspects are most characteristic of *Lucy*'s vocabulary, corresponding frequency lists were compiled based on the written component of the British National Corpus (BNC), a large and representative corpus of Present-day English (cf. Aston & Burnard 1998).[8] Rather

Table 8.3 The twenty most distinctive nouns in the response letters of 'Lucy Answers' (entire corpus; ranked by log-likelihood ratio)*

Noun	no. in 'Lucy Answers'	no. in BNC (written)	G^2
health	2,625	22,806	8,557
provider	1,001	387	7,920
sex	1,462	7,679	6,052
herpes	453	115	3,754
reader	833	3,587	3,735
penis	500	479	3,425
condom	446	222	3,412
symptoms	735	3,033	3,350
blood	1,013	9,227	3,218
orgasm	398	166	3,119
body	1,399	23,089	3,023
condoms	393	250	2,897
care	1,225	19,344	2,737
skin	769	6,340	2,577
percent	400	515	2,574
intercourse	429	891	2,446
foods	517	2,030	2,400
infection	541	2,636	2,310
vagina	326	264	2,305
pregnancy	449	1,525	2,196

* The nouns *Lucy* and reference to *AEI* have been removed from this list. It goes without saying that they are a distinctive part of the vocabulary used.

than merely comparing normalized frequency counts, however, it is also necessary to assess the probability that the observed differences are due to chance. For this purpose, a particularly useful measure of distinctiveness is given by the log-likelihood ratio – also known as G^2.[9] The higher the log-likelihood value, the more statistically significant the difference is between the observed raw frequencies. Here I will restrict my discussion to *Lucy*'s use of nouns.

Table 8.3 displays the twenty nouns which were calculated to be most distinctive in 'Lucy Answers'. The second column lists the total number of occurrences in *Lucy*'s responses while the third column shows their corresponding frequency in the BNC. The ranking of items is based on the log-likelihood value. The nouns in Table 8.3 obviously reflect the relatively limited range of topics discussed on 'Lucy Answers' and it will come as no surprise that health and relationship related nouns such as *health, provider*, and *sex* have a very high G^2 value. The high G^2 value for *reader* stems from the fact that *Lucy* often begins her replies with *Dear reader*. The list is nevertheless instructive with regard to the more specific question about the nature of the vocabulary employed. None of the nouns *Lucy* uses (with perhaps the exception of *herpes*) can be said to be particularly scientific or technical and no special knowledge would therefore be required to understand them. This finding is all the more striking since the frequency lists are based on the whole set of 2,286 records and the data consequently includes the entire topic categories of 'general health', 'fitness and nutrition', and 'sexual health' which might have been expected to require the use of scientific vocabulary. While *Lucy* certainly makes use of such vocabulary when necessary (e.g., *hirsutism, mammography, mescaline, serotonin, endometriosis*), these words feature much lower on the list of distinctive nouns and can thus not be considered typical elements of *Lucy*'s language. Furthermore, the advisor team always explain such terminology whenever the situation requires its use.

The lists of most distinctive verbs, adjectives and adverbs in *Lucy*'s vocabulary confirm the picture presented by the investigation of nouns.[10] In all cases, the items determined to be most characteristic of 'Lucy Answers' belong to fairly unspectacular everyday language. This quantitative finding is clear evidence for the claim that the makers of 'Lucy Answers' are fully aware of the implications of using special types of vocabulary.

While I have shown that frequency lists can offer useful information about the type of vocabulary used, a qualitative analysis must necessarily follow in order to provide a comprehensive picture. In this connection, I would like to concentrate briefly on *Lucy*'s use of informal language, which is perceived by some readers to be inappropriate, as exemplified in (8.18), in which a reader complains about *Lucy*'s use of *unoriginal slang*.

(8.18)   "Get serious – lose the slang!" (LA, general health, reader response)

> Dear Lucy,
>
> This is more of a comment, actually: Why do you feel you have to be vulgar and use unoriginal slang words when you answer questions (for example, calling a penis a 'hot dog' and using the phrase, 'whacking off')? Wouldn't you agree that most readers would take you more seriously if you used technical terms and answered questions in a more professional manner? People that write to you are looking for guidance, not comedy. However, most of your answers are competent, and you seem to be knowledgeable – just restrain yourself from being so vulgar.
>
> – JUST TRYING TO HELP

Since expressions such as *hot dog* are typically polysemous, frequency lists are unlikely to capture the true extent of their use, nor would such a collocation be recognized in the first place. Given their expressive nature, however, they may have a strong influence on the way *Lucy* is perceived by her readers. The other expression the reader complained about in (8.18) is used only once by *Lucy* in the entire corpus. In my qualitative analysis of the 280 records in the subcorpus, I found that

Lucy uses informal language, puns and humor but avoids language which might be offensive to readers. To strike an acceptable level of informality for the target audience is of course difficult. In my reading, *Lucy*'s style is characterized by a tendency to aim at a fairly neutral but accessible and informal style for young people.

I found several records in the reader response section, which show that the choice of appropriate vocabulary is also a topic among the readership. In (8.18) above, we saw a reader who believes that *Lucy* uses improper language. His criticism triggers three more responses by readers, see (8.19) and (8.20), who defend *Lucy*'s choice of vocabulary.

(8.19) (LA, general health, reader response)

> **(1)**
>
> Dear 'JUST TRYING TO HELP,'
>
> I believe this site is aimed at young people and, believe it or not, young people do not use expressions such as, 'Would you like me to indulge in a spot of cunnilingus?' or, 'I feel my penis extending with blood and feel that the release of semen may be imminent.'
>
> Young people need clear, honest, and relevant information and I recommend this site to all my clients in a British, male-only, sexual health session (the SPACEMAN). So lighten up, reader, and keep up the good work, Lucy.
>
> Felicitations for the season.
> [name]
>
> **(2)**
> Lucy,
>
> In response to 'Just trying to help's suggestion, he/she should note that Lucy is meant to be informative but not intimidating or pedagogical; the intention here to is to be more like an informed friend than a sex ed teacher or a doctor. Using slang adds a human element to the response without detracting from its credibility. Lucy doesn't use slang to be silly, or because she doesn't know better. Lucy uses slang to connect with the kids, dude. :)

(8.20) "Vulgar, Schmulgar!" (LA 2027, general health)

> Dear Lucy,
>
> About that reader's response about the slang – Get serious – Lose the slang! [Reader's Response]:
>
> Lucy, you rock. Everyone knows that you are a smart gal and a dependable source. You also happen to make your information very readable and light,

> although you broach some very heavy topics. Bravo on a great job, Lucy.
> You are not vulgar, so don't listen to that shmuck. No one in the world
> agrees with a shmuch [sic.]. Everyone loves you just the way you are.
>
> Love,
> Your #1 Fan

Notice that the two commentators in (8.19) have a clear understanding of the 'Lucy Answers' mission and consider language to be an important means to accomplish it. All three commentators share the view that *Lucy* uses language appropriately to connect with young people. The last reader's comment is the only one which received an answer from *Lucy*. The reason for this is the reader's use of the Yiddish word *shmuck*, which is a taboo word for 'penis' in its original translation. The reader is probably not aware of this ambiguity and he or she may indeed have aimed at its American English meaning of "contemptible or objectionable person, an idiot" (OED). *Lucy* takes the opportunity to mention this and to point out that

> the purpose of this response to your response is not to wash out your mouse
> [sic.] with soap. It's more of an example of the importance of word choices
> and effective communication for everything from persuasiveness to one's
> feelings about sex. (LA 2027, general health, "Vulgar, schmulgar!")

In the same answer, *Lucy* also admits that *it just ain't true that everyone loves Lucy just the way she is.* She thus comments on the difficulty in striking the right tone for the target audience.

In sum, *Lucy*'s answers are carefully constructed texts. We can assume that the choice of vocabulary is one of the elements discussed by members of the 'Lucy Answers' team. Both the quantitative as well as the qualitative analysis of the responses show that they make *Lucy* speak in an easily accessible, informal and inoffensive manner. On the one hand, language that may come across as too scientific is therefore avoided. On the other hand, the process of 'conversationalisation' (Fairclough & Mauranen 1997) in this public discourse does not go so far as to produce language similar to that employed by the peer advisors in the Studentcenter. This careful balance between colloquial and formal language use adds to the image of *Lucy* as an expert who fulfills a professional task, but is aware of the needs of the target audience.

8.2.5 *Lucy* has an opinion

In the introduction, the *Oxford English Dictionary* definition of advice which links advice to offering an opinion (as opposed to giving directions) was quoted. Indeed, it can be argued that giving advice is a fundamentally opinionated process. In the previous chapters it has been shown that *Lucy* certainly takes care not to be too directive in her realization of advice. In this section, I will demonstrate that the construction of her expert advisor identity is supported by the fact that *Lucy* presents herself to the reader as someone who also has 'personal' views about some of the issues under consideration. Rather than always offering advice in a neutral way, *Lucy* repeatedly shows emotions and takes a 'personal' stand. This manifests itself, for example, in explicit evaluations of the questioner's attitudes and actions. As shown in Chapters 6 and 7, both criticism and praise are used by *Lucy* to address the larger audience indirectly and to present the kind of behavior she considers commendable or objectionable. In her role as knowledgeable health educator, *Lucy* uses these evaluations to make her readers think – a strategy she has already been shown to pursue by using questions.

In the subcorpus, *Lucy* criticizes her questioners 51 times and she uses positive evaluations 65 times. In (8.21) *Lucy* comments on a questioner's willingness to abandon the habit of smoking marijuana.

(8.21)   You've mentioned that you find yourself continuing to use marijuana despite the fact that it no longer brings you pleasure. Recognizing this and looking for help quitting are two very important steps – which you've already taken. (LA 1579, drugs, praising, "Wants to stop smoking pot")

Lucy identifies two steps that she considers important in the process of quitting (*recognizing this and looking for help quitting*). While this could be read as a neutral summarizing comment, I argue that the relative clause introduced with the en-dash underlines the statement. The use of the adjective *important* then points out that the comment is meant as a compliment to the questioner for having taken the identified steps. The message to the wider readership is, in other words, that the questioner has taken the (desired) steps already, while many other readers who are in a similar situation might still need to do so. *Lucy* here emerges as having a positive opinion of the questioner's actions. This opinion is, of course, in line with the aim of 'Lucy Answers' to provide quality health care information and thus reflects this particular web site's ideology.

Lucy can also choose to voice a critical opinion, thus showing the readership what kind of behavior is deemed objectionable. An example of this was already presented in (8.13) above, in which *Lucy* criticized people who scare others by spreading rumors. In (8.22) from the category 'relationships', *Lucy* answers a questioner who asked *Know any good pick-up lines?*

(8.22)   How 'bout we call them conversation starters? This more general term may take away negative associations that some have with being "picked up," i.e., the only reason you're saying hello to them is so that you can say goodbye an hour or two later after you've had an orgasm. (LA 2041, relationships, criticizing, "Hey baby, got any good pick-up lines?")

Lucy makes clear that she considers the choice of words (*pick-up lines*) to be unfortunate and distances herself from it. Since *Lucy* goes into detail about how to start a conversation after this initial paragraph, the readers get the message that the topic as such is worth being answered, but that the advice-seeker's attitude is objectionable.

Lucy presents herself to her audience as someone who is involved and caring and as someone who does not hold back criticism when she considers it necessary. In the mission statement of 'Lucy Answers' the word *nonjudgmental* is used. At first sight it might therefore seem to be contradictory for *Lucy* to offer her own opinions. However, when the content of these opinions is investigated more closely, it becomes clear that *Lucy*'s evaluations remain in line with the site's ideology in that *Lucy* tries to provide information and advice which will facilitate the questioners' decision processes (and ultimately their well-being) regardless of their beliefs and practices.

8.2.6 *Lucy* shows awareness of difficult situations

Lucy not only provides information and advice, but also displays an awareness of the questioner's individual situation by offering empathy, as discussed in Chapter 6. I intend to demonstrate this once more with her answer to a person who needs help in finding a therapist. (8.23) represents the very beginning of the response in which *Lucy* acknowledges and explains that it is not easy to find a therapist who is suitable:

(8.23) Dedicating time to explore your thoughts and feelings with the help of a professional can be rewarding. *The process of finding someone who is a good match for you, however, may be daunting.* Just as you may not like or connect with everyone you meet at work, or at a party, the same can be true for first encounters with therapists. Given the nature of a therapeutic relationship, it makes sense to devote energy to this process *so that you can feel confident and comfortable* as you embark on your work together. (LA 2255, emotional health, "How to find a therapist", italics added)

Lucy clearly indicates that finding a good therapist can be difficult indeed (*daunting*), but also points out that it is worthwhile to spend time and effort so that the person can later feel *confident and comfortable*. *Lucy* then plunges into several units in which she gives helpful advice on how to go about organizing a search for a therapist. At the end, *Lucy* returns to discuss the daunting aspect of this search:

(8.24) *You may feel intimidated or awkward asking questions,* but ask away! If the person makes you feel uncomfortable, try out someone else. *Many compassionate and skilled counselors are out there.* With some effort, you can find someone

> with whom you can develop a meaningful working relationship. Good luck,
> Lucy (LA 2255, emotional health, "How to find a therapist", italics added)

Lucy acknowledges once more that feelings of intimidation may arise, but goes on
to reassure the questioner that he or she will surely find a *compassionate and skilled*
therapist. In this response, *Lucy* thus uses empathetic remarks to frame her advice.

In Chapter 6, I reported that empathy is mainly shown in the assessment
sections. This is where *Lucy* creates a connection with the advice-seeker and the
public readership. Through her use of empathy, *Lucy* is shown to have emotions
and emerges as being a caring and understanding advice-giver.

8.2.7 *Lucy* has a sense of humor

Humor is a stylistic means that adds a great deal to the tone of the particular response letter in 'Lucy Answers'. It is used to bond with the readers (mainly in the
assessment sections), to hedge a piece of advice or in rare cases to hedge criticism (cf. Chapter 6). Consider (8.25), in which *Lucy* reacts to the stenographic
style of the questioner by answering in an almost poetic style, thus outdoing the
questioner, which suggests that *Lucy* is not only knowledgeable but also clever
and witty:

(8.25)   "Girlfriend, bossy, dump?"(LA 1457, relationships)

Lucy,
I'll keep it simple: Girlfriend, bossy, dump?
Smile
Smile,
Talk, better, stay? Controlling, reason, understand? You, problem, change? Learn, compromise, fixed? Feelings, ignored, b-bye. New, better, happier?
Sentences, easier, later,
Lucy

In a few cases humor is also used in the titles to trigger the reader's interest as
shown in (8.26), in which we can see a word play, and (8.27), in which a humorous
rhyme is employed (cf. Section 7.2.2):

(8.26)   Should I cash in on hot banker? (LA 1602, relationships)

(8.27) Ain't got the giggles from crazy sex jiggles (LA 1465, relationships)

Overall, humor is used quite sparingly. That this is intentional can be seen in (8.28) in which *Lucy* explains her strategy in a response to a reader's complaint that *Lucy*'s answers have been lacking humor lately:

(8.28) "Yo, Lucy, lighten up" (LA 2099, general health)

> Lucy,
>
> I love the information you provide! But it seems as if things are getting a little boring? I recall that you used to be wittier, funnier, and more entertaining. And now, although you answer questions thoroughly, I feel like the Lucy personality has been lost! Lucy, please don't let down your loyal readers!
>
> ---
>
> Dear Reader,
>
> Yes, it's true that, overall, the guffaw factor in site pages is lower lately, but certainly not gone altogether.
>
> *Lucy Answers*'s goal is to increase access to accurate health info on a variety of issues while respecting the askers' situation and the emotion that can accompany it. Sometimes there can be humor, and sometimes the health issue is not a laughing matter. This poses a challenge for writers who believe that laughter, where appropriate, is pretty good medicine, and to readers who get off on a good giggle. Take nutrition, for example: 'Is that a partly-ripened banana in your pocket, or are you just happy to see me?' Well, that may be amusing, but *Lucy Answers* replies are based on real queries.
>
> Talking about serious subjects is just as important as maintaining funny bone density.
>
> Thanks for your thoughts,
>
> *Lucy*

The first comment I should make about (8.28) is, of course, that we here have an instance of an audience reaction which implies that the questioner shares my judgment that *Lucy* possesses a sense of humor. In the unlikely case indeed that the 'Lucy Answers' team invented this question to make its point, it is even more striking evidence that *Lucy* is conceived to possess a sense of humor, as well as also a sense of when its application is appropriate. Notice also that the reader refers to *the Lucy personality*, which implies that s/he considers *Lucy* to possess one particular *voice*. Apparently, the 'Lucy Answers' team considered the comment by this reader to be important enough to be published and answered in one of the topic categories of the site and not merely in the reader response section which is reserved for 'comments and corrections'. This in itself points to the importance of humor for 'Lucy Answers'.

Two more things can be observed about the construction of *Lucy*'s identity in (8.28). In the first paragraph, *Lucy* acknowledges that her answers have been less humorous lately, but she still maintains that she has not lost her sense of humor (*but certainly not gone altogether*). This means that she explicitly presents herself to the readers as an identity possessing a sense of humor. In the second and third paragraphs, *Lucy* then explains that humor may not be appropriate in all cases and presents herself as an advice-giver who takes the questioners' situation and fears into consideration. The members of the advisor team therefore draw a picture of *Lucy* as someone who does not use humor at the expense of others and who is considerate towards other people's feelings.

8.3 Summary

In this chapter I have explored the question of how the response letters created by a group of health educators, who write under the pseudonym *Lucy,* have the effect of creating a particular voice for the fictional female advisor persona (cf. the questions raised in Chapter 4). This voice is created with the help of several strategies. I have discussed *Lucy*'s name and her self-reference and address terms. I then focused on the way in which she presents herself as an expert and investigated how she makes readers think and gives them options when giving advice. I found that *Lucy* uses an easily accessible, informal and inoffensive range of vocabulary. *Lucy* also displays traits such as having an opinion of her own, showing an awareness of difficult situations by offering empathy and support, and having a sense of humor. In my opinion, all of these strategies combined contribute to the creation of a well-informed, trustworthy, and reliable expert advisor identity who takes the problems of her readers seriously. *Lucy*'s authority clearly stems from her status as expert in her roles as a knowledgeable source of accurate information and as an institutional helper. The other strategies identified, however, make her an attractive advice-giver, whom people can trust and turn to, as evidenced by the large weekly intake of questions.

The voice identified for *Lucy* shows interesting differences from that of other agony aunts who have received scholarly attention. For example, Mutongi (2000: 4) reports that the editors of the advice column 'Dear Dolly' in *Drum* (South Africa, 1960–1980) created the fictional advisor *Dolly* as an older female relative, aunt, or older sister. In addition, *Dolly* was crafted as a sensational and intriguing personality, who could flirt with her male advice-seekers (but did not do so with her female reader). The picture of an older sister is also evoked in McRobbie's (1978) and Talbot's (1992, 1995) work on the discourse strategies employed in *Jackie,* a magazine for teenage girls. In her investigation of the advice columnists *Cathy* and *Claire*, McRobbie (1978) critically evaluates how feminine knowledge is passed on to the target audience. She claims that, as (potentially) useful feminine knowledge is passed on as if by an older sister, a 'false sisterhood' is established, which is charged with ideological assumptions of how female teenagers ought to be. The issue of false or synthetic sisterhood is again taken up in Talbot's analysis of a 'consumer feature' on lipstick in the same magazine. She reports that "writer and reader ... are synthesized in a friendly relationship" in the text (1992: 193), which is achieved by "claiming common ground ...., by 'speaking the same language' and by showing that [the editor] knows what the reader is like, what she thinks" (1992: 180). When we compare *Dolly* and the advisors in *Jackie* to *Lucy*, it should be stressed that the target readerships as well as the general purposes of the advice columns differ. This explains why the identities created differ as well. *Lucy* clearly does not flirt with her readership (male or female) as *Dolly* does and she also does not seek to establish common ground with her female readership only, as is the case in *Jackie*. Neither strategy would be in line with the mission of 'Lucy Answers'. While some of the strategies discussed in the present chapter and in Chapter 6 certainly point to a strong element of bonding in 'Lucy Answers', the sisterly element is not present to a degree that would justify seeing *Lucy* as an older sister. *Lucy*'s role as a professional – albeit approachable and down-to-earth – health expert never quite fades into the background.

The strategies discussed in this chapter are in line with the mission stated by 'Lucy Answers', i.e. to provide information which will facilitate independent and responsible decision processes, rather than to be directive. It by no means necessarily follows that this mission would also be reflected in the actual linguistic realizations on the site. In my view, however, this is the case in 'Lucy Answers'. Using the strategies I have discussed, the health advisors have created an advisor identity for *Lucy* which corresponds to the overall aim 'to increase access to, and use of, health information by providing factual, in-depth, straightforward, and nonjudgmental information' (Lucy Answers 2004). My view is apparently one shared by the many readers who in their contributions to the reader response section compliment the site.

The attractive character of the advisor persona and the inherently entertaining nature of the format,[11] may be incentives for readers to read the problem and response letters in 'Lucy Answers' even if they do not have a particular problem themselves. 'Lucy Answers' is thus a valuable addition to the existing health care services at AEI because it passes on useful and easily accessible advice and information in a manner that is appealing to its members.

Finally, it is necessary to point out that not all strategies discussed as contributing to the identity of *Lucy* need occur in every response letter. Rather, it is the sum of these strategies within the discursive practice 'Lucy Answers' which form *Lucy*'s identity as a puzzle or a mosaic is formed, to use De Fina's metaphor (2003:224). I thus want to stress once again that *Lucy*'s identity only emerges in the readers' minds when they use the site repeatedly by reading the latest exchanges of questions and replies, browsing the archives or even by engaging in reader responses. My view admits the possibility that every reader will create a slightly different identity for *Lucy*. It will be one, however, that the strategies which I have identified have contributed to creating.

CHAPTER 9

The problem letters by the anonymous advice-seekers

9.1 Introduction

While the main focus of this study is on how the 'Lucy Answers' team gives advice, it is of course also important to look at the letters posted by the anonymous readership that solicit that advice. As I explained in Chapters 2 and 7, readers of the advice column are encouraged to browse the archive before they submit a question or a request for advice. The main reason for this is that only five, of the nearly 2000 letters submitted to 'Lucy Answers' each week, are answered online. A reader may therefore be more successful in finding an answer to his or her problem in a response in the archive than in being chosen as one of the few whose problem letter will be answered and published on the Internet. The team responsible for the advice column has the task of deciding which of the many letters to respond to. As previously argued, clearly the main criteria for inclusion are that the problem needs to be within the topic scope of 'Lucy Answers' and relevant to the larger readership rather than to only the individual advice-seeker.

In this analysis, it is important to recall that all the people whose problem letters are answered remain entirely anonymous. Their submittal information[1] is scrambled as soon as the letter reaches 'Lucy Answers'. By choosing to seek help from this site, the advice-seekers tacitly agree to have their problem published as there are no 'personal' responses to individual advice-seekers. Indeed, it is only by publication that they will receive an answer at all. Anonymity is, obviously, a very attractive feature of an Internet advice column such as 'Lucy Answers'. Alexander (2003:548), who investigates an advice column in the magazine *Men's Health*, makes the point that fears and embarrassment about health issues are the reason men write to the anonymous advice column. Van Roosmalen (2000:205), who studies the way adolescent women convey their experience in their letters to an advice column in *Teen Magazine*, also points out that problem pages are "forums for the unspeakable". In a similar way, the anonymity guaranteed by 'Lucy Answers' makes it easier for its readers to submit questions about touchy issues.

According to both personal communication with one of the 'Lucy Answers' team members and an examination of the records which deal with the worries about the authenticity of problem letters, the 'Lucy Answers' team does not summarize the letters or alter the text. The only exceptions to this are that "glaring typos and spelling errors are corrected, and personal identifying information, such as a person's last name or e-mail address, are deleted" (personal email communication).

When analyzing the responses in 'Lucy Answers', we can envisage a team that formulate and edit the answers that are then signed in the name of *Lucy*. In Chapter 8, I have demonstrated that they have created 'a voice' that belongs to *Lucy*. In the case of the problem letters, however, we are not confronting a homogeneous group of writers. On the contrary, we should assume that every problem letter is posted by a different person about whom we have no background information. The only details we are given are the ones revealed in the letter itself. Some advice-seekers mention their age and sex, while others (consciously, unconsciously or because it is not relevant to the topic) choose to withhold this information. Because of the heterogeneity of the advice-seekers we cannot look for a specific 'voice' as we did for *Lucy*. We can, however, investigate how their problem letters are formulated to express the concerns, worries, inflictions or simply curiosity in connection with the seven topic categories in 'Lucy Answers'.

9.2 Methodology

To study the questions raised in Chapter 4 about the problem letters in 'Lucy Answers' a catalogue of discursive moves was developed in order to capture the structure of the texts in a manner analogous to the method used in Chapters 5 and 6. These categories of discursive moves were then systematically applied to the 280 problem letters in the subcorpus. As already indicated in Chapter 5 (Table 5.1), the problem letter (or Question[2] with a capital Q) is split into 'address', 'unit' (one or more) and 'pseudonym'. Table 9.1 lists the discursive moves of the content structure level once again and adds the level of relational work that emerged in the analysis. In what follows I will illustrate the categories with examples.

Content structure level. There may be one or more units in the problem letter of the advice-seeker; and these units may consist of one or more discursive moves, just as was the case for the response letters. The discursive moves that make up a unit are apology, background information, comment on previous records, compliment, explanation, metacomment, problem statement, question, request for advice, and thanks. Table 9.2 gives an overview of the discursive moves by briefly defining them.

Apology. In several cases advice-seekers formulate apologies to *Lucy*. In (9.1) the writer apologizes for the length of the problem letter, and in (9.2) the advice-seeker

Table 9.1 The categories for the content structure and relational work in the problem letters of 'Lucy Answers'

Level 0	Level 1	Level 2	Level 3	Level 4
	Content structure level			Relational work
drugs emotional health fitness/nutrition general health relationships sexual health sexuality				
	Question	address		
		unit (one or more)	apology comment on previous record compliment explanation metacomment background problem statement question request advice thanks	appealing bonding humor-bonding boosting criticizing hedging humor-hedging
		pseudonym		appeal humor neutral none

Table 9.2 Discursive moves in the problem letters, level 3 (content structure; ordered alphabetically)

Discursive move	Explanation
apology	the advice-seeker apologizes for the 'intrusion'
background	background information
comment on previous record	a comment on a question-answer sequence previously published on *LA*
compliment	a compliment of *Lucy* or of the site in general
explanation	an explanation of a point just made; an extra type-tag indicates which element is further explained, namely 'apology', 'background', 'comment on previous record', 'compliment, 'metacomment', 'problem statement', 'question', 'request advice', 'thanks'
metacomment	a text-structuring comment
problem statement	a specific mention of a problem
question	an explicit question
request advice	a request for advice
thanks	thanks to *Lucy* for answering/helping

acknowledges that the question itself may be an imposition and gives her reason for approaching *Lucy* anyway. (Notice that this apology entails several lexical hedges: *I'm not sure, I thought.*)

(9.1) **apology** Sorry for the length of this letter, (LA 95, emotional health, "Family death five years ago")

(9.2) **apology** I'm not sure if this is the right place to ask, but since you just had a discussion on meeting grad students, I thought I'd give it a shot. (LA 81, fitness and nutrition, "Mountaineering grads?")

Comment on previous record. Readers who then become writers of problem letters, at times, acknowledge this fact specifically by referring to their reading of records in the 'Lucy Answers' archive. (9.3) and (9.4) exemplify this usage:

(9.3) **comment on previous record** I read a post from someone that you answered to which sounded a bit like my dilemma. (LA 957, sexual health, "More about bumps and lumps on penis")

(9.4) **comment on previous record** I was reading the question about male virginity recognition and got a doubt. (LA 1049, sexuality, "Is male virginity detectable: The full story")

Compliment and thanks. Advice-seekers compliment *Lucy* for the information on the site and thank her for the help that was either provided earlier or will be provided if the problem letter is accepted for publication. These discursive moves can be seen in (9.5) to (9.7):

(9.5) **compliment** Your site is very helpful. (LA 1532, drugs, "Friends say, 'Smoke!'")

(9.6) **thanks** Thanks so much, **compliment** your service is awesome! (LA 1251, sexuality, "Partner pleasuring through delaying orgasm")

(9.7) **thanks** Thanks for your help. (LA 331, sexuality, "Weight loss camps?")

Explanation, metacomment. Both of these categories correspond to their counterparts in the responses. 'Explanation' is further categorized by a type-tag which indicates which discursive move is further explained. As a case in point, consider (9.8) in which a question is followed by an explanation. This is indicated with the tag 'explanation type=question':

(9.8) **question** Is alcoholism an habitual addiction or can it also be a chemical one? **explanation type=question** I have heard that it is not chemical, but have lived with people who needed the alcohol every night. (LA 3, drugs, "Drinking addiction – psychological or physical?")

Metacomments help the advice-seekers to structure their text. In (9.9), for example, the advisee announces that there are two parts to his or her problem:

(9.9) **metacomment** I have two items that I'd like to address: (LA 206, drugs, "Coffee-nauseous? and marijuana facts")

Background and problem statement. The discursive moves of 'problem statement' and 'background' are closely related. A 'problem statement' is an explicit mention of the problem that requires advice, while the category 'background' denotes moves in which an advice-seeker gives additional information about a problem. (9.10) and (9.11) contain both categories:

(9.10) **background** Like many others during this season, I have been suffering from allergies for past week or so. I have the usual indications such as runny nose, sneezing, and watery eyes. I have been taking over-the-counter medicine, and it seems to work well for sneezing and runny nose. **problem statement** However, I often find my eyes very itchy and watery. It bothers me a lot since I need to study. But, with my irritated eyes, it is sometimes difficult to read for a long time. **question** Do you know of any medicine that would help me? (LA 265, general health, "Allergy eye relief?")

(9.11) **background** We have a case in our family where our sister has bone fractures at age 30 due to low bone density. At age 34 she was diagnosed as having a gluten allergy. It seems like that was the root cause of poor calcium absorption, which led to the bone fractures. **problem statement** It is difficult to get a hold of good information on food allergies. **question** Can you provide any that is at your disposal? (LA 462, fitness and nutrition, "Gluten allergy")

In both examples the advice-seeker first outlines the background to his or her problem (allergies/low bone density), specifies one particular problem (irritated eyes/no information) and proceeds to ask a question.

Questions and request for advice. In examples (9.8), (9.10) and (9.11) we have already encountered questions which asked for advice. No further illustration of the move is needed as the syntactic structure of the question allows us to identify this request for advice quite easily. The category 'request advice' accounts for realizations other than questions. The distinction is therefore only a syntactic one and not one of function. Examples are given in (9.12) to (9.15):

(9.12) **request advice** Any suggestions would be greatly appreciated. (LA 2354, general health, "I got the nose wiping and blowing blues")

(9.13) **request advice** I'm hoping that you can help!! (LA 1306, drugs, "Dealing with a brother addicted to heroin")

(9.14) **request advice** Your answer may save our relationship. Please Lucy, I need your help. (LA 1738, relationships, "Girlfriend gets scared every time I say, 'I love you'")

(9.15) **request advice** I do not know what to do. (LA 25, fitness and nutrition, "Bulimic?")

Relational work. In the examples just quoted we can, of course, see that there is much more entailed in each letter than a simple request for information. The authors also display their emotions and *appeal* to *Lucy* for help. To account for this and other relational aspects of the problem letters I have formulated the categories presented in Table 9.3. Only the category 'appealing' is new; all the others were already applied to analogous contexts in the response letters.

Appealing. With the exception of (9.12), the three requests for advice quoted in the previous section ((9.13)–(9.15)) have all been assigned to the category 'appealing'. (9.15) is presented again here:

(9.15) **request advice** <**appealing**> I do not know what to do. </**appealing**> (LA 25, fitness and nutrition, "Bulimic?")

'Appealing' is in some sense a counterpart to 'empathizing' in the answers in that it may act as an invitation to the advisor to feel sympathy for the advice-seeker. It is also used to stress to *Lucy* the urgency of the request for advice. The writers thus reveal their emotions.

Boosting, criticizing, hedging, humor-hedging, bonding, humor-bonding. The categories of these very different types of relational work are already familiar from my analysis in Chapter 6. Here I have chosen to present only a few examples to illustrate their use in the problem letters of 'Lucy Answers'. (9.16) represents an

Table 9.3 Relational work in the problem letters, level 4 (ordered alphabetically)

Level 4-category	Explanation
appealing	the advice-seeker displays emotions, distress and (at times indirectly) appeals to *Lucy* for sympathy
bonding	the advice-seeker seeks to establish a connection with *Lucy*
humor-bonding	humor which aims at bonding with *Lucy* or the readership
boosting	a word or phrase used to give a point more weight
criticizing	criticism of other readers or of a previous answer by *Lucy*
hedging	the use of downtoners/mitigators
humor-hedging	humor which mitigates the advice-seeker's (distressing) situation or the imposition on *Lucy*

instance of boosting; the advice-seeker emphasizes that there was only *one* time she could have been infected with AIDS:

(9.16) **background** I've been married for five years; the rape was **<boosting>** the ONLY possibility **</boosting>** I have had of being exposed to the AIDS virus. (LA 559, sexual health, "Raped – HIV status?")

The advice-seeker uses the capital letters functioning as a boosting device to emphasize the singular experience. By doing this she both asserts that she is aware of how dangerous AIDS is, and she demonstrates that she can account for her sexual activities. The booster may thus be intended to increase her credibility.

Criticizing was discussed as a face-threatening strategy in Chapter 6. In (9.17) we see a reader who takes up comments by *Lucy* made in a previous record and corrects her: *your point* [...] *is deceptive; you neglect to state*:

(9.17) **comment on previous record** **<criticizing>** Your point concerning the "best high" is deceptive in that holding the smoke for longer than a few seconds does not add to the intensity of the high. **</criticizing>** Notwithstanding this information, you are generally correct in stating that MJ smoke contains more tar and hydrocarbons than tobacco, **<criticizing>** but you neglect to state **</criticizing>** that the quantity of MJ per user typically smoked is less than tobacco by a factor of ten. One rarely hears of "pack-a-day" pot smokers. Also note that in over 10,000 years of use, there are no documented fatalities attributed to the consumption of marijuana. (LA 206, drugs, "Coffee-nauseous? and marijuana facts")

Criticism is therefore not a move used only by *Lucy* and addressed to an advice-seeker. Readers also criticize *Lucy* and in doing so they may refer to the contributions in the entire 'Lucy Answers' archive. This shows that the discursive practice of 'Lucy Answers' cannot be understood just by looking at the most recent problem and response letters. 'Lucy Answers' must be seen as a site with a history that influences the composition of new problem and response letters (cf. also Section 7.3).

Hedging has been defined as a face-saving strategy. In both (9.18) and (9.19) the writers use lexical hedges to mitigate their requests for information (*I was wondering if you could; I just wrote asking about how I might*):

(9.18) **question** **<hedging>** I was wondering if you could **</hedging>** tell me what the cigarette with the lowest tar and nicotine is on the market or if there is one with no nicotine? (LA 508, drugs, "Low tar and nicotine cigarette?")

(9.19) **question** **<hedging>** I just wrote asking about how I might **</hedging>** prolong my orgasm so that my girlfriend might be able to reach hers. (LA 1251, sexuality, "ner pleasuring through delaying orgasm")

Acknowledging the face-threatening character of the advice situation can also be achieved in a humorous way: humor-hedging mitigates the advice-seeker's (distressing) situation (9.20) or the imposition on *Lucy* (9.21):

> (9.20)   **question** What is mucous <**humor-hedging**> (besides another word i probably can't spell) </**humor-hedging**> and what is its function? (LA 1503, general health, "Much ado about mucus")

> (9.21)   **question** How much calcium do college-age women need in order to avoid osteoporosis and other such problems in later life? **question** What's the best way to get it? <**humor-hedging**> (Calcium, I mean, not osteoporosis.) </**humor-hedging**> (LA 92, fitness and nutrition, "Women, calcium, and osteoporosis?")

The discursive moves of apologies and thanks have been interpreted as hedging devices in general since they acknowledge the imposition on the 'Lucy Answers' team that is caused when advice is requested (examples are given in (9.1)–(9.2) and (9.6)–(9.7) above).

Finally, all instances of complimenting have been interpreted as bonding, i.e., as attempts to establish a connection with *Lucy* (see (9.5) above). Bonding is also achieved by means of humor, as can be seen in (9.22):

> (9.22)   **background** <**humor-bonding**> We have an ice cream wagered on this one! I hope I'm right! </**humor-bonding**> (LA 1509, general health, "Tongue brushing")

The advice-seekers' pseudonyms. The last categories that need to be introduced are those used to define the pseudonym which the writer of the problem letter chooses for him- or herself. The pseudonyms have been divided into four categories: 'appeal' (which has the function described above), 'humor' (containing word play), 'neutral' (ascribed to matter-of-fact pseudonyms) or 'none' (no pseudonym chosen). Table 9.4 gives examples to illustrate each of these categories.

Table 9.4 Examples of the pseudonym categories

category	pseudonym	record number	topic category
appeal	Dazed and Confused…	113	emotional health
appeal	Signed, Suffering from allergies	265	general health
humor	Curious Carrot	926	fitness and nutrition
humor	Edward Scissorhands	795	general health
neutral	Hiker	81	fitness and nutrition
neutral	Taller than B/F	1728	relationships

Presentation of entire problem letters. The discursive moves and relational work categories for the problem letters have now been introduced in isolation. Before I move on to a discussion of results, two brief examples of entire question texts will be presented to show how the discursive moves interact with each other.

In Figure 9.1 we can see a very short problem letter that consists of a brief problem statement, followed by a question. There is no relational work categorized, nor did the author of this text choose a pseudonym (hence "none" as a type tag).

Figure 9.2 represents a somewhat longer problem letter, also from the category 'general health'. The author starts out with background information (presented in the form of a short narrative), followed by two questions. One of them is hedged with *I was wondering.* Notice that this record does not contain a problem statement

```
Question
├─ address
│     └─ Lucy,
├─ unit 1
│     ├─ problem statement
│     │  When I wake up in the morning, I have a layer of stringy white stuff lining my
│     │  bottom gums.
│     └─ question
│        Can you help me identify this?
└─ pseudonym type=none
```

Figure 9.1 The problem letter in "White stuff on gums?" (LA 1028, general health)

```
Question
├─ address
│     └─ Lucy-
├─ unit 1
│     ├─ background
│     │  My roommate infected me with some kind of virus that he had (actually still has
│     │  it) and I got over it in one day. He, on the other hand, went out with his friends,
│     │  drank insanely, stayed out all night, and consequently got sicker and sicker. Now,
│     │  he's left for a few days to recover at home.
│     ├─ question
│     │  <hedging> I was wondering </hedging>, since he got so sick (he was ill for over
│     │  eight days, was coughing, vomiting, etc.), is it possible that he may have contracted
│     │  mono, or even pneumonia?
│     └─ question
│        And if it is, should I be concerned for myself?
└─ pseudonym type=neutral
      └─ Signed, Curious
```

Figure 9.2 The problem letter in "Mono?" (LA 23, general health)

per se. The background information is not presented as a problem, but as merely a description of an event in the past, the outcome of which is still open and topical at the moment of writing. This time, the advice-seeker has chosen *Curious* as a pseudonym, which has been categorized as neutral.

In this chapter, the content structure and the relational work of the 280 problem letters in the subcorpus of 'Lucy Answers' will be examined. I will present my results starting with a discussion of the number of words and number of units per answer (Section 9.3.1). Then I will look at the number and type of discursive moves overall (Section 9.3.2) and at how many discursive moves can be typically found in a unit (Section 9.3.3). Finally, I will report on the sequence of discursive moves within units (Section 9.3.4). A summary of these investigations, which are by necessity rather technical, is presented in Section 9.3.5. After this I will discuss relational work (Section 9.4) and present a discussion of the linguistic realization of a selected number of discursive moves (Section 9.5). I will end by presenting a selection of complete problem letters in order to reassemble the information gained from the previous analyses (Section 9.6).

9.3 The composition of the problem letter

9.3.1 Number of words and number of units in a problem letter

In Alexander's data from an advice column in the magazine *Men's Health* the problem letter "is usually just one or two sentences long, followed by the advice-seeker's initials and place of residence" (2003:548). The problem letter in the question-answer exchange in 'Lucy Answers' may sometimes be as short as that, but it can also be considerably longer – assuming that Alexander's sentences are fairly modest in length. Table 9.5 shows the length of the problem letters in the entire corpus in number of words. We can see that, on average, the categories 'relationships' (n = 124) and 'emotional health' (n = 107) contain the longest problem letters, while the other categories have a fairly similar number of words (n = 61 – 77). Of these, letters in 'fitness and nutrition' are considerably shorter (n = 61). However, as was the case in our examination of the response letters, the standard deviation tells us that there is great variance in length within the categories as well.

If we turn to the subcorpus and look at the problem letters with 'unit' (N = 323) as our point of reference, the seven topic categories present a strikingly similar picture. Table 9.6 shows that in each category more than 80 percent of the problem letters contain only one single unit. This means that only 27 problem letters are composed of more than one unit.

Table 9.5 Problem letters in 'Lucy Answers' (ranked by average number of words in problem letters; entire corpus)

Topic categories	no. of records	%	no. of words in all Questions	average no. of words per Question	*sd
relationships	274	12	34,106	124	107
emotional health	150	7	16,069	107	95
sexuality	392	17	30,199	77	67
drugs	155	7	11,673	75	74
sexual health	469	21	32,695	70	56
general health	499	22	32,129	64	62
fitness and nutrition	347	15	21,103	61	51
total	2,286	100	177,974	78	

*sd = standard deviation.

Table 9.6 The number of problem letters according to number of units (by category; subcorpus)

no. of units per Question → topic categories ↓	1	2	3	4	5	total
drugs	36	1	1	2		40
emotional health	32	4	3	1		40
fitness and nutrition	37	3				40
general health	39	1				40
relationships	38	1	1			40
sexual health	36	3			1	40
sexuality	35	3	2			40
total	253	16	7	3	1	280
%	90	6	3	1	0	100

9.3.2 Number and type of discursive moves overall

There are 1,033 discursive moves in all of the 280 problem letters. Table 9.7 presents the percentages of discursive moves in each topic category. The last two rows show that the largest share of discursive moves is of the question type (n = 391, 38%), followed by background information (n = 216, 21%) and problem statements (n = 216, 21%). Explicit requesting of advice and thanking occur in seven percent of all discursive moves (n = 69, 70). Explanations, metacomments, comments on previous records and compliments are rare indeed (1 to 2%).

Table 9.7 The percentage of discursive moves in each topic category (subcorpus)

discursive moves → topic categories ↓	100% =	question	background	problem statement	request advice	thanks	EXPL**	metacomment	apology	comment on prev. rec.	compliment	total
Group 1:												
drugs	n = 141	43	23	15	7	6	2	1		2	1	100
fitn./nutrition	n = 121	37	22	22	7	9	1		1		1	100
gen. health	n = 153	39	22	17	7	8	3	3	1		1	101
sexual health	n = 153	45	23	18	3	6	1	1	1	2	1	101
Group 2:												
emot. health	n = 174	32	20	26	7	5	3	3	3			99
relationships	n = 154	31	21	27	10	6	3	1	1			100
sexuality	n = 137	40	15	20	7	7	2	3	2	1	1	98
% of total (N = 1,033)		38	21	21	7	7	2	2	1	1	1	101
total no. dm*	1,033	391	216	216	70	69	22	19	14	8	8	

* dm = discursive move. ** The category Explanation contains subcategories.

In Table 9.7 the percentages that correspond to a topic category's most frequent discursive moves have been highlighted in dark gray and the second most
frequent moves are highlighted in light gray. We can see that all categories use
questions most. The second most frequent move once more varies according to the
two clusters of the categories already established for the responses. 'Drugs', 'fitness
and nutrition', 'general health' and 'sexual health' (Group 1) feature more background information moves, while 'emotional health', 'relationships' and 'sexuality'
(Group 2) have a larger share of explicit problem statements. 'Fitness and nutrition', however, features an equal number of problem statements and background
information. As we saw with the content of the response letters, the content of the
problem thus influences the composition of the text.

9.3.3 Number of discursive moves in a unit

Let us now turn to a consideration of the internal composition of the units. Table 9.8 shows that the number of discursive moves in a single unit ranged from
one to eight. (Remember that by definition a unit needs to contain at least one
discursive move.) The row totals show an equal overall distribution of the 1,033
discursive moves into 323 units for all the topic categories (13–16%). The column
totals and their percentages tell us that more than six discursive moves per unit
are rare (30 instances, 9%), while units consisting of two, three, or four discursive
moves are more frequent and equally distributed (21–23%).

Table 9.8 The number of units according to number of discursive moves (subcorpus; N units = 323)

no. of dm* per unit → categories ↓	1	2	3	4	5	6	7	8	Row total	%
Group 1:										
drugs	10	13	10	10	2	3	1		49	15
fitness/nutrition	7	15	9	8	1	1	2		43	13
general health	5	6	7	9	9	2	2	1	41	13
sexual health	10	11	5	7	8	4	2		47	15
Group 2:										
emotional health	9	10	13	10	5	3	1	2	53	16
relationships	4	5	12	14	3	2	3		43	13
sexuality	6	13	13	10	4	1			47	15
total	51	73	69	68	32	16	11	3	323	100
%	16	23	21	21	10	5	3	1	100	

* dm = discursive move.

A more varied picture emerges when we consider Table 9.8 again and focus on the distribution within the categories – the highest number of units in each category is highlighted in gray. In general, the categories 'emotional health', 're-lationships' and 'sexuality' use more units per problem letter. Again, the topic categories group together in the same way they did in the answers. Only 'general health' leaves the group it was part of in the answers because it uses more units per problem letter than 'drugs', 'fitness and nutrition' and 'sexual health'.

9.3.4 Sequence of discursive moves

In this section the focus is on the sequence of discursive moves within units. It is of interest to find out which discursive move starts or ends the problem letter, or a unit, and which compositions of discursive moves are likely to make up a typical unit. As I did in the discussion in Chapter 5, I will first focus on the very first and very last position in the problem letters. Since 90 percent of all problem letters contain only one unit, and since these units contain only one to four discursive moves in 81 percent of all cases, this discussion will already tell us a great deal about the overall composition of the problem letters.

Table 9.9 shows that, overall, questions, background information and prob-lem statements are equally frequent (28–30%) in the very first position. The table also tells us which discursive moves are more frequently used to start the body of a problem letter in each topic category (highlighted in gray). It is interesting to note that there is no clear pattern which would allow us to group topic cate-gories. The category 'drugs', for example, seems to go together with 'general health' because both frequently use background information and questions. Their third

Table 9.9 The number of discursive moves in the very first position of a problem letter by topic category (subcorpus)

discursive moves → topic categories ↓	question	background	problem statement	metacomment	request advice	apology	compliment	comment on prev. rec.	thanks	EXPL*	total
Group 1:											
drugs	13	22	2	1	1		1				40
fitn./nutrition	12	12	13		2	1					40
gen. health	13	14	10		2		1				40
sexual health	16	11	8	1	1	1	1	1			40
Group 2:											
emot. health	11	8	17	2	1	1					40
relationships	7	12	16	2	1	2					40
sexuality	13	3	13	3	1	2	1	2		2	40
total	85	82	79	9	9	7	4	3		2	280
%	30	29	28	3	3	3	1	1		1	99

* Explanation contains subcategories.

most frequent move, however, differs since there are fewer problem statements in the category 'drugs' than in 'general health'. The category 'emotional health' appears to be in a group with 'fitness and nutrition', 'relationships' and 'sexuality' because of their preference for problem statements. However, while the category 'fitness and nutrition' uses all three discursive moves equally, 'emotional health' has fewer background information moves (n = 8) and 'sexuality' even fewer than that (n = 3). There is thus no clear pattern in the use of discursive moves that could be explained according to topic category.

Table 9.10 focuses on the very last discursive move in a question. The main discursive moves used for this position are questions (n = 144, 51%), thanks (n = 64, 23%) and explicit requests for advice (n = 28, 10%). This general sequence of frequency for the last discursive move is the same for all topic categories. There seems to be a consensus in the community of problem letter writers to prefer questions in final position over statements that request advice. The use of background information and problem statements to conclude a question occurs only seventeen times each (6%). It is also interesting to see that thanking *Lucy* appears in all topic categories, but only 64 times overall. Nevertheless, since 64 of the 69 total occurrences of thanking occur as the last move in the problem letter, thanking can be argued to be a typical closing move.

I will now turn to the internal composition of units within the problem letters. Table 9.11 displays the number of discursive moves that follow each other in individual units. In the row headings the first discursive move of a sequence is

Table 9.10 The number of discursive moves in the very last position of a problem letter by topic category (subcorpus)

discursive moves → topic categories ↓	question	thanks	request advice	background	problem statement	EXPL*	compliment	comment on prev. rec.	apology	metacomment	total
Group 1:											
drugs	23	8	4	1	1	1	1	1			40
fitness/nutrition	20	11	3	3	2		1				40
gen. health	20	11	1	5	1	2					40
sexual health	22	9	3	3	2			1			40
Group 2:											
emot. health	19	9	6	3	2				1		40
relationships	19	9	8	1	3						40
sexuality	21	7	3	1	6	1	1				40
total	144	64	28	17	17	4	3	2	1		280
% (N = 280)	51	23	10	6	6	1	1	1			99

* Explanation contains subcategories.

Table 9.11 The sequence of discursive moves within units (row is first element; column is second element; subcorpus)

2nd discursive move → 1st discursive move ↓	'end of unit'	apology	comment on prev. rec.	compliment	EXPL*	metacomment	background	problem st.	question	request advice	thanks	total
'start of unit'		7	7	5		13	92	91	91	11	6	323
apology	1				1		4	2	2	3	1	14
comment on prev. rec.	5							1	2			8
compliment	3						2	2	1			8
EXPL*	6						2	2	7	2	3	22
metacomment							7	4	5	3		19
background	31	1			1	5	1	78	73	18	8	216
problem st.	29	3			9	1	50		103	19	2	216
question	152	2	1	1	8		45	31	101	13	37	391
request advice	32	1			3		11	5	6		12	70
thanks	64			2			2			1		69
total	323	14	8	8	22	19	216	216	391	70	69	†1,356

* The category explanation contains subcategories. † The 323 start/end positions of units need to be subtracted to obtain the total number of discursive moves (N = 1,356 − 323 = 1,033).

listed, while the column headings contain the second discursive move. The first row entitled 'start of unit' and the column entitled 'end of unit' indicate when the discursive move following or preceding it is in first or last position in a unit. These numbers include the very first and last discursive moves in a problem letter. These positions are the ones which have just been discussed in the previous paragraphs.

The combinations that occur more than 30 times are highlighted in Table 9.11. They are problem statement-question (n = 103), question-question (n = 101), background-problem statement (n = 78), background-question (n = 73), problem statement-background (n = 50), question-background (n = 45), question-thanks (n = 37), and question-problem statement (n = 31). Two combinations dominate. The first is problem statements followed by questions (n = 103). We have seen earlier that problem statements rarely occur at the end of a problem letter or a unit. It seems logical that a question follows an identified problem since the author of the problem letter is writing to 'Lucy Answers' to ask for advice in the first place. However, it is striking that this sequence is clearly preferred to problem statements followed by a request for advice (n = 19). The second strong combination consists of one question followed by another one. Questions therefore often appear in clusters. Background information precedes a problem statement or question more often than the other way around. It is also interesting to see that thanks follows a question most often. Since thanks was identified as a very last discursive move in 64 cases in Table 9.10 and since there are no additional instances of thanks as a unit closing move noted in Table 9.11, it follows that combinations with thanks as a second discursive move are used to end the problem letter. However, the completion of a problem letter by means of thanking never occurs in much more than 25 percent in any topic category.

To see whether the different topic categories prefer one of these eight combinations, I have studied their distribution. The results can be seen in Table 9.12, in which the percentages of each individual combination type is given by topic category. Percentages scoring nine and higher are highlighted in the table. Starting with the most frequent combination, Table 9.12 shows that the categories 'drugs', 'general health', 'sexual health' and 'sexuality' all use questions in clusters to a large extent (9–13%). There is, however, no clear indication as to whether these topic categories form a group since their other preferences do not coincide. The categories 'emotional health' and 'relationships' have a high percentage of the background-problem statement (as does the category 'drugs') and the problem statement-question combinations. The category 'sexuality', which, as we saw, forms a group in the responses of 'Lucy Answers' with the latter two categories, only joins them here in the frequency of the combination of problem statement-question, but there are almost no background-problem statement combinations at all. This category has fewer background information moves overall (only fifteen percent, as opposed to more than twenty percent in all the other categories,

Table **9.12** Combinations of discursive moves in units in percent (subcorpus)

topic categories → discursive move combinations ↓ 100% =	all categories	Group 1				Group 2		
		drugs	fitness/ nutrition	gen. health	sexual health	emotional health	relationships	sexuality
	n = 1,033	n = 141	n = 121	n = 153	n = 153	n = 174	n = 154	n = 137
background – problem statement	8	10	7	7	6	9	12	1
background – question	7	9	7	5	11	5	5	7
problem statement – background	5	1	6	4	5	6	8	3
problem statement – question	10	8	12	12	9	9	10	10
question – background	4	3	2	5	8	3	3	7
question – problem statement	3	2	3	3	3	3	3	3
question – question	10	13	7	11	13	8	7	9
question – thanks	4	3	6	3	3	3	5	2

Table 9.7) and can therefore also combine them less frequently. Most often, problem statements (10%) as well as questions (9%) are followed by questions in the category 'sexuality'. Apart from the few patterns mentioned, there are no clear tendencies with respect to a possible grouping of categories. Within every individual category, however, certain preferences for combinations could be found (see highlighting).

9.3.5 Summary

As in the discussion of the response letters in Chapter 5, the focus in this section has been on establishing the content structure of the 280 problem letters in the subcorpus of 'Lucy Answers', by looking at the number of units per problem letter, the number and type of discursive moves making up these units, and the sequence of discursive moves within units. Once again, there was an attempt to determine whether patterns across the topic categories existed. The results of this analysis are summarized below:

– A problem letter contains only one unit in 90 percent of all cases, which means that only 27 problem letters have more than one unit (Table 9.6).

–   There is no consistent pattern according to topic categories that explains the distribution of the number of discursive moves per unit (81% range from one to four, Table 9.8).

–   Three discursive moves are the most frequently used in the realization of problem letters: questions (38%), background information (21%) and problem statements (21%). Requesting advice and thanking account for seven percent of all discursive moves. The other moves are rare (Table 9.7).

–   All categories use questions most frequently. The same grouping of topic categories as for the responses emerges when second-most frequent moves are examined: 'drugs', 'fitness and nutrition', 'general health' and 'sexual health' (Group 1) prefer background information; 'emotional health', 'relationships' and 'sexuality' (Group 2) have a larger share of explicit problem statements.

–   The very first discursive move in the body of a problem letter is equally likely to be either a question, background information or a problem statement (Table 9.9). The topic categories do not form groups according to their preferences, but do have favorite realizations.

–   The very last discursive move in a problem letter is likely to be a question (51%), thanks (23%), or a request for advice (10%, Table 9.10). This sequence is seen in all topic categories. Thanking is almost entirely used only in this closing position.

–   Two combinations of discursive moves dominate the formation of the sequences in a unit: problem statement-question (n = 103), and question-question (n = 101, Table 9.11). This means that the combination of problem statements with questions is clearly preferred to problem statements followed by requests for advice (n = 19) and that questions appear in clusters. The topic categories did not form groups in their use of discursive moves in sequence.

A summary of the results of the study of the characteristics of the content structure of the problem letters for each topic category is presented in Table 9.13.

9.4 Aspects of relational work in the advice-seekers' problem letters

Before turning to a discussion of the linguistic realizations of discursive moves, I will examine the way relational work (appealing, boosting, criticizing, hedging, humor-hedging, bonding and humor-bonding) is used in the problem letters. As was pointed out in the analogous sections in Chapter 6, this kind of analysis aims at identifying tendencies of how and where relational work manifests itself. I do not want to give the impression that the seven chosen types cover all aspects of relational work which emerge in individual readings of every single problem letter, nor do I wish to imply that there is no relational work involved when the categories

Table 9.13 Summary of the typical content structures in problem letters in 'Lucy Answers' by categories and groups (subcorpus)

characteristics → topic categories ↓	typical n. of units	typical n dms* per unit and typical range	preferred types of dms* (first two)	typical first dm* in a Question	typical last dm* in a Question	typical sequence
Group 1						
drugs	1	2; 1 to 4	question background	background question	question	question-question background-problem statement
fitness and nutrition	1	2; 1 to 4	question background problem statement	problem statement question background	question	problem statement-question
general health	1	4 or 5; 1 to 5	question background	background question	question	problem statement-question question-question
sexual health	1	2; 1 to 5	question, background	question background	question	question-question background-question
Group 2						
emotional health	1	3; 1 to 4	question problem statement	problem statement question	question	background-problem statement problem statement-question
relationships	1	3 or 4; 1 to 4	question problem statement	problem statement background	question	background-problem statement problem statement-question
sexuality	1	2 or 3; 1 to 4	question problem statement	problem statement question	question	problem statement-question question-question

* dm = discursive move.

Table 9.14 Number of relational work moves in all problem letters by topic category (subcorpus)

relational work → topic categories ↓	hedging	humor-hedging	appealing	bonding	humor-bonding	boosting	criticizing	total	%
Group 2:									
emotional health	50		57			1		108	23
relationships	33	1	39	1		2		76	16
sexuality	45	1	20	2		3		71	15
Group 1:									
drugs	36		16	2		2	3	59	13
general health	35	2	17	1	1	1		57	12
sexual health	26	1	14	2	2	1	2	48	10
fitness/nutrition	27	2	15		1			45	10
total	252	7	178	8	4	10	5	464	99
%	54	2	38	2	1	2	1	100	

chosen for analysis are not found in an individual problem letter (cf. especially Section 6.2). The categories discussed here should, however, give us a good idea of the way relational work is used since they were developed by studying the problem letters in the first place.

Overall, I identified 464 instances of the use of relational work and categorized them, as can be seen in Table 9.14. The largest number occurs in the topic category 'emotional health' (n = 108, 23%), followed by 'relationships' (n = 76, 16%) and 'sexuality' (n = 71, 15%). The other four topic categories all have between 45 and 59 occurrences (10–13%). The same two groups of topic categories can be seen in this distribution of relational work as were observed in the responses. The reason for this may be the sensitivity of the topics in the three aforementioned categories which deal with more personal and intimate matters. The categories 'drugs', 'fitness and nutrition', 'general health' and 'sexual health', by their very nature, may allow the writers to formulate their problem letters in a more distanced and technical way to obtain factual information.

Only two of the six relational work categories investigated turn out to be used frequently. These are hedging with 252 instances (54%) and appealing with 178 occurrences (38%). Table 9.14 also tells us that the topic categories 'emotional health' (n = 57) and 'relationships' (n = 39) contain appealing far more often than the other categories. Hedging is used most often in the category 'emotional health' (n = 50), followed by the category 'sexuality' (n = 45). All other topic categories feature between 26 to 36 instances of hedging, thus, the differences in use by category are not very pronounced.

Table 9.15 Number of relational work moves in discursive moves (subcorpus)

relational work → discursive moves ↓	hedging	humor-hedging	appealing	bonding	humor-bonding	boosting	criticizing	total rel. work	% rel. work	in total dm*
problem statement	26	2	81		1	9	1	120	26	216
question	60	3	26					89	19	391
request advice	45		33					78	17	70
thanks	69		2					71	15	69
background	30	2	27		2	1		62	13	216
EXPLANATION**	5		9				1	15	3	22
apology	14							14	3	14
compliment				7	1			8	2	8
comment on prev. rec.	1						3	4	1	8
metacomment	2			1				3	1	19
total	252	7	178	8	4	10	5	464		1,033
% (N = 464)	54	2	38	2	1	2	1	100		

* dm = discursive move; ** The category Explanation contains subcategories.

The next question to ask is in which kind of discursive moves is relational work found. Table 9.15 tells us that problem statements (n = 120, 26%) and questions (n = 89, 19%) have the largest share of relational work, followed by requests for advice (n = 78, 17%), thanks (n = 71, 15%) and background information (n = 62, 13%). The last column in Table 9.15 shows the total number of the discursive moves in which relational work could have occurred.[3] From this we can see that questions contain fewer instances of the relational work categorized than requests for advice. This is striking since these two discursive moves are comparable in the force of their imposition. Table 9.15 also shows that problem statements are more likely to occur in combination with appealing than with hedging. Conversely, questions, requests for advice, and thanks are more prone to instances of hedging than appealing. Background information contains both appealing and hedging in almost equal numbers.

Since hedging and appealing are the dominant relational work categories, I will concentrate my discussion on them and on the discursive moves in which they appear most frequently. Table 9.16 shows the number of discursive moves that contain hedging (first column in every block), and the overall number of discursive moves (second column) in which they occur for five discursive moves categories. Hedging is used in two different ways. In background information and problem statements, the hedges are primarily employed to save the face of the advice-seekers by, for example, pointing out that the information given is subjective or from sources that the advice-seekers do not trust. Overall, there are only

Table 9.16　Hedging in five types of discursive moves by topic category (subcorpus)

| topic categories ↓ | face-saving of the advice-seeker's face | | | | face-saving addressed to *Lucy* | | | | | |
| | background | | problem statement | | question | | request advice | | thanks | |
	no. of hedging	no. of dm*	no. of hedging	no. of dm*	no. of hedging	no. of dm*	no. of hedging	no. of dm*	no. of hedging	no. of dm*
Group 1:										
drugs	7	32	1	21	11	60	6	10	9	9
fitn./nutrition	4	27	1	27	6	45	4	8	11	11
gen. health	4	33	1	26	10	60	7	11	12	12
sexual health	2	35	2	27	12	69	1	5	9	9
Group 2:										
emot. health	7	35	9	45	9	55	8	12	9	9
relationships	4	33	4	42	4	47	10	15	9	9
sexuality	2	21	8	28	8	55	9	9	10	10
total	30	216	26	216	60	391	45	70	69	69

* dm = discursive move.

a handful of such hedges in background information and problem statements in each topic category, which shows that this type of hedging is rather rare.

More frequent is the second type of hedging which aims at mitigating the imposition which the request for advice places on *Lucy*. The categories 'drugs', 'general health', 'sexual health' and 'emotional health' appear to use hedging in questions more than the other topic categories do. Requests for advice are most often mitigated in the category 'relationships', followed by 'sexuality' and 'emotional health'. Since the number of discursive moves (n = 70) in which these hedges (n = 45) occur is much smaller than in the questions, we can say that requests for advice are not only more often mitigated than are the questions, but they also seem more likely to require hedging. Thanks, finally, is argued to constitute an act of hedging in general in 'Lucy Answers' because it specifically acknowledges that *Lucy* is offering a service by answering the problem letters.

An identical investigation was also carried out on acts of appealing. Table 9.17 shows that, in the case of background information, the category 'emotional health' features the most appealing (n = 8), followed by 'relationships' (n = 5) and 'fitness and nutrition' (n = 4). Only the category 'sexuality' shows very little appealing combined with background information (n = 1). On the other hand, 'sexuality' is the only topic category in which appealing appears with questions to a noteworthy extent (n = 10). For problem statements it is striking that the category 'emotional health' features frequent use of appealing (n = 34, in 45 discursive moves), followed by 'relationships' (n = 15, in 42 discursive moves). In the case of 'emotional

Table 9.17 Appealing in four types of discursive moves by topic category (subcorpus)

disc. move →	background		problem statement		question		request advice	
topic categories ↓	no. of appealing	no. of dm*	no. of appealing	no. of dm*	no. of appealing	no. of dm*	no. of appealing	no. of dm*
Group 1:								
drugs	3	32	7	21	3	60	3	10
fitness/nutrition	4	27	7	27	1	45	3	8
general health	3	33	4	26	5	60	2	11
sexual health	3	35	7	27	2	69	2	5
Group 2:								
emotional health	8	35	34	45	1	55	8	12
relationships	5	33	15	42	4	47	13	15
sexuality	1	21	7	28	10	55	2	9
total	27	216	81	216	26	391	33	70

* dm = discursive move.

health', appealing often seems to be linked with problem statements as such. Finally, appealing in requests for advice occurs most in the categories 'relationships' (n = 13, in 15 discursive moves) and 'emotional health' (n = 8, in 12 discursive moves), thus it is safe to say that appealing is an integral part of requesting advice. Overall, it should be stressed that the number of occurrences per discursive move category is so small that the tendencies we are discussing are weak.

The analysis of the relational work types appealing, boosting, criticizing, hedging, humor-hedging, bonding and humor-bonding has yielded the following results:

- An examination of the overall number of instances of the relational work categories in all problem letters shows that the topic categories divide into the same two groups as they did in the examination of the responses: Group 2 with the categories 'emotional health' (n = 108, 23%), 'relationships' (n = 76, 16%) and 'sexuality' (n = 71, 15%) contains more relational work than the other four categories in Group 1 (45–59 instances; 10–13%, Table 9.14).
- Of the six relational work categories, only hedging (n = 252, 54%) and appealing (n = 178, 38%) are frequent (Table 9.14).
- Overall, questions contain far fewer examples of the relational work categories analyzed than requests for advice; these two discursive moves are thus treated differently despite the fact that both impose on *Lucy*. Thanks is interpreted to be a face-saving strategy in the context of asking for advice in 'Lucy Answers'.
- Appealing is used most often in the topic categories 'emotional health' and 'relationships' and it occurs predominantly in the problem statements.

It is important to stress again that the categories chosen for the analysis are meant to indicate only *tendencies* of how relational work may manifest itself in the problem letters written by the anonymous advice-seekers of 'Lucy Answers'.

9.5 The linguistic realization of discursive moves

The discussion will now turn to the actual linguistic realizations of discursive moves. Since some of the discursive moves turned out to be used more frequently, they will also receive most attention (questions, requests for advice, background information, problem statements). I will, however, also briefly discuss the other discursive moves that play a role in the problem letters.

9.5.1 The address form and mention of *Lucy* in the body of the problem letter

The writers who address *Lucy* choose different ways of beginning their problem letters. Mainly, they select a variant of *Dear Lucy* (n = 186), or the name *Lucy* on its own (n = 71). The variation within these two main options is due to punctuation (the comma is the preferred option; see Table 9.18). Fifteen records start either with *Hi Lucy* (n = 12), or *Hey Lucy* (n = 5). There are three more variants that occur only once and in three cases there is no address form at all (zero). The vast majority of writers thus comply with the format of advice columns in which the agony aunt is addressed with *Dear {name}*. It is also interesting to see that there are only four records in which the name *Lucy* does not appear. There is thus an orientation towards the advisor persona from the very beginning and also to the genre of advice columns and their letters that traditionally start in this way (cf. *Dear Abby* or *Ann Landers,* among many).

 Lucy is also at times directly addressed in the body of the problem letter. With only ten occurrences, these instances are rare and clearly noticeable, because they

Table 9.18 The address form in the problem letters in 'Lucy Answers' ('subcorpus; N = 280)

Dear Lucy,	172	Lucy,	55	Hi Lucy,	12
Dear Lucy	5	Lucy –	15	Hey Lucy,	3
Dear Lucy-	3	Lucy…	1	Hey Lucy…	1
Dear Lucy –	3			Hey Lucy –	1
Dear Lucy:	2			Hi there!	1
Dear Lucy!	1			Okay Lucy,	1
				To Lucy,	1
				'zero'	3
total	186		71		23

emphasize a special link between the writer and the advisor *Lucy*. Examples to illustrate this are given in (9.23) to (9.25):

(9.23)   This is the reason that I am here, Lucy. (LA 0027, general health, metacomment, "Hair loss")

(9.24)   Your answer may save our relationship. Please Lucy, I need your help. (LA 1738, relationships, request advice, appealing, "Girlfriend gets scared every time I say, 'I love you'")

(9.25)   Thanks, Lucy! (LA 0744, sexual health, thanks, "Warts from oral sex?")

9.5.2 Questions

Questions are the main way in which advice is asked for in 'Lucy Answers' (the other is a 'request for advice' in statement form) and is one of the three main discursive moves overall (n = 391, 38%, Table 9.7). As Table 9.11 has shown, questions are part of all the large sequence combinations: problem statement-question (n = 103), question-question (n = 101), background-question (n = 73), question-background (n = 45), question-thanks (n = 37), and question-problem statement (n = 31). Questions are as likely to start a problem letter as background information or problem statements are, but are more likely to end one than the others.

A look at the type of question that appears in 'Lucy Answers' reveals that the writers prefer to use *yes/no*-questions in 212 instances (54%, Table 9.19). *Wh*-questions are used in 153 instances (39%), while alternative questions are rare with only 19 occurrences (5%). Only the topic category 'relationships' features more *wh*- than *yes/no*-questions (see highlighting).

Table 9.19 Question types in the problem letters of 'Lucy Answers' by topic category (subcorpus)

question type → topic categories ↓	yes/no	row %	wh-	row %	alternative	row %	total
Group 1:							
drugs	39	64	18	30	4	7	61
fitness and nutrition	24	53	17	38	4	9	45
general health	31	52	27	45	2	3	60
sexual health	34	49	31	45	4	6	69
Group 2:							
emotional health	31	56	23	42	1	2	55
relationships	19	41	25	54	2	4	46
sexuality	34	62	12	22	2	4	55
total	212	54	153	39	19	5	391

In most cases the *yes/no*-questions function as invitations to *Lucy* to elaborate on the issues raised. Examples (9.26) to (9.30) show such usage and also represent types of questions that occur several times:

(9.26) Can you help?
        (LA 1665, drugs, "Mysterious meds arrive in the mail")

(9.27) Could you comment?
        (LA 645, sexuality, "Prozac and male libido")

(9.28) Should I be concerned?
        (LA 1166, general health, "Eye mucus")

(9.29) Is this true?
        (LA 1898, fitness and nutrition, "A bowl of oatmeal a day keeps the cholesterol at bay?")

(9.30) Is this normal?
        (LA 200, sexuality, "New heterosexual sex")

The last question is telling since many of the concerns that come to light in 'Lucy Answers' are of a sensitive nature. To ask whether something is 'normal' reflects the writers' concern with establishing whether they conform to norms – either of a physical or a moral nature. However, an explicit mention of such concerns only oc-curs in 21 cases (cf. Section 6.3.2 on the reaction to such worries). Advice-seekers also specifically asked for advice, insight, help, comments and clarifications.

The *wh*-questions range from expressing more general invitations to *Lucy* to elaborate on a given topic, as in (9.31) and (9.32) to posing quite specific concerns, as represented in (9.33) to (9.35):

(9.31) What can I do?
        (LA 0451, relationships, "Curfews on break")

(9.32) What should I do?
        (LA 1339, relationships, "Close friends – take it to the next level?")

(9.33) What does the latest research explain on the CAUSES of stuttering?
        (LA 2447, emotional health, "Causes of stuttering?")

(9.34) Why can't I stop if this "soft drug" is not addictive?
        (LA 1579, drugs, "Wants to stop smoking pot")

(9.35) And where does one draw the line if mutual consent is established?
        (LA 0646, sexuality, "S/M roleplaying")

My analysis of relational work has shown that questions only rarely contain acts of appealing and are only rarely mitigated (especially in comparison with requests for advice). In addition, there is a clear preference not to address *Lucy* directly in the question (n = 350), such as shown in (9.28) to (9.35), in which the focus is either on the advice-seeker (*What can I do?*) or on the issue at hand (*Is this true?*). For this reason, questions that address *Lucy* directly with *can you* (n = 15) or *could you* (n = 13) are considered to be hedged, because they differ from the vast majority of questions that do not show any face-saving considerations (see (9.26) and (9.27) above).[4] The other important hedge consists of instances of *I am/was wondering* (n = 20).

In rare cases problem statements can take over the function of a question or a request for advice. This is the case in only four problem letters in 'Lucy Answers' in which neither questions nor requests for advice are to be found. In these cases the mere mention of the problem at hand is interpreted by *Lucy* as a request for advice, which can, of course, be explained by the orientation of both the advice-seeker as well as the advisor to the contextual frame of the advice column. In general, however, advice-seekers use either explicit questions or requests for advice, which shows that they take account of the dialogic character of the question-answer format of advice columns. Biber et al. (1999:211) report that questions are characteristic of conversations rather than writing. The dominance of questions in what is after all a written advice column thus underlines the 'interactive' appeal that advice columns have.

9.5.3 Requests for advice

The category 'request advice' refers to statements (as opposed to questions) which explicitly ask for help/advice/information from *Lucy*. With 70 occurrences overall, this discursive move is clearly only the second choice when compared to the number of questions. Requests for advice follow problem statements (n = 19), background information (n = 18) and questions (n = 13) most often. One other important finding from the analysis of relational work is that requesting advice occurs in conjunction with hedging and appealing in many cases (cf. Tables 9.16 and 9.17). I have chosen a number of examples from the category 'relationships' to illustrate this combination:

(9.36) Please help.
        (LA 1465, relationships, "Ain't got the giggles from crazy sex jiggles")

(9.37) I need your help!
        (LA 1602, relationships, "Should I cash in on hot banker?")

(9.38) I'm in desperate need of help!
        (LA 1627, relationships, "Help me stop stalking my ex and his new partner")

(9.39) Please help me get over this obsession!
        (LA 1627, relationships, "Help me stop stalking my ex and his new partner")

Help as a noun or verb appears in 26 of the 70 requests for advice and is catego-rized as a case of appealing (the total number of appealing is 33). Other instances of appealing in requests for advice consisted of descriptions of emotional states such as *Please suggest another solution because it really hurts me.* In thirteen cases *help* is combined with *please,* which is categorized as a hedge (see (9.36) and (9.39) above). In addition, *please* appears fourteen more times in combination with other words than *help* in the discursive move of requesting advice. Other hedges are *X would be appreciated* (n = 6) or *I would like to know/...* (n = 3). In twenty cases appealing and hedging occur together. It is clear that requesting advice in 'Lucy Answers' is considered to be a discursive move that requires face-saving strategies, while the questions previously discussed are usually formulated without consideration of the face-threatening aspect of advice-seeking.

If we turn once more to the linguistic realization of requests for advice in general, it should be pointed out that writers do not only ask for *help.* They also simply want to *know* or *understand* a problem (n = 7), use the expression *tell me how/where* to get *Lucy* to answer (n = 6), or want the solution to *questions* and *problems* (n = 5), and *answers* and *solutions* to problems (n = 3). They ask *Lucy* for *advice* (n = 4), *suggestions* (n = 3), *ideas* (n = 3), *tips and tricks* (n = 2), *observations* (n = 1), and *information* (n = 1). They want *resources* (n = 1), *guidance* (n = 1), *reassurance* (n = 1) or are simply *wondering* and *curious* (n = 2).

9.5.4 Background information

The writers of the problem letters are not merely asking for advice in a straightfor-ward and matter-of-fact manner. They also tell stories and illustrate their particu-lar dilemmas. When they do so, this is categorized as giving background informa-tion. Such information is usually provided in a very concise and condensed way. As pointed out in my previous analysis, it is rare that a problem letter has more than one unit; and, in general, a unit in turn has only one to four discursive moves. We know, however, that, together with problem statements, background information ranks second after questions in the frequency of occurrence of discursive moves (n = 216, 21%, Table 9.7), and that it is followed by either a problem statement or a question, and is often used to start the problem letter/unit.

In fact, examples (9.10) and (9.11) given above showed background informa-tion followed by problem statements. Figure 9.3 shows the second most frequent pattern: background information followed by a question. The first two sentences do not identify the habit of the advice-seeker's sister to smoke marijuana as prob-lematic *per se,* but serve as background information to the actual question, which is then phrased in a neutral and detached way. The only indications of involvement on the part of the advice-seeker are the phrase *and I don't know what* (hedge) in the background information move, which points to some insecurity on the part of

```
Question
  ├─ address
  │     └─ Dear Lucy,
  ├─ unit 1
  │     ├─ background
  │     │   I have a sister who just told me that she occasionally smokes marijuana. She's used
  │     │   weeds, bongs, and I don't know what.
  │     └─ question
  │         Is there any danger of her becoming addicted and what are the effects of smoking
  │         pot?
  └─ pseudonym type=appeal
        └─ Worried and Burned
```

Figure 9.3 The problem letter in "Sister smokes dope" (LA 225, drugs)

the advice-seeker about her/his sister's behavior, and the pseudonym *Worried and Burned* (appeal). The latter immediately gives the entire problem letter a more urgent tone and reveals that the advice-seeker is in fact quite worried and not that neutral after all. The choice of pseudonym may thus greatly influence the overall tone of a problem letter.

Every writer of a problem letter will decide for him- or herself how much factual background to give and how much to reveal of his or her personal views of the problem. In Section 9.4, I found that appealing (n = 27) and hedging (n = 30) are used rather sparingly in the 216 background information moves. The hedges are used to save the face of the advice-seeker, by, for example, prefacing a statement with *I heard* or *it has been said* to indicate that the source of the following statement is not the writer him- or herself, or by qualifying information about themselves and their problems with *I think, in my opinion* or *perhaps* to show that other interpretations may be possible as well.

Appealing in background sections is seen most in the category 'emotional health' (n = 8; cf. Table 9.17). As a final example of the way background information is used, I have thus chosen an illustration for this use. In Figure 9.4, a reader whose father has just died is distressed by this situation and does not know where to turn for help. Sentences that are considered to contain appealing are italicized. The advice-seeker in Figure 9.4 starts by identifying the reason for his or her question right away and leaves no doubt that the loss of his or her father has left him or her in a state of depression (problem statement). The ensuing background information explains the nature of this depression and also specifies that he or she is looking for someone to turn to for help. The appeal to *Lucy* is shown most clearly in the expression *but I'm afraid to approach my friends* and in the explanation that *Lucy* is *the first person that I've said anything to about this.* (Notice also that *Lucy* is addressed as a *person.*) Since the advice-seeker negates a number

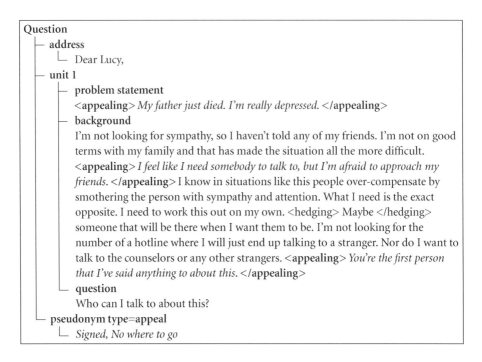

Figure 9.4 The problem letter in "Father died" (LA 191, emotional health, italics added)

of options for help (friends, family, a hotline, counselors, strangers in general), this makes the appeal to *Lucy* even stronger. If we compare the last two problem letters, it is striking that the background information in Figure 9.4 already clearly reveals the emotional point of view of the advice-seeker in the body of the problem letter and not just at the end in the pseudonym (*Signed, No where to go*). The pseudonym just serves to reinforce the character of appeal in the main part of the problem letter.

9.5.5 Problem statements

Problem statements occur 216 times (21%) in the subcorpus of 'Lucy Answers' (Table 9.7). They are the second most frequently used discursive move after questions in the categories 'emotional health', 'relationships' and 'sexuality', and occur equally frequently as background information in the category 'fitness and nutrition'. Problem statements rarely end a letter, but are equally likely to open one as background information or questions. Problem statements are found to form a sequence with questions that follow them (n = 103), or background information that precedes them (n = 78, Table 9.11). Problem statements were already seen in Figures 9.1 and 9.4, and in examples (9.10) and (9.11):

- When I wake up in the morning, I have a layer of stringy white stuff lining my bottom gums. (from Figure 9.1)
- My father just died. I'm really depressed. (from Figure 9.4)
- However, I often find my eyes very itchy and watery. It bothers me a lot since I need to study. But, with my irritated eyes, it is sometimes difficult to read for a long time. (from example (9.10))
- It is difficult to get a hold of good information on food allergies. (from example (9.11))

A look at relational work tells us that, overall, hedging is rather infrequent in problem statements (n = 26, Table 9.16). For a further illustration of problem statements I have thus chosen an example from the category 'emotional health' to demonstrate how they can combine with appealing, since this type of relational work is most prominent in this topic category (n = 34, in 45 discursive moves, Table 9.17).

Figure 9.5 represents the problem letter in "Divorce pain". With six discursive moves, this letter is uncharacteristically long. It starts with a problem statement that is neutrally formulated and gives background information immediately after.

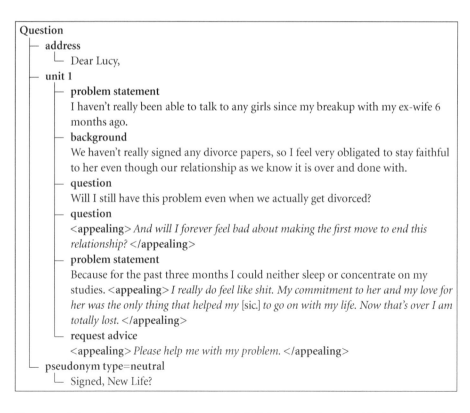

Figure 9.5 The problem letter in "Divorce pain" (LA 31, emotional health, italics added)

Then two questions follow which lead to another problem statement. This time, the writer is quite clear about his emotional state: he feels *like shit* and is *totally lost* (see italics). This clear appeal to *Lucy* is reinforced by the ensuing request for advice in which the writer uses the words *please*, *help* and *problem*. The pseudonym *Signed, New Life?*, however, was not categorized as containing appeal.

9.5.6 Apology, comments on previous records, compliments, explanations, metacomments, and thanks

The remaining discursive moves all occur only rarely (Table 9.7): explanations (n = 22), metacomments (n = 19), apologies (n = 14), comments on previous records (n = 8), and compliments (n = 8). Only thanks reaches as high a frequency as seven percent (n = 69) of all discursive moves, which is why I will focus my discussion on them. Thanking is considered to be an act of hedging since it explicitly acknowledges *Lucy*'s efforts, in that the advice-seeker is asking *Lucy* to do work. We have seen earlier that it completes the problem letters and thus usually appears in the very final position.

Table 9.20 shows that a simple *thanks* on its own is used in the majority of cases (n = 37; variation only being due to punctuation). The more formal form of *Thank you* (n = 11) and the more personalized *thanks Lucy* (n = 2) are rarer. More elaborate forms are used nineteen times. In Table 9.20 four instances of thanking have been categorized as a special type of 'elaboration'. These are instances of thanking that consist of entire sentences in which the writers express their gratitude:

(9.40)   Thanks for any help you can give me!!!!!!!!!!!!
         (LA 2255, emotional health)

(9.41)   First, I'd like to thank you for this service!
         (LA 200, sexuality)

(9.42)   I wanted to thank you for the information on your site [but I have a question.]
         (LA 1633, sexuality)

Table 9.20 Realizations of thanks in the problem letters of 'Lucy Answers' (subcorpus; N = 69)

on its own	n =	*Lucy* is addressed	n =	more elaborate	n =
Thanks,	15	Thank you!	2	Thanks for helping/your help/your time	6
Thanks.	8	Thank you,	4	Thanks in advance.	2
Thanks!	6	Thank you.	5	Thanks so much.	2
Thanks	6	Thanks Lucy,	1	Thank you so much.	2
Thanx	2	Thanks, Lucy!	1	Thanks a lot.	3
				"elaboration"	4
Total	37		13		19

(9.43) Thank you very much for any help you can give me.
        (LA 1926, fitness & nutrition)

With only four instances, these types of thanking are rare. The majority of writers to 'Lucy Answers' who choose to express their gratitude at all make do with just a simple *thanks*. However, as pointed out before, 75 percent of all answers contain no thanks at all.

9.5.7 The pseudonyms of the advice-seekers

The very last (optional) move in a writer's problem letter is the choice of a pseudonym to sign. As it turns out, in 37 percent of the letters (n = 103), the writers prefer not to sign at all. The other 177 pseudonyms are formulated in different ways. Table 9.21 shows that 93 entail a form of appeal (33% of 280); 74 are formulated neutrally in a matter-of-fact way (26%), and ten strike a humorous note (4%), i.e., they contain word play.

 If we look at how pseudonyms are chosen in the problem letters in the different topic categories, we can see that the category 'sexuality' features pseudonyms most often (i.e., there are only eight instances in which the writer chooses not to create one). In the category 'relationships', conversely, less than 50 percent of the records have pseudonyms. For once, these two categories do not form a group. The categories 'sexual health' and 'drugs', which usually behave in a similar way to 'general health' and 'fitness and nutrition', also feature appeal pseudonyms more frequently than the other two categories, where neutral realizations are more often used. This means that they behave similarly to 'emotional health', which also prefers no pseudonyms and appealing to the other options (see gray highlighting in Table 9.21). This pattern thus does not reflect the split into the two content groups

Table 9.21 Pseudonyms (40 in each category)

type of pseudonym → topic category ↓	none	appeal	neutral	humor
Group 1:				
drugs	15	15	8	2
fitness and nutrition	13	9	15	3
general health	14	8	17	1
sexual health	15	17	7	1
Group 2:				
emotional health	13	18	9	
relationships	25	10	3	2
sexuality	8	16	15	1
total	103	93	74	10
% (N = 280)	37	33	26	4

Table 9.22 Examples of typical pseudonyms chosen by the advice-seekers

type	pseudonym	topic category
appeal	Wish I Were a Loner	emotional health
appeal	Emotion-laden	emotional health
appeal	An AIDS paranoid	sexual health
appeal	Slightly embarrassed.	sexual health
appeal	Concerned	sexuality
appeal	Somewhat insecure about sexuality	sexuality
appeal	Sincerely, Totally Confused	relationships
appeal	Sad and Unhappy	relationships
neutral	Sis living without wheat	fitness and nutrition
neutral	Ab man	fitness and nutrition
neutral	Bellyache	general health
neutral	Thirsty	general health

that has been witnessed time and again in other aspects. However, if we disregard the possibility of using no pseudonym, then the categories 'emotional health', 're-lationships' and 'sexuality' have appeal as their first preference – which might have been expected because of the likelihood of an appeal due to the sensitive topics treated. The categories making up the more factually oriented group of topic categories remain split. But the more technical and information oriented categories 'fitness and nutrition' and 'general health' feature more neutral pseudonyms than do the categories 'drugs' and 'sexual health'. Topic sensitivity can therefore also be seen as a factor in the choice of pseudonyms, although not in such a distinct way as in previous discussions. Table 9.22 offers a few examples of what these pseudonym realizations may look like.

Humor in pseudonyms is rare with only ten occurrences. However, as stressed many times before, humor is, of course, a very subjective phenomenon, and it may well be that other readers would categorize less conservatively than I have. Nonetheless, I believe that the general ranking of preferences would not be affected to any significant degree by a more tolerant interpretation.

9.6 Discussion of a selection of problem letters

In this chapter we have seen one typical specimen of a problem letter from the category 'drugs' (cf. Figure 9.3), two from the category 'general health' (cf. Figures 9.1 and 9.2), and two from the category 'emotional health' (cf. Figure 9.4 and 9.5). In what follows, I will present one example each from the other categories as a way of reassembling all the bits and pieces of the analyses carried out in this chapter.

The first example is taken from the category 'fitness and nutrition' (Figure 9.6). Like most other typical cases in this category, this problem letter consists

```
Question
 ├─ address
 │   └─ Lucy,
 ├─ unit 1
 │   ├─ problem statement
 │   │   My friend recently got a blood test back from her doctor and she was told she was
 │   │   deficient in Vitamin B12. She is a vegetarian.
 │   └─ question
 │       What can she do to supplement this vitamin if she does not eat meat?
 └─ pseudonym type=neutral
     └─ – Animal lover
```

Figure 9.6 The problem letter in "Vegetarian – Vitamin B-12?" (LA 677, fitness and nutrition)

```
Question
 ├─ address
 │   └─ Dear Lucy,
 ├─ unit 1
 │   └─ question
 │       Could you tell me what risks are involved in sharing accommodation and/or
 │       working with someone who has Hepatitis C?
 └─ pseudonym type=neutral
     └─ – Uninfected
```

Figure 9.7 The problem letter in "Hep-C" (LA 565, sexual health)

of one unit, containing two discursive moves: a problem statement in the first and a question in the final position. The pseudonym is neutral. After addressing *Lucy*, the writer first identifies the problem of her/his friend (a deficit in vitamin B12) and adds that the friend is a vegetarian, which the writer considers to be part of the problem. Then the writer proceeds to ask a *wh*-question to find out how to supplement one's diet if one is both a vegetarian and has a vitamin B12 deficiency. Notice also that the pseudonym *Animal lover* gives rise to the assumption that the advice-seeker is also a vegetarian and that an answer to this problem letter may not only be relevant to the advice-seeker's friend, but to her- or himself as well.

In Figure 9.7 we see a problem letter typical of the category 'sexual health'. It consists of one unit and just one discursive move (a question). Questions are likely to be in the first as well as in the last position, which is the case here. The advice-seeker of the record "Hep-C" addresses *Lucy* with *Dear Lucy* before he or she formulates a question about the risks of infection with Hepatitis C that is hedged with *could you tell me*. The pseudonym *Uninfected* and the question both point to the writer's interest in protecting him- or herself.

```
Question
├── address
│   └── Dear Lucy,
├── unit 1
│   ├── problem statement
│   │   My super-paranoid parents went krazy when they caught me kissing my boyfriend.
│   │   They say that you can get diseases (!) from kissing alone, even AIDS. <appealing>
│   │   And here I was thinking I was being safe by not having sex! </appealing>
│   ├── question
│   │   Is there any real danger in kissing someone with no sores or cuts or anything like
│   │   that in or around their mouth?
│   └── request advice
│       <appealing> Please help! </appealing>
└── pseudonym type=appeal
    └── – Petrified Pucker
```

Figure 9.8 The problem letter in "Can you get any diseases from kissing?" (LA 1714, sexuality)

Figure 9.8 from the category 'sexuality' is longer than the previous two problem letters. The letter also consists of one unit, but of three discursive moves (the majority of records in this category have either two or three discursive moves per unit). The first discursive move in a problem letter in the category 'sexuality' is likely to be a problem statement or a question, and the last a question. In Figure 9.8, however, we see a request for advice in final position. In "Can you get any diseases from kissing?" a young person complains about her parents, who did not approve of her kissing her boyfriend and told her that she could get diseases from doing so. The writer feels clearly upset by her parents' reason: note the adjectives *super-paranoid, krazy*, the exclamation mark and the final sentence in the problem statement, in which the writer expresses her fear that she was wrong in feeling safe. Her parents' comments clearly left the writer feeling insecure and she conveys this to *Lucy* (appealing). The resulting question is formulated with a hedge that mitigates factual content (*or anything like that*) and seeks clarification about the likelihood of catching a disease from kissing. This question is followed up by a plea for help that also contains a hedge (*please*).

The final example of an entire letter is taken from the category 'relationships', which usually features problem letters that consist of one unit with three or four discursive moves. Background information, questions and problem statements are likely to appear in first position, while questions most often end a problem letter. Figure 9.9 represents the problem letter for the record entitled "Happy Anniversary ideas". It consists of one unit with three discursive moves and a pseudonym. The writer of the problem letter in "Happy Anniversary ideas" begins by providing background information about her age and length of relationship with her

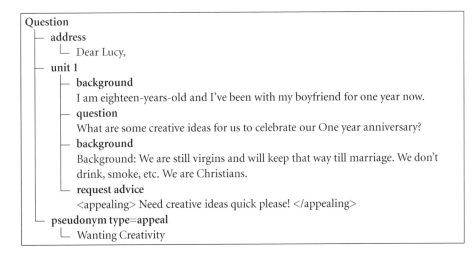

```
Question
  ├── address
  │     └── Dear Lucy,
  ├── unit 1
  │     ├── background
  │     │   I am eighteen-years-old and I've been with my boyfriend for one year now.
  │     ├── question
  │     │   What are some creative ideas for us to celebrate our One year anniversary?
  │     ├── background
  │     │   Background: We are still virgins and will keep that way till marriage. We don't
  │     │   drink, smoke, etc. We are Christians.
  │     └── request advice
  │         <appealing> Need creative ideas quick please! </appealing>
  └── pseudonym type=appeal
        └── Wanting Creativity
```

Figure 9.9 The problem letter in "Happy Anniversary ideas" (LA 1527, relationships)

boyfriend. She then asks, in a matter-of-fact way, the question of how to celebrate their first anniversary, and follows this question up with more background information. In this case the writer even marks this as *Background*. The final discursive move is a request for advice, that contains the hedge *please*. At this point, a sudden note of urgency and appeal (which was not present beforehand) enters the problem letter with the words *Need creative ideas quick please!* The pseudonym, *Wanting Creativity*, once more reinforces the appeal voiced in the request for advice.

9.7 Summarizing remarks and the links between the problem and response letters

With the same methodology I used to study the response letters (cf. Section 5.1), I developed a coding system that allowed me to analyze the content structure of the problem letters in 'Lucy Answers'. While Mininni (1991:79) identified strategies such as volunteering identity markers, stating the core question, making room for emotions, and a summarizing formulation in his study of two Italian and two British advice columns in women's magazines, the advice-seekers in 'Lucy Answers' are shown to make use of apologies, comments on previous records, compliments, explanations, metacomments, background information, problem statements, questions, requests for advice and thanks. The majority of these discursive moves are questions (n = 391, 38%), followed by background information (n = 216, 21%) and problem statements (n = 216, 21%, Table 9.7). DeCapua and Dunham (1993:524) report that advice-seekers use "explanation, elaboration, and narration" when seeking help in the radio shows investigated. The discursive move in the problem letters of the advice-seekers in 'Lucy Answers' that I have categorized as background information or problem statements can be compared to this finding, but questions are the most important discursive move in the problem letters. For each topic category I established the typical number of units, the number of discursive moves per unit, the most frequent discursive moves in all the texts, the typical sequences of discursive moves, as well as the most frequent first and last discursive moves in a problem letter. A summary of this investigation was presented in Table 9.13 above.

My discussion of relational work in the problem letters showed that appealing and hedging are the most frequently used types, and that, overall, these types of relational work are more frequently found in the topic categories of Group 2 than the other topic categories. A summary of the findings with respect to relational work can be found at the end of Section 9.4. After the discussion of the linguistic realization of the discursive moves primarily found in the problem letters of 'Lucy Answers', I presented several problem letters to illustrate how the typical features listed in Table 9.13 interact with each other. Instances of hedging and appealing, the two types of relational work used most often, were no longer looked at only in isolation but in their specific contexts as well. In general, the split of the topic categories into two groups is less pronounced in the problem letters than in the response letters. Nevertheless, a general similarity in the topic categories of the two groups could also be stated with respect to aspects of the content structure as well as relational work in the problem letters.

Now that the problem letters as well as the response letters have been discussed, I will look at the connections between them. The most obvious link is, of course, their content. In my subcorpus there is not a single answer in which *Lucy* does not respond to the advice-seeker's concerns. In some cases, the answers are rather short as when the reader is given a link to a previously answered problem. In other responses, as discussed in Chapter 7, the scope of the answer is broadened to accommodate the wider readership's needs and to fulfill the educational aims of 'Lucy Answers'. By choosing to have the question-answer exchange appear in a publicly available form on the Internet, the 'Lucy Answers' team has already demonstrated that the topic is considered relevant for its readership, and it is therefore not surprising that the topic link is also there by default.

I also examined whether there are connections between long and short problem letters and response letters, between relational work in the problem letter and relational work in the response letter, and, more particularly, whether appealing in the problem letter is matched by empathy in the response letter. The first research question has to be answered in the negative, since 90 percent or 253 of all problem letters contain only one unit anyway, while there is a range from one to seven units per response letter (256 answers, or 91%, Table 5.3).

Table 9.23 Cross tabulation of appealing in problem letter and empathizing in response letter (appealing > 0)|(empathizing > 0)

	no empathizing in response	empathizing in response	total
no appealing in problem letter	127	36	163
appealing in problem letter	46	71	117
total	173	107	280

$Chi^2 = 42.97623$ d.f. = 1 (p = 5.540901e-011)

The second question is whether relational work in the problem letters triggers relational work in the responses. This question has to be answered in the negative both for the entire subcorpus as well as for the individual topic categories. It should be pointed out, however, that the numbers for relational work categories do not include the syntactic information gained about hedging in the analysis of the advisory moves. However, if we specifically investigate whether an appeal in the problem letter triggers empathy in the response letter, a different picture emerges. Table 9.23 shows the number of records in which the problem letter contains (or does not contain) an appeal and the number of records in which the response letter contains (or does not contain) empathy. In 198 records (127 + 71) there is a match of 'no appealing and no empathizing' and 'appealing and empathizing', while there is no correlation in only 82 records.

The individual categories show a significant correlation for 'emotional health' and 'sexuality', but not for 'relationships'. In the more factually oriented group of topic categories, only in 'general health' is appealing matched with empathizing in a significant way. This may be because appealing is so rare in the problem letters in this category that the 'Lucy Answers' team considers empathy an appropriate response.

Gough and Talbot (1996) report that the "[p]roblem page letters and replies contain conventional activity-structures such as the Request – Reason for Request and constitute a generic activity-type". In Section 9.5.2, I reported that there are only four problem letters that do not contain a question or a specific request for advice. In these four cases, problem statements take over the function of indirectly requesting advice. These rare instances can be said to correspond to what Heritage and Sefi (1992: 372) have classified as the description of a problematic state of affairs in order to trigger advice. This examination of the content structure of the problem letters in 'Lucy Answers' has shown that the texts of the advice-seekers correspond to the format of an advice column or a question-answer service. Thus, the advice-seekers can be said to participate along with the advisor team in the construction of this genre.

PART IV

CHAPTER 10

Factors constituting the discursive practice in 'Lucy Answers'

In the literature review for this study I quoted Leppänen (1998:210), who maintains that "the study of advice should both carefully explicate the details of the production of advice and show how these details are systematic products of the interactants' orientations to specific features of the institutions". It is thus important to look for patterns of advice-giving and to discuss the reasons for the choices made by the advice-seekers and advice-givers. These features that constitute advice-giving can then be compared to the variety of advice-giving reported on in the literature. In the preceding chapters, I have identified and discussed some of the constituting features that are of importance for 'Lucy Answers', and I have demonstrated how the interactants in this particular discursive practice jointly construct the genre of an advice column and together create its meaning. I refer readers to the summary sections of the individual chapters for detailed results of this study and for comparisons to the studies on advice used as background for this project. In what follows, I will recapitulate the main points that emerged in my analysis of 'Lucy Answers' and will connect them to as complete a picture of this discursive practice as possible within the frame of the present study.

'Lucy Answers' belongs to the genre of written advice columns and to the advisory discourse of expert health care on the Internet. The following factors emerged as those constituting this site's practice and shaping its discourse:

- The content and mission of 'Lucy Answers'
- The appeal of anonymity for the advice-seekers
- The archive as a source of information
- The declared ideal of non-directiveness
- The need for an attractive advisor voice to appeal to the target readership
- The orientation to the format of an advice column
- The restriction to only 'one turn' for the advice-seeker and the advice-givers
- Constant awareness of the public readership in the composition of the response letters
- Topic sensitivity

These factors work together to influence what is posted on the site. They are closely connected and it would also have been possible to arrange them in a different sequence. The one chosen here begins with the more general factors and then proceeds to those that have an immediate impact on the content and the language used. I will discuss them in turn.

The content and mission of 'Lucy Answers'. The first important observation is that 'Lucy Answers' belongs to a health education program that is part of the health services of an educational institution. This means that it is bound by the clear mandate of this organization. There is a mission statement that can be read if the hyperlink 'about Lucy Answers' is clicked on. That statement describes both the content and the way in which this content should be imparted:

> [The LA mission is] to increase access to, and use of, health information by providing factual, in-depth, straight-forward, and nonjudgmental information to assist readers' decision-making about their physical, sexual, emotional, and spiritual health.   (Lucy Answers 2004)

Since the interactional power of decision about what kind of questions will be responded to lies with the producers of 'Lucy Answers' (cf. Thibault 1988 on advice columns in general), it follows that only requests for advice that are within its topic scope receive attention. The mission statement also defines the way in which these answers ought to be formulated. I will comment on this further below.

The Internet advice column must be seen as a complement to the other services offered by the health education program. The choice to make it publicly available on the Internet makes use of the target audience's familiarity with this communication medium and its availability on campus or via home computers. The text type of a question-answer service or of an advice column is also one known to the readership from the print media or from other Internet forums. By publishing genuine requests for help from the target audience, the 'Lucy Answers' team invites the readership to identify with the advice-seekers (Franke 1997). One of the appeals of such an advice column is therefore that personalized advice is offered in such a way that more than just the original advice-seeker can benefit from the advice offered. Two further advantages of 'Lucy Answers' are that this advice is also stored and easily accessible in the archives of the site and that there is the guarantee of anonymity for the advice-seekers.

The appeal of anonymity for the advice-seekers. It is not possible for the 'Lucy Answers' team to contact the advice-seekers since they are entirely anonymous. The guarantee of anonymity may be one of the reasons why the readers turn to 'Lucy Answers', after the genuine need for advice and the desire for the entertainment the site offers. The site was conceived as an addition to the existing health care services provided at AEI. It offers a possibility of obtaining information and help to target students who may be too afraid to approach the health services in person because they are embarrassed to talk about their concerns. This may be especially true for students with questions about delicate taboo issues in the categories 'sexuality' and 'sexual health', but also for students with difficult emotional or relationship problems, or those with dilemmas in the category 'drugs', who may be insecure about legality or dangerous side effects. The attraction of anonymity in advice columns is stressed by Van Roosmalen (2000:205), who points out that problem pages are "forums for the unspeakable", and Alexander (2003:548), who sees fears and embarrassment about health issues as the reason men turn to the anonymous advice column in *Men's Health*. The anonymity guaranteed by 'Lucy Answers' is bound to reduce the advice-seeker's inhibition to submit questions about touchy issues to the expert advisor team. At the same time, the public availability of the problem and response letters enables a large number of people to access the site's information without asking questions themselves. The anonymity thus not only facilitates the posting of questions to advice-seekers but allows the far greater number of people who do not contribute actively to the site to comfortably search for solutions to their problems.

The archive as a source of information. 'Lucy Answers' is not just an advice column such as those which can be found in weekly or monthly newspaper print media. Its purpose is to educate and to offer an easily accessible source of information for the target audience. The latter aspect is achieved by making available in an archive all the letter exchanges that appeared in the past. This collection is organized into seven topic categories and can be searched with keywords. The archive is conceived as an integral part of the site's practice, since advice-seekers are encouraged to consult the archive first before submitting a question to 'Lucy Answers'. As a consequence, the responses have to be checked regularly to ensure that they still meet the quality standards. The archive demonstrates most clearly that the discursive practice 'Lucy Answers' is influenced by its being published on the Internet. My analysis of the updated response letters in the archive in Chapter 7 has shown that not only are certain stylistic changes (e.g., with respect to *Lucy*'s voice) made, but there are also changes in content. The latter partly consist of updates of information. In addition, the existence of previously published response letters also influences the way in which the new answers are composed, in that they may be expanded or shortened as a consequence. The history of the site, present and available in the response letters already published, thus influences the manner in which the old response letters are updated and the way in which the new responses are composed. The archives are thus an ever-growing and ever-changing corpus of question-answer exchanges without which 'Lucy Answers' would not be able to offer the wealth of advice or cover the range of problems that it presently does.

The declared ideal of non-directiveness. The site's declared ideal of non-directiveness, which is stated in the mission statement quoted above, clearly influences how advice is given. As I have shown in Chapters 5 and 6, this ideal results in linguistic realizations of advice that are often mitigated to indicate that it is the responsibility of the readers to decide whether or not to adopt the advice. This mitigation is achieved by the syntactic form of the advisory moves (interrogatives and declaratives are considered more mitigated than imperatives[1]) and additional lexical hedges. Moreover, the interpretations of the advice-seekers' situation in the assessment sections or the rendition of general information are used to point out for whom the ensuing advice is relevant. This means that advice is rarely just offered on its own, but is embedded in the overall composition of the response texts. Thus, a 'stepwise entry' to advice, as witnessed, for example, by Heritage and Sefi (1992) in their interactional face-to-face data, can also be observed in the composition of the response letters in 'Lucy Answers.'

The ideal of non-directiveness is also followed in other advisory contexts, such as student or health care risks counseling. He (1994), Sarangi and Clarke (2002), and Vehviläinen (2001, 2003) focus on the particular dilemma of counselors who are told to be non-directive by their institutions, while at the same time they are asked by the counselees to share their (personal) opinions. In 'Lucy Answers' this dilemma is less pronounced since the format of only 'one turn' each (only one problem letter and only one response letter) means that issues cannot be jointly developed as they can in face-to-face advisory contexts, in which questions may come up that the counselors have to fend off. Since the response text is created asynchronically, there is time to carefully construct and design it in such a way as to guide the readership in a non-directive manner. This non-directive manner, however, does not mean that the content of advice is ambiguous. The messages of the individual responses are in fact quite clear, but are packaged in such a way that the reader gets the impression that the decision to take the advice is up to him or her.

The need for an attractive advisor voice to appeal to the target readership. The decision to maintain a question-answer service in addition to the other services of the health education program clearly also involves consideration as to how expert advice should be given there. The voice of the advisor is important since the way in which advice is imparted may affect its reception by the target readership. The 'Lucy Answers' team decided to use the fictional advisor persona *Lucy* as their mouthpiece. This decision places this online advice column in the well-established American tradition of print advice columns with female advisors. In Chapter 8, I have analyzed how the strategies for advice-giving discussed in Chapters 5 to 7 contribute to *Lucy*'s voice. I have shown that *Lucy* is constructed as a well-informed, trustworthy, and reliable expert advisor, who uses an appropriate level of not too scientific and not too informal vocabulary, who possesses a sense of humor, and who takes the problems of her readers seriously by showing support and empathy. The tone in which advice is given in 'Lucy Answers' is established by showing an awareness of the face-threatening aspect of advice by means of mitigation, by the involvement strategies (empathizing, bonding, praising, the use of humor) which are used to create rapport with the readership, and by the face-threatening strategies (boosting and criticizing). The advisor team thus manage to strike a balance between stressing their expertise when they offer help and writing in such a way that the advisor persona emerges as an approachable 'person' whom the students can trust and turn to. The weekly intake of almost 2,000 inquiries proves that they are successful in this endeavor.

The orientation to the format of an advice column. 'Lucy Answers' declares itself to be a "health Q&A Internet site". Investigating the 'questions' and 'answers', we find that they are formulated in the form of letters, just as in many traditional print advice columns. If we look in more detail at the problem letters, we can say that interrogatives are indeed the means most frequently used to ask for advice. Explicit requests for advice in the form of statements are much rarer, and only four of the 280 problem letters do not contain a question or a request for advice at all. My analysis of the response letters has shown that they not only include information giving but also advice. The fact that there are only four response letters in which there is no advice or referral move to be found suggests that this question and answer health service aims at giving advice and not just at providing information. This makes 'Lucy Answers' an advice column not only in format but also in content. By adhering to the format of advice columns, both the advice-seekers and the advisor team construct this genre of interaction. (It should be stressed, however, that the advisor team is the more powerful partner in this interaction since they decide which problem letters to answer and publish.)

The restriction to only 'one turn' for the advice-seeker and the advice-givers. The fact that there is only 'one turn' for the advice-seekers and the advisors represents an important constraint on the creation of the texts. The advice-seekers are often quite sparing in the amount of background information that they reveal and offer only very short presentations of problems. In a face-to-face counseling situation, clarifications can be requested with follow-up questions. In the case of an advice column, however, the responses are often created on the basis of very little background information. This means that the 'Lucy Answers' team has to make up for this lack when composing their answers by providing interpretations of the advice-seeker's situation to make advice relevant. These interpretations are offered mainly in the assessment sections, but also in the advisory moves when conditional clauses specify for which case the ensuing advice is relevant, or when questions are employed to engage the reader in thinking about his or her particular situation. By offering these interpretations (often in a hedged form) the advisor team thus leaves it to the reader to establish for him- or herself how relevant the advice is. Since in the majority of cases the response letters adhere to the format of overtly addressing only the original advice-seeker, the format of a letter exchange transpires as a form of mitigation itself, as members of the wider readership can always claim not to be the intended recipients of the particular messages conveyed.

The creation of the problem and response letters is thus clearly influenced by the fact that there is only 'one turn' for both parties. However, it is important to stress the Internet specificity of 'Lucy Answers'. The Internet allows this discursive practice to expand beyond the 'one turn' in two ways. First, the 'Lucy Answers' team composes its responses in close consideration of the response letters already published in the archive and also refers the reader to these prior texts, which are only a mouse click away. The 'communication' with a particular advice-seeker thus does not necessarily end with the completion of the reading process of one particular question-answer sequence. Second, the advice-seeker is also invited to comment on a response. However, such reader responses only appear as a hyperlink outside of the frame of the actual question-answer sequence (cf. Figure 2.3) and are only rarely made use of and reacted to by *Lucy* (see below). In this way, the limit of 'one turn' does hold.

Constant awareness of the public readership in the composition of the response letters. The published question-answer pairs are of course not meant to reach just the original advice-seeker. The site's declared mission and its role as part of a health education program are clearly communicated. In Chapter 7 I demonstrated that the choice of a 'personalized' letter exchange that aims at reaching a wider readership has consequences for the composition of the response letters. In general, the format of a 'personal' reply to an advice-seeker is upheld, but there are strategies employed to ensure that the primary goal is reached, i.e., to be as relevant to as large a number of the target students as possible. The first of these strategies is the choice of which problem letter to answer. Others consist in designing the hyperlinked titles as teasers, broadening the scope of the answer, and, in a few rare cases, addressing the wider readership directly. Evaluations of the questioner's attitudes and actions, and the display of awareness of and support for the questioner's situation demonstrate to the wider readership that the advice-seeker's problem is important. The letter exchange thus offers advice and information to the target readership by means of a personalized reply to the genuine request of one of their (assumed) peers.

Topic sensitivity. Many of the issues discussed in 'Lucy Answers' are of a sensitive nature. This has an influence on how the response letters are designed. The way the content is presented in the topic categories 'general health', 'sexual health', 'fitness and nutrition' and 'drugs' (Group 1) differs from the manner adopted in the categories 'emotional health', 'relationships' and 'sexuality' (Group 2). There are more assessment and advice sections in Group 2 than in Group 1, which in contrast contains more general information. The sensitive and personal nature of the interpersonal problems raised in Group 2 thus call for more interpretation (assessments), while the more fact-centered problems in Group 1 trigger the giving of more information. The analysis in Chapter 6 showed that the categories 'emotional health' and 'relationships' also form a group with respect to relational work, since they feature more empathy and hedging than the other categories. This can be explained by their need to address sensitive issues. It was argued that the topic category 'sexuality' uses empathy to a smaller degree as a way of avoiding embarrassment for the advice-seeker.

Concluding comments. In Chapter 4, I presented the questions that I developed out of the study of the literature on advice-giving and through analyzing the records in 'Lucy Answers'. In the analysis chapters I then offered answers to this list of questions. These have been summarized in this chapter. I would like at this point to make a few comments on methodology since my approach was both a qualitative and a quantitative one. After assessing the individual problem and response letters in the pilot study phase (Locher & Hoffmann 2003), I found it necessary to develop a schema which would allow a systematic investigation of the individual texts. Using specifically Miller and Gergen's (1998) study, but also other studies on advice that are interested in interactional sequences, I settled on the concept of 'discursive move' to identify the typical content structures and the aspects of relational work in both the problem and response letters. This means that I not only used close readings to analyze each individual text qualitatively, but that the systematic methodology I employed allowed me to later carry out a comparison of the 280 chosen records (40 in each topic category). The resulting quantitative analysis gives far more support to my argument that there is a frequent division of the topic categories into two groups and my statements about the linguistic realizations I found. The discussions of my results in Chapters 5 and 6 then formed the backbone for the more qualitative considerations in Chapters 7 and 8. In Chapter 9 I once more employed qualitative and quantitative methods for analysis. The methodology used and the number of records analyzed resulted in a thorough description of the discursive practice in 'Lucy Answers'.

Just as I have adjusted the catalogue of discursive moves from Miller and Gergen (1998) to suit the 'Lucy Answers' data, it will be necessary for other researchers to develop their own set of discursive moves for their own data. The reason for this is that the categories proposed in my framework were developed out of the data itself. Therefore it may well be that other data, especially if it has a different interactional frame, will require other categories of discursive moves to capture the discursive practice at hand adequately. I still hope, however, that the manner in which this study was carried out may serve as an example for others.

Since my main aim in this study has been to contribute to the understanding of expert advice-giving, in my analysis I have concentrated first on the expert advice in the response letters and second on the construction of the problem letters. However, 'Lucy Answers' also offers its readers the opportunity to react to the advice given. At the beginning of the site's history, such reactions were only accessible by clicking on a hyperlink that was not very noticeable. After the latest redesign of the site's layout which occurred after my data collection, this option is presented in a more prominent place and previous reactions are thus more easily accessible than before (cf. Chapter 2). In 2004, however, there were only 446 individual responses to 257 records. This is a small number if one considers that, in theory, all of the 2,286 records could have triggered a response. It remains to be seen whether this number will increase and whether peer advice will take on a more important role in 'Lucy Answers'. This is clearly a project for future research that is worth pursuing.

As a final point, I would like to return to the notion of Community of Practice, which I introduced in Chapter 3, and explain why I consider 'Lucy Answers' to constitute one. Meyerhoff (2002: 527–528) reports three criteria taken from Wenger (1998) which, if fulfilled, are essential constituents of a Community of Practice:

1. "mutual engagement of the members",
2. "some jointly negotiated enterprise", and
3. "the members' shared repertoire"

(Meyerhoff 2002: 527–528; emphasis removed)

All three points can be shown to be true for 'Lucy Answers'. There clearly is mutual engagement of its members in the sense that they 'get together', not in a physical space but in a space on the Internet that is reserved for their jointly negotiated enterprise. This enterprise can be described as seeking and receiving advice for a clearly defined set of topics. I have also shown that the participants involved in the social practice 'Lucy Answers' work together to construct this site by participating in the genre of advice columns and together use a particular repertoire which I identified in my discussions.

That 'Lucy Answers' fulfills the criteria of points 2 and 3 may not be controversial; the argument that it fulfills point 1 perhaps requires some more elaboration. The individuals who access 'Lucy Answers', who read the previously posted problem and response letters, and who may become letter writers themselves do not know each other in the same sense as members of face-to-face Communities of Practice. There is, in fact, no way to establish whether the 'Lucy Answers' community is always composed of the same individuals or whether its composition is constantly changing. People frequenting this site, however, have a common interest and may share problems and concerns. The format of 'Lucy Answers' allows them to identify with other advice-seekers and to access the 'history' of the site by means of the archive. The members therefore know of each other in the sense that together they form a group of people who ask *Lucy* for advice about mutual concerns. Their choice to use a publicly accessible forum instead of, for example, personal and private counseling sessions indicates their willingness to be part of a community of advice-seekers. The team of advisors, as I have shown in Chapter 8, emerges as adopting a particular voice with which they address their target readership. This contributes to the participants' feeling that they are addressing someone they know, whether people respond to *Lucy* as a 'person' or as the team behind her. A Community of Practice is thus not necessarily restricted to forms of interaction in which members meet face-to-face, know each other personally and interact synchronically. My study thus suggests that the notion of Community of Practice can be successfully applied to asynchronic and written forms of communication as well.

I chose to analyze 'Lucy Answers' because of its popularity among the professionally managed health care sites on the Internet. This study has explored how 'Lucy Answers' imparts advice to its target audience of young American students through a service that functions as a supplement to already existing ways of offering advice on campus. I hope that my analysis has contributed to the understanding of how this Community of Practice functions and, more broadly, that it will contribute to the literature on advice-giving. I also hope that I have been able to awaken readers' interest in the topic of advice and that my work will encourage more studies of discursive practices similar to 'Lucy Answers', and studies of other ways advice is given such as peer-to-peer counseling. Advice is such an integral part of our daily lives in so many different contexts that it merits further investigation.

Notes

Chapter 1

* This study was accepted as a post-doctoral thesis ('Habilitationsschrift') by the Faculty of Arts of the University of Berne in the winter semester 2005/2006 on the recommendation of Prof. Dr. Richard J. Watts, Prof. Dr. Elke Hentschel, Prof. Dr. Bruno Moretti, Prof. Dr. Peter Trudgill and Prof. Dr. Sandra Harris.

1. At the request of the Internet site in question, I have changed the names of the site and the institution that produces it, as well as used a pseudonym for the team of advisors. (The questioners who write to 'Lucy Answers' are already anonymized.) Any correspondence to possible Internet sites that may happen to be called 'Lucy Answers' or that sound similar is unintentional. At this point, I also wish to express once more my gratitude to 'Lucy Answers' for allowing me to research the language used on their site.

2. The terms 'question' and 'answer' for the problem and response letters are taken over from the site's practice of referring to questions and answers (Q&A). With the same reasoning I also use the terms 'advice-seeker' and 'questioner' interchangeably, without wishing to imply that advice-seekers use only the syntactic form of interrogatives when they ask for advice.

3. Hernández-Flores (1999:42) reports that advice has positive connotations in Spanish colloquial conversation and is not necessarily face-threatening. Hinkel (1994, 1997) also maintains that the topics on which it is appropriate to give advice differ from culture to culture. How advice is valued and what function it is assigned in everyday interaction is thus bound to differ from culture to culture. Wierzbicka (1985), for example, reports different realizations, functions and perceptions of advice for English and Polish interactants.

4. See Section 6.1 for a definition of the concepts 'face' and 'face-threatening'.

Chapter 3

1. The total is not 260 (10 times 26) because some answers were counted in more than one category.

2. *The Athenian Mercury* can now also be visited online (*AthenianMercury* 1 September 2000).

3. "Wenn jemand/man (HS) einen bestimmten Zustand herbeiführen will (HZ), dann kann/sollte (HMOD) er/man die Handlung/Handlungsabfolge (H/HA) ausführen" (Franke 1997: 194).

4. There are some (online) advice columns, such as 'Dear Abby' and also 'Lucy Answers', that allow for a limited kind of interaction between their readers in the reader response sections.

5. Santhakumaran (2004) observes in her questionnaire data of British female readers of women's magazines that reading the advice sections in a group rather than on one's own is a common practice.

Chapter 4

1. Recall that Franke looks at the dialogic form of the presentation of advice merely as one variant of advisory texts that could also be rendered in a different form. The dialogic presentation, however, offers the possibility for the reader to identify with the advice-seeker (Franke 1997:226).

Chapter 5

1. The terms 'Question' and 'Answer' to denote the problem and response letters are adopted from the site's practice of referring to these as questions and answers (Q&A). With the same reasoning I also use the terms advice-seeker and questioner interchangeably, without wishing to imply that advice-seekers use only the syntactic form of interrogatives to ask for advice. Since I focus on the responses in this chapter, there is no danger of confusing the main Question with a particular syntactic question and I will therefore use question and answer without capitals to refer to the problem and response letters. In general, however, I will prefer the latter terms.

2. In the example *You might also want to* I focus on the personal pronoun and the modal verb as agentive. I am aware of the fact that *want* never has an agentive subject since it is thematic (Watts, personal communication). For my analysis here, I consider it as a hedge. The use of the modal *might* is also considered as a hedge, as will be explained in Chapter 6.

3. Extraposition of a clausal subject means that the original sentence structure 'subject + predicate' is changed into '*it* + predicate + subject' (cf. Quirk et al. 1985:1391–1392; Biber et al. 1999:155). In the case of *it's time to leave*, however, such a restructuring is impossible.

4. In this record *Lucy* answers a reader who wonders *Is it true that a man's erect penis size can be predicted by dividing his shoe size in half?* The answer is a clear *Certainly not – no more than big hands and a big nose mean anything more than large gloves and extra room to store boogers.* This was categorized as assessment, while the next move did not fit any of the other discursive moves and thus received the label 'open category' (*If there's research out there based on something other than fantasy, which counters this declaration, please pass it along*). Their usage will be discussed in Section 5.3.2.

5. The remaining instances are the rendition of entire poems which are copied into *Lucy's* response.

6. There is, however, the possibility for any reader of 'Lucy Answers' to respond to any given Q&A record by using the reader response function. These contributions are only hyperlinked and do not appear together with the actual question and response letters on the screen. It is clear that this possibility is not taken advantage of very often as there are only 446 contributions, while there are 2,286 question-answer pairs that could have triggered a response.

7. In all topic categories the sequences of advice-advice and advice-explanation are even more frequent (cf. Section 5.2.4)

Chapter 6

1. For references on the face-threatening character of advice-giving in the Anglo-Western context see the introduction and Section 4.2.

2. The interpretation of whether something was, for example, meant to be humorous, followed by an analysis of what kind of function humor has in the context given, is by definition debatable. Judgments about relational work will always rely on the values and norms of the individual who reads and interprets the text. People who share similar values and norms *may* arrive at similar interpretations, but since these concepts are discursive by nature, i.e., since they are continually in flux and shaped by members of a society rather than static and carved in stone, judgments are bound to vary.

3. I have decided against incorporating this information into Table 6.4 so as to avoid giving the impression that relational work can be numerically added up in a straightforward way. I will comment on the more indirect syntactic realizations of advice and also on the use of modals in Section 6.3.1 on hedging.

4. Please note, however, that I have said nothing about whether these realizations are more or less polite. The level of indirectness *per se* does not allow any conclusions of this kind (cf. Locher 2004; Locher & Watts 2005). In the case of 'Lucy Answers' the fact that 36 percent of the advisory discursive moves are realized in the syntactic form of imperatives tells us that they are part of the norm of advice-giving established in this discursive practice and should not be regarded as inappropriate.

5. *You need to, you must* and the combination with the semi-auxiliary *you have to* are counted as boosting in the context of 'Lucy Answers' since their force emphasizes urgency rather than mitigation of the face-threatening act. The other modals were regarded as instances of hedging in the appropriate contexts.

6. Since I only established the *occurrence* of relational work rather than the number of words realizing these instances, I cannot take the overall number of words per topic category or per discursive move as a point of reference. Nor can I use the number of units or discursive moves because the relational work types tagged can appear more than just once in a discursive move. The overall appearance of the relational work moves analyzed can still be compared since the number of response letters is the same for each topic category.

7. See Note 5 in Chapter 6.

8. By absence of limitations, MacGeorge et al. (2004:46) mean that "policy advocates must also . . . show that the drawbacks of the policy are not too severe or numerous".

Chapter 7

1. It is, of course, also conceivable that staffing and time problems are the primary reasons to re-use previous records. The choice of records will still, however, be guided by their usefulness to the readers.

2. 'Lucy Answers' is not an emergency or instant response service and can also not directly contact its advice-seekers. As pointed out in Chapter 2, the site has a disclaimer on the main entry page to refer readers in urgent situations to other support services.

3. In *Lucy*'s words swing clubs "are businesses that provide an environment for partners to have sex with each other, with someone else, with many people, with partner swapping, and even have solo sex" (LA 831, sexuality, "More on commercial party houses").

4. "Obviously, a swing club is an environment where it would be easy to pass and receive sexually transmitted diseases, such as herpes or HIV. Condoms are available at many of the clubs, but it is difficult to say how careful the clients are with protection" (2002, LA 831) **is changed to** "Because a visitor may have sex with several partners and not know each partner's sexual history, a swing club provides an environment where it's easy to pass and receive sexually transmitted infections (STIs), such as herpes or HIV. Condoms are available at many clubs, but it is difficult to say how careful and consistent guests are with using protection. Of course, participants are not eager to get or give an STI, so many are careful about their health" (2004, LA 831).

Chapter 8

* Many thanks to Sebastian Hoffmann who worked with me on this topic in the pilot study phase of this research project (Locher & Hoffmann 2003), and to whom I am indebted for the comparisons with the BNC data in this chapter. I published an earlier version of this chapter together with Sebastian Hoffmann in *Text and Talk* in 2006. My thanks also go to the anonymous referees whose helpful and constructive comments contributed to strengthening this chapter/paper's line of argumentation.

1. This statement appears not to be true of some current television and radio shows where the hosts take on the role of a 'relentless tormentor' of their guests. It is safe to assume that these shows do not represent genuine advice exchanges. Instead, the conventional format is diverted from its intended function to satisfy the voyeuristic demands of the audience.

2. In this sense, associations evoked by the name *Lucy* that might tap into the cultural world of post-60s young adults are supported.

3. These numbers include double counting of relational work combinations, such as empathizing-hedging.

4. That *Lucy* is treated as if she were alive can be seen time and again in the reader responses, in which the writers address, praise, criticize and defend *Lucy* (e.g., *Hi Lucy, have been reading your post for years now. I feel as if you are one very close friend of mine that I can talk about anything with*). While it is not possible to establish whether these commentators believe in *Lucy* as a real person, it is safe to say that their comments contribute to the construction of *Lucy* as a 'person'.

5. It is rare for 'Lucy Answers' to publish more than one question in sequence in one record. In this specific record *Lucy* pays tribute to the concern which many readers voiced and reflects this by listing several questions.

6. The Studentcenter in its 'Teenadvice' section offers informal non-professional peer counseling and claims to have no official mission other than to offer help to fellow teenagers. This makes this site very different from 'Lucy Answers' which strives to provide researched quality information.

7. In order to compile these lists, the EngCG tagger was used to automatically annotate the responses in 'Lucy Answers' with part-of-speech tags. See Voutilainen (2004) for further information on the EngCG tagger. Many thanks to Sebastian Hoffmann for his help in this vocabulary analysis.

8. Since the BNC contains almost exclusively British English, a direct comparison with 'Lucy Answers' raises some methodological problems. However, apart from having to account for obvious differences in spelling, the impact of comparing data from two different varieties of English was deemed to be negligible for the present purposes.

9. See Dunning (1993) for further information about the log-likelihood ratio and Leech et al. (2001) for its application on the basis of data from the BNC.

10. The twenty most distinctive verbs (disregarding the modals and auxiliary verbs) are: *help, cause, feel, try, need, talk, check, call, experience, eat, use, make, causes, masturbate, ask, get, might, want, include, prevent*. The twenty most distinctive adjectives are: *dear, sexual, vaginal, healthy, genital, oral, menstrual, contraceptive, anal, medical, over-the-counter, psychological, pregnant, pubic, allergic, physical, comfortable, pelvic, cervical, safe*. The twenty most distinctive adverbs are: *sexually, also, usually, how, often, more, likely, maybe, sometimes, commonly, typically, especially, physically, probably, when, medically, while, daily, longer, possibly*.

11. Consider Hendley (1977:345), who maintains that from their first appearance English advice columns were immediately successful because this format is 'naturally appealing' for two reasons: people need advice and are curious and nosy by nature (cf. Chapter 3).

Chapter 9

1. By submittal information I mean the hidden script that may lead back to the user's computer. Advice-seekers are not asked to supply any information about themselves.

2. See Note 1 in Chapter 5.

3. See Note 6 in Chapter 6 for a comment on why a straightforward normalization of these numbers is not possible.

4. There are thirteen cases of questions that address *Lucy*, but which are not considered to be hedged (for example, *do you know where I can get a copy?* (LA 574)) since they do not show any face-saving considerations.

Chapter 10

1. See Note 4 in Chapter 6.

Appendix

Sample of an XML file

"Anxiety attacks from moving … again" (LA 1245, emotional health)
<?xml version="1.0" encoding="UTF-8"?>
<LA xmlns:xsi="http://www.w3.org/2001/XMLSchema-instance"
xsi:noNamespaceSchemaLocation="file:/E:/Miriam/Lucy%20Data%202004/XML/LA.xsd"
category="emotHealth" record="1245">
<questionM>
    <address> Dear Lucy, </address>
    <unit>
        <problemStatement> The last week or so I've been having anxiety attacks <hedging> or at least that's what I think they are. </hedging> I've been tossing and turning at night. </problemStatement>
        <background> We have just moved, which isn't unusual. My husband's job moves us around a lot. I've never had this problem before and <appealing> I'm starting to get worried.</appealing></background>
        <question> Should I see a doctor? </question>
    </unit>
    <pseudonym type="appeal"> Worried </pseudonym>
</questionM>
<answer>
    <address> Dear Worried, </address>
    <unit>
        <assessment><empathizing> It's not at all uncommon to experience some degree of anxiety when you move, change jobs, graduate, get married, etc. – even if these big life events are positive ones. </empathizing></assessment>
        <referral type="decl"> If change-related angst continues well after you've settled into your new situation, then you might consider a visit to your doctor or a counselor. </referral>
        <explanation type="referral"> Your poor sleep <hedging> may be </hedging> a normal stress-related symptom, not anxiety attacks which are usually characterized by heart palpitations, difficulty breathing, fear, a need to escape, and feelings of impending doom. Health care providers can be very helpful if or when concerns and worries (including frequent moves) impair your regular routine: sleep; work; studying; etc. </explanation>
        <referral type="imp-a"><empathizing> But, if a trip to the doctor now would help rest your mind and body, then make that appointment. </empathizing></referral>
    </unit>

```
<unit>
     <referral type="imp-a"> For more info about anxiety, browse these websites and/or
     call these hotlines: Anxiety-Panic Internet Resource – National Mental Health
     Association – Anxiety Disorders Association of America – The National Institute of
     Mental Health (NIMH) – NIMH Anxiety Information Line – (xxx)-x-ANXIETY /
     -xxx-xxxx – NIMH Panic Information Line – (xxx)-xx-PANIC / -xxx-xxxx
     </referral>
</unit>
<signature> Lucy </signature>
</answer>
</LA>
```

References

Adelswärd, Viveka, & Nilholm, Claes (2000). "Who is Cindy? Aspects of identity work in a teacher-parent-pupil talk at a special school." *Text, 20*, 545–568.

Aijmer, Karin (1986). "Discourse variation and hedging." In Jan Aarts & Willem Meijs (Eds.), *Corpus Linguistics II. New Studies in the Analysis and Exploitation of Computer Corpora* (pp. 1–18). Amsterdam: Rodopi.

Alexander, Susan M. (2003). "Stylish hard bodies: Branded masculinity in *Men's Health* magazine." *Sociological Perspectives, 46*, 535–554.

Aston, Guy, & Burnard, Lou (1998). *The BNC Handbook. Exploring the British National Corpus with SARA*. Edinburgh Textbooks in Empirical Linguistics. Edinburgh: Edinburgh University Press.

Athenian Mercury. 1 September 2000. Nulton Kemmerer, Kathleen (Ed.). Available: http://www. hn.psu.edu/faculty/kkemmerer/18thc/periodicals/mercury1.htm [2004, 16 February].

Bakhtin, M. (1981). *The Dialogic Imagination: Four Essays*. Austin: University of Texas Press.

Biber, Douglas, Johansson, Stig, Leech, Geoffrey, Conrad, Susan, & Finegan, Ed (Eds.). (1999). *Longman Grammar of Spoken and Written English*. Harlow: Longman.

Bresnahan, Mary (1992). "The effects of advisor style on overcoming client resistance in the advising interview." *Discourse Processes, 15*, 229–247.

Brown, Penelope, & Levinson, Stephen C. (1987). *Politeness. Some Universals in Language Usage*. Cambridge: Cambridge University Press. [1978]

Bulcaen, Chris (1997). "Discourses and counselling: HIV counselling as social interaction." *Pragmatics, 7*, 648–649.

Collins Concise Dictionary Plus (1989). London and Glasgow: Bath Press.

Currie, Dawn (2001). "Dear Abby: Advice pages as a site for the operation of power." *Feminist Theory, 2*, 259–281.

Davies, B., & Harré, R. (1990). "Positioning: The social construction of self." *Journal for the Theory of Social Behavior, 20*, 43–63.

De Fina, Anna (2003). *Identity in Narrative. A Study of Immigrant Discourse*. Amsterdam: John Benjamins.

DeCapua, Andrea, & Dunham, Joan Findlay (1993). "Strategies in the discourse of advice." *Journal of Pragmatics, 20*, 519–531.

DeCapua, Andrea, & Huber, Lisa (1995). "'If I Were You …': Advice in American English." *Multilingua, 14*, 117–132.

Duke, L. L., & Kreshel, P. J. (1998). "Negotiating femininity: Girls in early adolescence read teen magazines." *Journal of Communication Inquiry, 22*, 48–71.

Dunning, Ted (1993). "Accurate methods for the statistics of surprise and coincidence." *Computational Linguistics, 19*, 61–74.

Durkheim, Emile (1915). *The Elementary Forms of the Religious Life*. London: G. Allen & Unwin.

Eckert, Penelope, & McConnell-Ginet, Sally (1992a). "Think practically and act locally: Language and gender as community-based practice." *Annual Review of Anthropology, 21,* 461–490.

Eckert, Penelope, & McConnell-Ginet, Sally (1992b). "Communities of practice: Where language, gender, and power all live." In Kira Hall, Mary Bucholtz, & Birch Moonwomon (Eds.), *Locating Power. Proceedings of the Second Berkeley Women and Language Conference* (pp. 89–99). Berkeley, CA: Women and Language Group.

Erickson, Frederick, & Shultz, Jeffrey (1982). *The Counselor as Gatekeeper: Social Interaction in Interviews.* New York: Academic Press.

Fairclough, Norman, & Mauranen, Anna (1997). "The conversationalisation of political discourse. A comparative view." In Jan Blommaert & Chris Bulcaen (Eds.), *Political linguistics* (pp. 89–119). Amsterdam: John Benjamins.

Fleischhacker, Andrea M. (1987). *Zeitschriftenberatung in 'Lebensfragen'. Textanalyse unter pragmatischen Gesichtspunkten.* Münster: Magisterarbeit.

Franke, Wilhelm (1996). "Ratgebende Aufklärungstexte. Überlegungen zur linguistischen Beschreibung ratgebender Beiträge der Massenmedien." *Zeitschrift für Germanistische Linguistik, 24,* 249–272.

Franke, Wilhelm (1997). *Massenmediale Aufklärung eine sprachwissenschaftliche Untersuchung zu ratgebenden Beiträgen von elektronischen und Printmedien.* Bern: Lang.

Gaik, Frank (1992). "Radio talk-show therapy and the pragmatics of possible worlds." In Alessandro Duranti & Charles Goodwin (Eds.), *Rethinking Context. Language as an Interactive Phenomenon* (pp. 271–290). Cambridge: Cambridge University Press.

Goffman, Erving (Ed.). (1967). *Interactional Ritual: Essays on Face-to-Face Behavior.* Garden City, NY: Anchor Books.

Goldsmith, Daena J., & MacGeorge, Erina L. (2000). "The impact of politeness and relationship on perceived quality of advice about a problem." *Human Communication Research, 26,* 234–263.

Goodwin, Marjorie Harness (1990). *He-said-she-said: Talk as Social Organization among Black Children.* Bloomington: Indiana University Press.

Gough, Val, & Talbot, Mary (1996). "'Guilt over games boys play': Coherence as a focus for examining the constitution of heterosexual subjectivity on a problem page." In Carmen Rosa Caldas-Coulthard & Malcolm Coulthard (Eds.), *Texts and Practices. Readings in Critical Discourse Analysis* (pp. 214–230). London: Routledge.

Grice, H. Paul (1982). "Meaning revisited." In N. V. Smith (Ed.), *Mutual Knowledge* (pp. 223–245). London: Academic Press.

Hay, Jennifer (2000). "Functions of humor in the conversations of men and women." *Journal of Pragmatics, 32,* 709–742.

Hayashi, Takuo (1996). "Politeness in conflict management: A conversation analysis of dispreferred message from a cognitive perspective." *Journal of Pragmatics, 25,* 227–255.

Hays, Charlotte (1984). "The evolution of Ann Landers: From prim to progressive." *Public Opinion,* December/January, 11–13.

He, Agnes Weiyun, & Keating, Elizabeth (1991). "Counselor and student at talk: A case study." *Issues in Applied Linguistics, 2,* 183–209.

He, Agnes Weiyun (1993). "Exploring modality in institutional interactions: Cases from academic counselling encounters." *Text, 13,* 503–528.

He, Agnes Weiyun (1994). "Withholding academic advice: Institutional context and academic practice." *Discourse Processes, 18,* 297–316.

He, Agnes Weiyun (1995). "Co-constructing institutional identities: The case of student counselees." *Research on Language and Social Interaction, 28*, 213–231.

He, Agnes Weiyun (1996a). "Narrative processes and institutional activities: Recipient guided storytelling in academic counseling encounters." *Pragmatics, 6*, 205–216.

He, Agnes Weiyun (1996b). "Stories as academic counseling resources." *Journal of Narrative and Life History, 6*, 107–121.

Health Services at AEI [The source cannot be indicated for legal reasons.]

Hendley, W. Clark (1977). "Dear Abby, Miss Lonelyhearts, and the Eighteenth Century: The origins of the newspaper advice column." *Journal of Popular Culture, 11*, 345–352.

Herbert, Robert K. (1990). "Sex-based differences in compliment behavior." *Language in Society, 19*, 201–224.

Heritage, John, & Sefi, Sue (1992). "Dilemmas of advice: Aspects of the delivery and reception of advice in interactions between health visitors and first-time mothers." In Paul Drew & John Heritage (Eds.), *Talk at Work. Interaction in Institutional Settings* (pp. 359–417). Cambridge: Cambridge University Press.

Heritage, John, & Lindström, Anna (1998). "Motherhood, medicine, and morality: Scenes from a medical encounter." *Research on Language and Social Interaction, 31*, 397–438.

Hernández-Flores, Nieves (1999). "Politeness ideology in Spanish colloquial conversation: The case of advice." *Pragmatics, 9*, 37–49.

Hinkel, Eli (1994). "Appropriateness of advice as L2 solidarity strategy." *RELC Journal, 25*, 71–93.

Hinkel, Eli (1997). "Appropriateness of advice: DCT and multiple choice data." *Applied Linguistics, 18*, 1–26.

Holmes, Janet (1995). *Women, Men and Politeness*. New York: Longman.

Holmes, Janet (2000). "Politeness, power and provocation: How humour functions in the workplace." *Discourse Studies, 2*, 159–185.

Hudson, Thom (1990). "The discourse of advice giving in English – 'I wouldn't feed until spring no matter what you do'." *Language and Communication, 10*, 285–297.

Hutchby, Ian (1995). "Aspects of recipient design in expert advice-giving on call-in radio." *Discourse Processes, 19*, 219–238.

Janoschka, Anja (2004). *Web Advertising. New Forms of Communication on the Internet*. Amsterdam: John Benjamins.

Jefferson, Gail, & Lee, John R. E. (1992). "The Rejection of advice: Managing the problematic convergence of a 'troubles-telling' and a 'service encounter'." In Paul Drew & John Heritage (Eds.), *Talk at Work. Interaction in Institutional Settings* (pp. 521–548). Cambridge: Cambridge University Press.

Jessner, Ulrike (1996). "Female empathy: Linguistic implications of a 'Restricted Code'?" In Gudrun Grabher & Ulrike Jessner (Eds.), *Semantics of Silences in Linguistics and Literature* (pp. 89–98). Heidelberg: Universitätsverlag C. Winter.

Johnson, Donna M., & Roen, Duane H. (1992). "Complimenting and involvement in peer reviews: Gender variation." *Language in Society, 21*, 27–57.

Joseph, John Earl (2004). *Language and Identity. National, Ethnic, Religious*. Basingstoke: Palgrave Macmillan.

Kinnell, A. M., & Maynard, D. (1996). "The delivery and receipt of safer sex advice in pretest counseling sessions for HIV and AIDS." *Journal of Contemporary Ethnography, 24*, 405–437.

Kinnell, A. M. (2002). "Soliciting client questions in HIV prevention and test counseling." *Research on Language and Social Interaction, 35*, 367–393.

Kissling, Elizabeth (1991). "Street harassment: The language of sexual terrorism." *Discourse and Society, 2*, 451–460.

Kotthoff, Helga (1993). "Disagreement and concession in disputes: On the context sensitivity of preference structures." *Language in Society, 22*, 193–216.

Kreuz, Roger J., & Graesser, Arthur C. (1993). "The assumptions between questions in letters to advice columnists." *Text, 13*, 65–89.

Labov, William, & Fanshel, David (1977). *Therapeutic Discourse.* New York: Academic Press.

Lebow, J. (1998). "Not just talk, Maybe some risk: The therapeutic potentials and pitfalls of computer-mediated conversation." *Journal of Marital and Family Therapy, 24*, 203–206.

Leech, Geoffrey, Rayson, Paul, & Wilson, Andrew (2001). *Word Frequencies in Written and Spoken English: Based on the British National Corpus.* London: Longman.

Leppänen, Vesa (1998). "The straightforwardness of advice: Advice-Giving in interactions between Swedish district nurses and patients." *Research on Language and Social Interaction, 31*, 209–239.

Lewandowska-Tomaszczyk, Barbara (1989). "Praising and complimenting." In Wieslaw Olesky (Ed.), *Contrastive Pragmatics* (pp. 73–100). Amsterdam: John Benjamins.

Locher, Miriam A. (2004). *Power and Politeness in Action: Disagreements in Oral Communication.* Berlin: Mouton de Gruyter.

Locher, Miriam A., & Hoffmann, Sebastian (2003). "Constructing authority in two Internet advice columns." Paper presented at the *Georgetown University Round Table on Languages and Linguistics (GURT 03)*, Washington DC.

Locher, Miriam A., & Hoffmann, Sebastian (2006). "The emergence of the identity of a fictional expert advice-giver in an American Internet advice column." *Text and Talk, 26*, 67–104.

Locher, Miriam A., & Watts, Richard J. (2005). "Politeness theory and relational work." *Journal of Politeness Research, 1*, 9–33.

Lucy Answers [The source cannot be indicated for legal reasons.]

Lumby, Malcolm E. (1976). "Ann Landers' advice column: 1958 and 1971." *Journalism Quarterly, 53*, 129–132.

MacGeorge, Erina L., Feng, Bo, Butler, Ginger L., & Budarz, Sara K. (2004). "Understanding advice in supportive interactions." *Human Communication Research, 30*, 42–70.

McLelland, Mark (2001). "Live life more selfishly: An on-line gay advice column in Japan." *Journal of Media & Cultural Studies, 15*, 103–116.

McRobbie, Angela (1978). *Jackie: An Ideology of Adolescent Femininity.* Birmingham, UK: The Centre for Contemporary Cultural Studies.

McRobbie, Angela (1991). *Feminism and Youth Culture: From "Jackie" to "Just Seventeen".* Boston: Unwin Hyman.

Meyerhoff, Miriam (2002). "Communities of practice." In J. K. Chambers, Peter Trudgill, & Natalie Schilling-Estes (Eds.), *Handbook of Language Variation and Change* (pp. 526–548). Oxford: Blackwell.

Miller, D., & Bor, R. (1988). *AIDS: A Guide to Clinical Counselling.* London: Science Press.

Miller, John, & Gergen, Kenneth J. (1998). "Life on the line: The therapeutic potentials of computer-mediated conversation." *Journal of Marital and Family Therapy, 24*, 189–202.

Mininni, Giuseppe (1991). "Diatextual analysis of the advice column." *Rassegna Italiana di Linguistica Applicata, 23*, 73–81.

Mutongi, Kenda (2000). "'Dear Dolly's' advice: Representations of youth, courtship, and sexualities in Africa, 1960–1980." *International Journal of African Historical Studies, 33*, 1–24.

Peräkylä, Anssi, & Silverman, David (1991). "Reinterpreting speech-exchange systems: Communication formats in HIV counselling." *Sociology, 25*, 627–651.

Peräkylä, Anssi (1993). "Invoking a hostile world: Discussing the patient's future in AIDS counselling." *Text, 13*, 291–316.

Peräkylä, Anssi (1995). *Aids Counselling: Institutional Interaction and Clinical Practice.* Cambridge: Cambridge University Press.

Pilnick, Alison (1999). "'Patient counseling' by pharmacists: Advice, information, or instruction?" *Sociological Quarterly, 40*, 613–622.

Pilnick, Alison (2001). "The interactional organization of pharmacist consultations in a hospital setting: A putative structure." *Journal of Pragmatics, 33*, 1927–1945.

Pomerantz, Anita (1978). "Compliment responses. Notes on the co-operation of multiple constraints." In Jim Schenkein (Ed.), *Studies in the Organization of Conversational Interaction* (pp. 79–112). New York: Academic Press.

Pomerantz, Anita (1984). "Agreeing and disagreeing with assessments: Some features of preferred/dispreferred turn shapes." In John Maxwell Atkinson & John Heritage (Eds.), *Structures of Social Action. Studies in Conversation Analysis* (pp. 75–101). Cambridge: Cambridge University Press.

Quirk, Randolph, Greenbaum, Sidney, Leech, Geoffrey, & Svartvik, Jan (1972). *A Grammar of Contemporary English.* Harlow: Longman.

Quirk, Randolph, Greenbaum, Sidney, Leech, Geoffrey, & Svartvik, Jan (1985). *A Comprehensive Grammar of the English Language.* London: Longman.

Richardson, Kay P. (2003). "Health risks on the Internet: Establishing credibility on line." *Health, Risk and Society, 5*, 171–184.

Santhakumaran, Dharshi (2004). "'It would have to be somebody desperate': taking advice from a women's magazine." Paper presented at *Sociolinguistics Symposium 15, Culture – Contact – Change*, Newcastle, England.

Sarangi, Srikant, & Clarke, Angus (2002). "Zones of expertise and the management of uncertainty in genetics risk communication." *Research on Language and Social Interaction, 35*, 139–171.

Schiffrin, Deborah (1984). "Jewish argument as sociability." *Language in Society, 13*, 311–335.

Schiffrin, Deborah (1996). "Narrative as self-portrait. Sociolinguistic constructions of identity." *Language in Society, 25*, 167–203.

Scollon, Ron, & Scollon, Suzanne W. (2001). *Intercultural Communication: A Discourse Approach.* Oxford: Blackwell.

Searle, John R. (1969). *Speech Acts. An Essay in the Philosophy of Language.* Cambridge: Cambridge University Press.

Silverman, David (1989). "Making sense of a precipice: Constituting identity in an HIV clinic." In Peter Aggleton, Graham Hart, & Peter Davies (Eds.), *AIDS: Social Representations, Social Practices* (pp. 101–126). New York: Falmer Press.

Silverman, David (1990). "The social organization of HIV counselling." In Peter Aggleton, Peter Davies, & Graham Hart (Eds.), *AIDS: Individual, Cultural and Policy Dimensions* (pp. 191–214). London: Falmer Press.

Silverman, David, & Peräkylä, Anssi (1990). "AIDS counselling: The interactional organization of talk about 'delicate' issues." *Sociology of Health and Illness, 12*, 293–318.

Silverman, David, Bor, Robert, Miller, Riva, & Goldman, Eleanor (1992a). "'Obviously the advice is then to keep to safer sex' – advice-giving and advice reception in AIDS counselling." In Peter Aggleton, Peter Davies, & Graham Hart (Eds.), *AIDS: Rights, Risk and Reason* (pp. 174–191). London: Falmer Press.

Silverman, David, Peräkylä, Anssi, & Bor, Robert (1992b). "Discussing safer sex in HIV counselling: Assessing three communication formats." *AIDS Care, 4*, 69–82.

Silverman, David (1994). "Describing sexual activities in HIV counselling: The cooperative management of the moral order." *Text, 14*, 427–453.

Silverman, David (1997). *Discourses of Counselling: HIV Counselling as Social Interaction.* London: Sage.

Smith, Terry, & Levin, Jack (1974). "Social change in sex roles: An analysis of advice columns." *Journalism Quarterly, 51*, 525–527.

Stoll, Pamela (1998). "Text as conversation: An interpretative investigation of utterances in a women's magazine." *Journal of Pragmatics, 29*, 545–570.

Studentcenter (2004). Available: http://teenadvice.studentcenter.org/ [2004, March 11].

Sunderland, Jane, & Litosseliti, Lia (2004). "Gender identity and discourse analysis. Theoretical and empirical considerations." In Jane Sunderland & Lia Litosseliti (Eds.), *Gendered Discourses* (pp. 1–39). Basingstoke: Palgrave Macmillan.

Talbot, Mary (1992). "The construction of gender in a teenage magazine." In Norman Fairclough (Ed.), *Critical Language Awareness* (pp. 174–199). London: Longman.

Talbot, Mary (1995). "A synthetic sisterhood. False friends in a teenage magazine." In Kira Hall & Mary Bucholtz (Eds.), *Gender Articulated* (pp. 144–165). New York: Routledge.

Tannen, Deborah (1990). *You Just Don't Understand. Women and Men in Conversation.* New York: William Morrow and Company.

Tannen, Deborah (1993). "What's in a Frame?: Surface evidence for underlying expectations." In Deborah Tannen (Ed.), *Framing in Discourse* (pp. 14–56). Oxford: Oxford University Press.

The American Heritage Dictionary of the English Language (2000). Available: http://www.bartleby.com/ [2005, 9 May].

The Oxford English Dictionary (1989). Oxford: Oxford University Press. Available: http://www.oed.com/ [2005, 9 May].

Thibault, Paul (1988). "Knowing what you're told by the agony aunts: Language function, gender difference and the structure of knowledge and belief in personal columns." In David Birch & Michael O'Toole (Eds.), *Functions of Style* (pp. 205–233). London: Pinter.

Thibault, Paul (2002). "Interpersonal meaning and the discursive construction of action, attitudes and values: The Global Modal Program of one text." In P. H. Fries, M. Cummings, & D. Lockwood (Eds.), *Relations and Functions within and around Language* (pp. 56–116). London: Continuum.

Tyler, Leona (1961). *The Work of a Counselor.* New York: Appleton Century Crofts.

van der Meij, H. (1987). "Assumptions in information-seeking questions." *Questioning Exchange, 1*, 111–118.

van Dijk, Teun A. (1997). "Discourse as interaction in society." In Teun A. van Dijk (Ed.), *Discourse as Social Interaction* (pp. 1–37). Thousand Oaks, CA: Sage.

van Roosmalen, Erica (2000). "Forces of patriarchy: Adolescent experiences of sexuality and conceptions of relationships." *Youth & Society, 32*, 202–227.

Vehviläinen, Sanna (2001). "Evaluative advice in educational counseling: The use of disagreement in the 'stepwise entry' to advice." *Research on Language and Social Interaction, 34*, 371–398.

Vehviläinen, Sanna (2003). "Avoiding providing solutions: Orienting to the ideal of students' self-directedness in counselling interaction." *Discourse Studies, 5*, 389–414.

Voutilainen, Atro (2004). *The EngCG-2 tagger.* Available: http://www.ling.helsinki.fi/~avoutila/cg/index.html [2004, 2 November].

Watzlawick, Paul, Beavin, Janet Helmick, & Jackson, Don D. (1967). *Pragmatics of Human Communication. A Study of Interactional Patterns, Pathologies and Paradoxes.* New York: Norton.

Wenger, Etienne (1998). *Communities of Practice: Learning, Meaning, and Identity.* Cambridge: Cambridge University Press.

West, Nathanael (1933). *Miss Lonelyhearts.* New York: J. Laughlin.

Wierzbicka, Anna (1985). "Different cultures, different languages, different speech acts." *Journal of Pragmatics, 9,* 145–178.

Wierzbicka, Anna (1987). *English Speech Act Verbs: A Semantic Dictionary.* New York: Academic Press.

Wolfson, Nessa (1983). "An empirically based analysis of complimenting in American English." In Nessa Wolfson & Elliot Judd (Eds.), *Sociolinguistics and Language Acquisition* (pp. 82–95). Rowley, MA: Newbury House.

Index

Pragmatics & Beyond New Series

A complete list of titles in this series can be found on the publishers' website, *www.benjamins.com*

118 **CHENG, Winnie:** Intercultural Conversation. 2003. xii, 279 pp.

117 **WU, Ruey-Jiuan Regina:** Stance in Talk. A conversation analysis of Mandarin final particles. 2004. xvi, 260 pp.

116 **GRANT, Colin B. (ed.):** Rethinking Communicative Interaction. New interdisciplinary horizons. 2003. viii, 330 pp.

115 **KÄRKKÄINEN, Elise:** Epistemic Stance in English Conversation. A description of its interactional functions, with a focus on *I think*. 2003. xii, 213 pp.

114 **KÜHNLEIN, Peter, Hannes RIESER and Henk ZEEVAT (eds.):** Perspectives on Dialogue in the New Millennium. 2003. xii, 400 pp.

113 **PANTHER, Klaus-Uwe and Linda L. THORNBURG (eds.):** Metonymy and Pragmatic Inferencing. 2003. xii, 285 pp.

112 **LENZ, Friedrich (ed.):** Deictic Conceptualisation of Space, Time and Person. 2003. xiv, 279 pp.

111 **ENSINK, Titus and Christoph SAUER (eds.):** Framing and Perspectivising in Discourse. 2003. viii, 227 pp.

110 **ANDROUTSOPOULOS, Jannis K. and Alexandra GEORGAKOPOULOU (eds.):** Discourse Constructions of Youth Identities. 2003. viii, 343 pp.

109 **MAYES, Patricia:** Language, Social Structure, and Culture. A genre analysis of cooking classes in Japan and America. 2003. xiv, 228 pp.

108 **BARRON, Anne:** Acquisition in Interlanguage Pragmatics. Learning how to do things with words in a study abroad context. 2003. xviii, 403 pp.

107 **TAAVITSAINEN, Irma and Andreas H. JUCKER (eds.):** Diachronic Perspectives on Address Term Systems. 2003. viii, 446 pp.

106 **BUSSE, Ulrich:** Linguistic Variation in the Shakespeare Corpus. Morpho-syntactic variability of second person pronouns. 2002. xiv, 344 pp.

105 **BLACKWELL, Sarah E.:** Implicatures in Discourse. The case of Spanish NP anaphora. 2003. xvi, 303 pp.

104 **BEECHING, Kate:** Gender, Politeness and Pragmatic Particles in French. 2002. x, 251 pp.

103 **FETZER, Anita and Christiane MEIERKORD (eds.):** Rethinking Sequentiality. Linguistics meets conversational interaction. 2002. vi, 300 pp.

102 **LEAFGREN, John:** Degrees of Explicitness. Information structure and the packaging of Bulgarian subjects and objects. 2002. xii, 252 pp.

101 **LUKE, Kang Kwong and Theodossia-Soula PAVLIDOU (eds.):** Telephone Calls. Unity and diversity in conversational structure across languages and cultures. 2002. x, 295 pp.

100 **JASZCZOLT, Katarzyna M. and Ken TURNER (eds.):** Meaning Through Language Contrast. Volume 2. 2003. viii, 496 pp.

99 **JASZCZOLT, Katarzyna M. and Ken TURNER (eds.):** Meaning Through Language Contrast. Volume 1. 2003. xii, 388 pp.

98 **DUSZAK, Anna (ed.):** Us and Others. Social identities across languages, discourses and cultures. 2002. viii, 522 pp.

97 **MAYNARD, Senko K.:** Linguistic Emotivity. Centrality of place, the topic-comment dynamic, and an ideology of *pathos* in Japanese discourse. 2002. xiv, 481 pp.

96 **HAVERKATE, Henk:** The Syntax, Semantics and Pragmatics of Spanish Mood. 2002. vi, 241 pp.

95 **FITZMAURICE, Susan M.:** The Familiar Letter in Early Modern English. A pragmatic approach. 2002. viii, 263 pp.

94 **McILVENNY, Paul (ed.):** Talking Gender and Sexuality. 2002. x, 332 pp.

93 **BARON, Bettina and Helga KOTTHOFF (eds.):** Gender in Interaction. Perspectives on femininity and masculinity in ethnography and discourse. 2002. xxiv, 357 pp.

92 **GARDNER, Rod:** When Listeners Talk. Response tokens and listener stance. 2001. xxii, 281 pp.

91 **GROSS, Joan:** Speaking in Other Voices. An ethnography of Walloon puppet theaters. 2001. xxviii, 341 pp.

90 **KENESEI, István and Robert M. HARNISH (eds.):** Perspectives on Semantics, Pragmatics, and Discourse. A Festschrift for Ferenc Kiefer. 2001. xxii, 352 pp.

89 **ITAKURA, Hiroko:** Conversational Dominance and Gender. A study of Japanese speakers in first and second language contexts. 2001. xviii, 231 pp.

88 **BAYRAKTAROĞLU, Arın and Maria SIFIANOU (eds.):** Linguistic Politeness Across Boundaries. The case of Greek and Turkish. 2001. xiv, 439 pp.

87 **MUSHIN, Ilana:** Evidentiality and Epistemological Stance. Narrative Retelling. 2001. xviii, 244 pp.

86 **IFANTIDOU, Elly:** Evidentials and Relevance. 2001. xii, 225 pp.

85 **COLLINS, Daniel E.:** Reanimated Voices. Speech reporting in a historical-pragmatic perspective. 2001. xx, 384 pp.

84 **ANDERSEN, Gisle:** Pragmatic Markers and Sociolinguistic Variation. A relevance-theoretic approach to the language of adolescents. 2001. ix, 352 pp.